BRUTAL NATURE

COVER ART BY
ARIEL OLIVETTI

COLLECTION EDITS BY
JUSTIN EISINGER AND
ALONZO SIMON

COLLECTION DESIGN BY
CHRIS MOWRY

PUBLISHER
TED ADAMS

THE AUTHORS WISH TO ACKNOWLEDGE THE SUPPORT
OF SOME PEOPLE WITHOUT WHOM THE ROAD WOULD
HAVE BEEN THAT MUCH STEEPER: MARTÍN CANALE,
ALEJANDRO VIKTORÍN, VALE LAGNA FIETTA,
GABRIEL & MARTÍN OLIVETTI, MALENA SARACINO,
JOSÉ ANTONIO VILCA, GLADYS OCHARAN,
EDUARDO RISSO, AXEL ALONSO AND THE ENTIRE
IDW TEAM, FOR MAKING US FEEL AT HOME.

ISBN: 978-1-63140-764-2   19 18 17 16   1 2 3 4

Become our fan on Facebook facebook.com/idwpublishing
Follow us on Twitter @idwpublishing
Subscribe to us on YouTube youtube.com/idwpublishing
See what's new on Tumblr tumblr.idwpublishing.com
Check us out on Instagram instagram.com/idwpublishing

Ted Adams, CEO & Publisher
Greg Goldstein, President & COO
Robbie Robbins, EVP/Sr. Graphic Artist
Chris Ryall, Chief Creative Officer/Editor-in-Chief
Laurie Windrow, Senior VP of Sales & Marketing
Matthew Ruzicka, CPA, Chief Financial Officer
Dirk Wood, VP of Marketing
Lorelei Bunjes, VP of Digital Services
Jeff Webber, VP of Licensing, Digital and Subsidiary Rights
Jerry Bennington, VP of New Product Development

For international rights, please
contact licensing@idwpublishing.com

WRITTEN BY
LUCIANO SARACINO

ART BY
ARIEL OLIVETTI

LETTERS BY
CHRIS MOWRY AND
ANDWORLD DESIGN

TRANSLATION AND SERIES EDITS BY
CARLOS GUZMAN

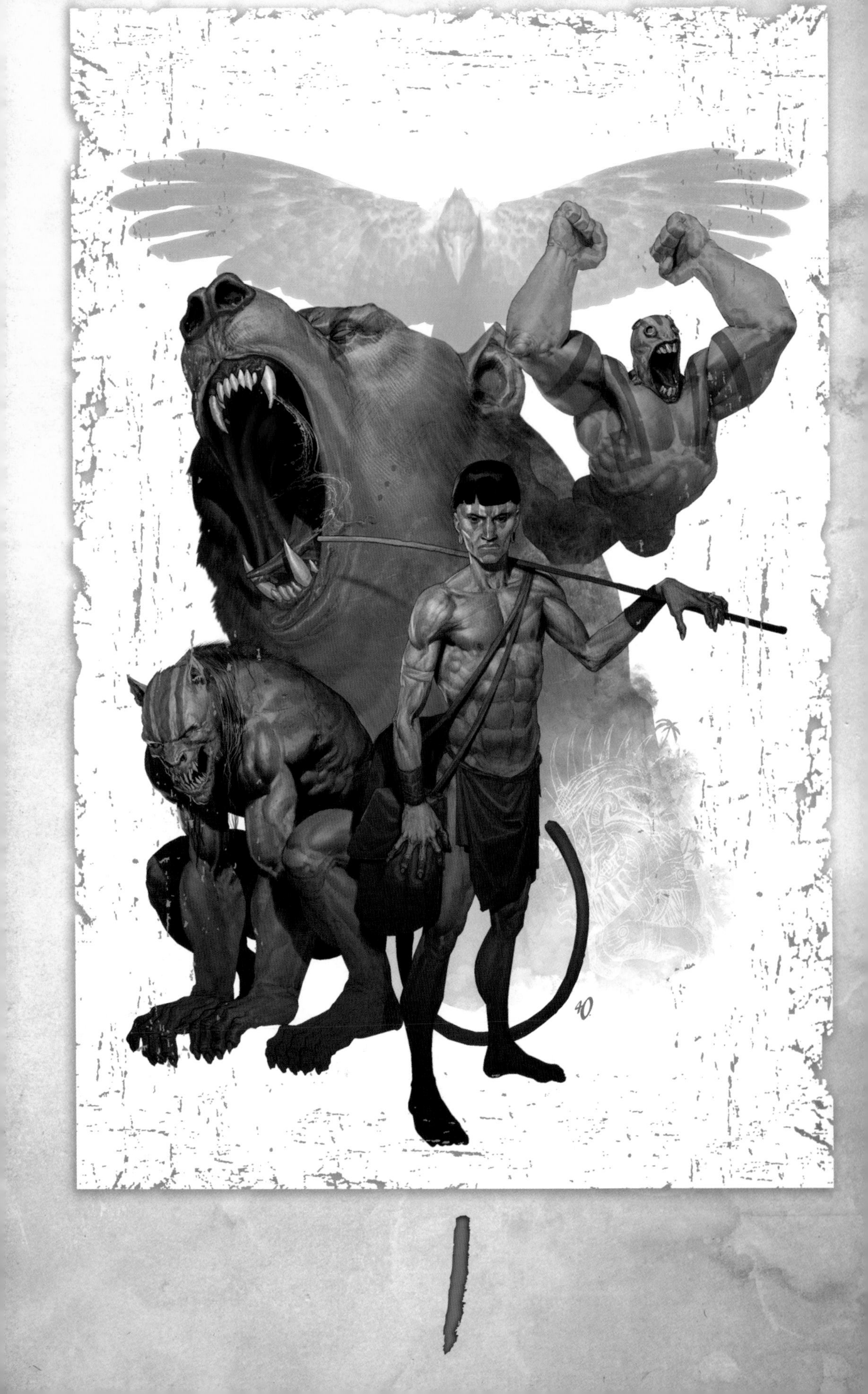

I

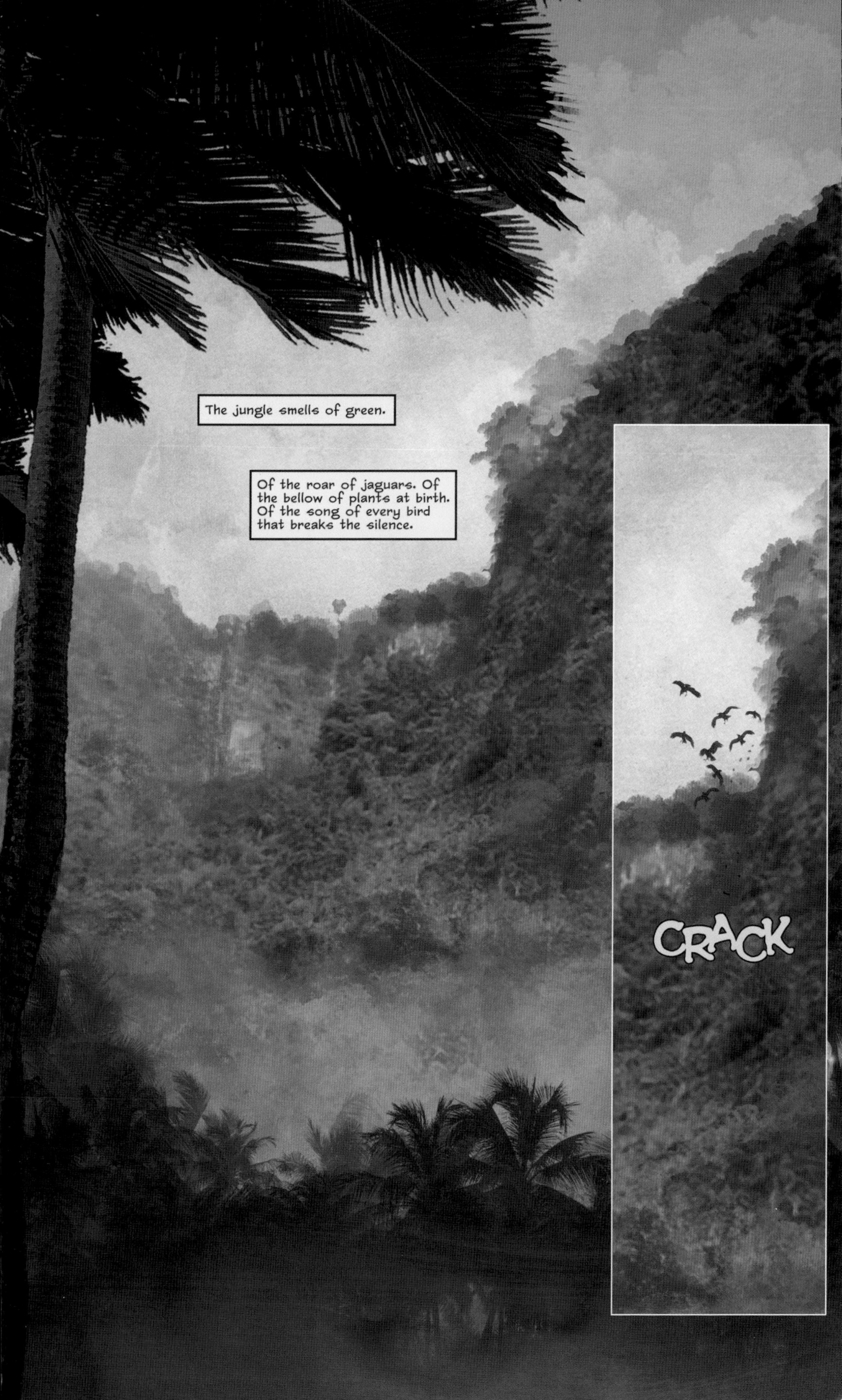
The jungle smells of green.
Of the roar of jaguars. Of the bellow of plants at birth. Of the song of every bird that breaks the silence.
CRACK

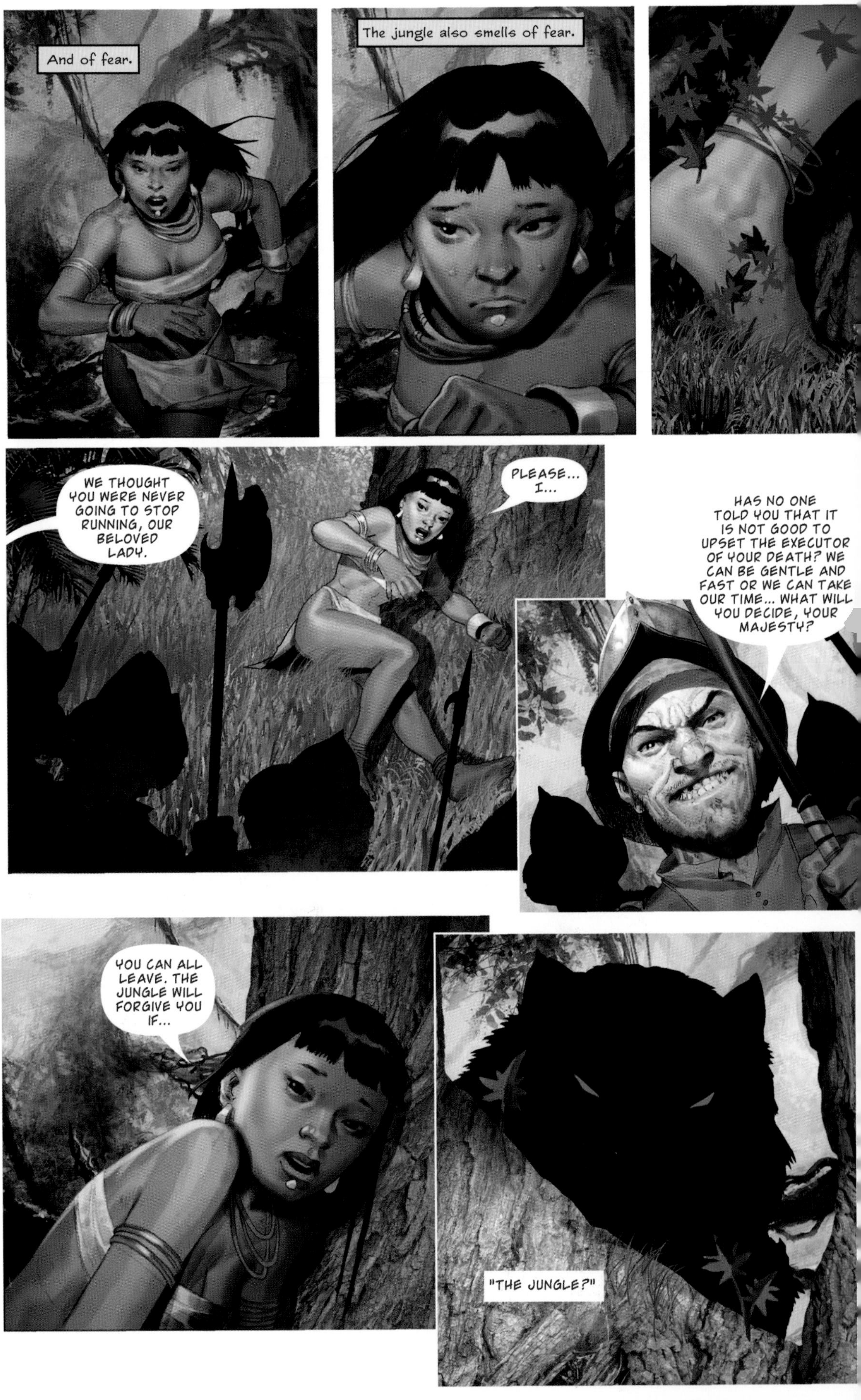

And of fear.
The jungle also smells of fear.
WE THOUGHT YOU WERE NEVER GOING TO STOP RUNNING, OUR BELOVED LADY.
PLEASE... I...
HAS NO ONE TOLD YOU THAT IT IS NOT GOOD TO UPSET THE EXECUTOR OF YOUR DEATH? WE CAN BE GENTLE AND FAST OR WE CAN TAKE OUR TIME... WHAT WILL YOU DECIDE, YOUR MAJESTY?
YOU CAN ALL LEAVE. THE JUNGLE WILL FORGIVE YOU IF...
"THE JUNGLE?"

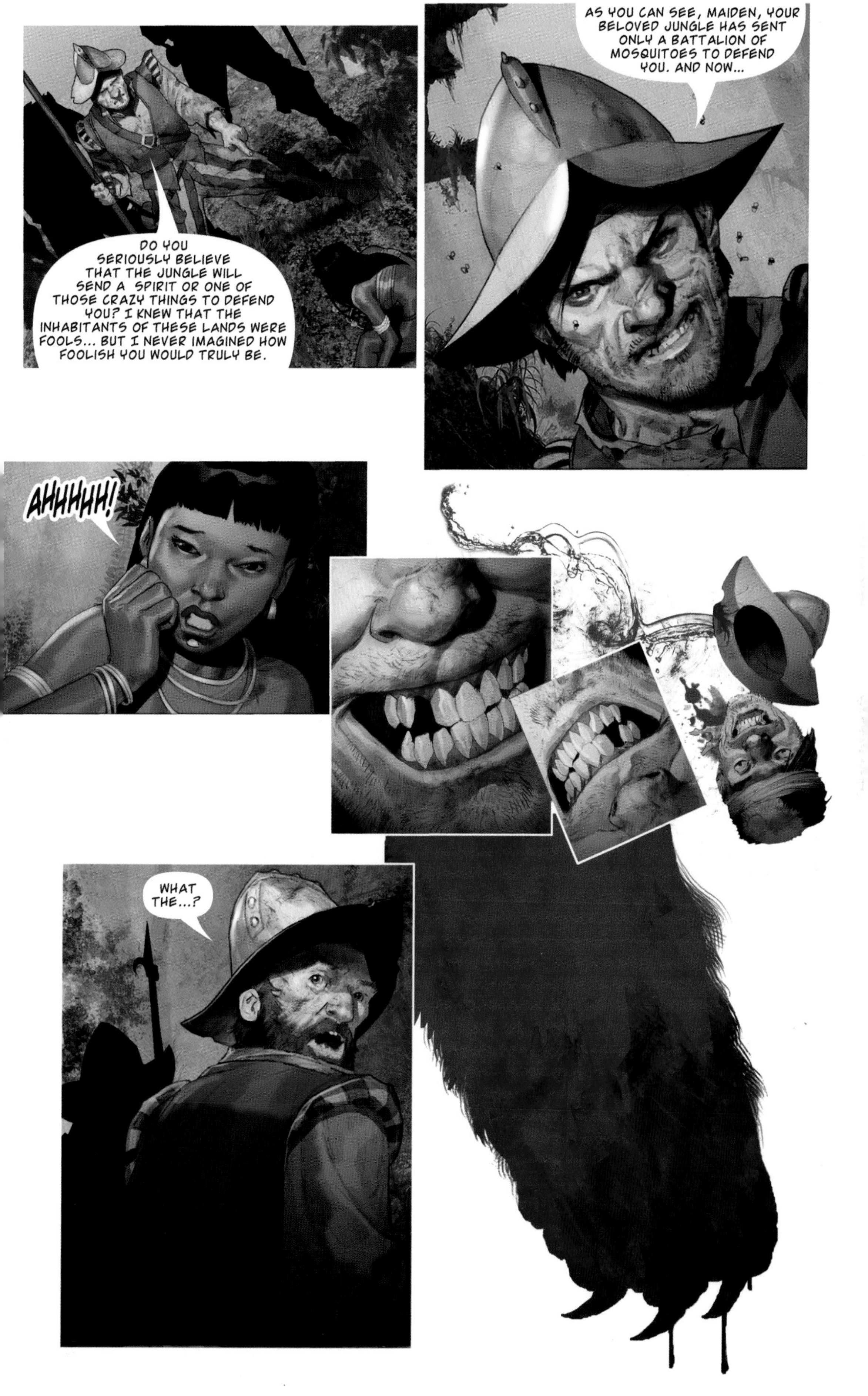
DO YOU SERIOUSLY BELIEVE THAT THE JUNGLE WILL SEND A SPIRIT OR ONE OF THOSE CRAZY THINGS TO DEFEND YOU? I KNEW THAT THE INHABITANTS OF THESE LANDS WERE FOOLS... BUT I NEVER IMAGINED HOW FOOLISH YOU WOULD TRULY BE.
AS YOU CAN SEE, MAIDEN, YOUR BELOVED JUNGLE HAS SENT ONLY A BATTALION OF MOSQUITOES TO DEFEND YOU. AND NOW...
AHHHHH!
WHAT THE...?

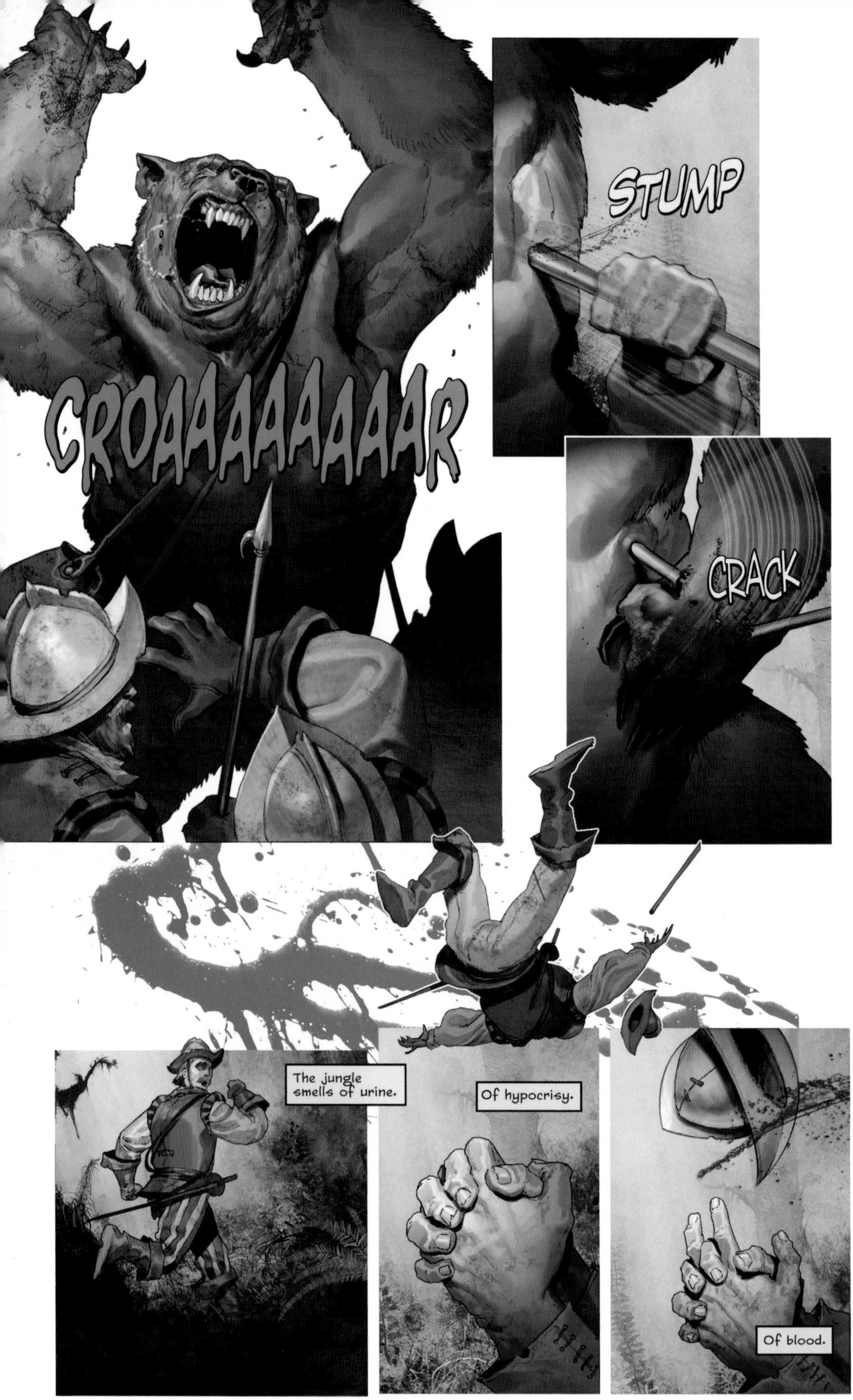

CROAAAAAAAAR
STUMP
CRACK
The jungle smells of urine.
Of hypocrisy.
Of blood.

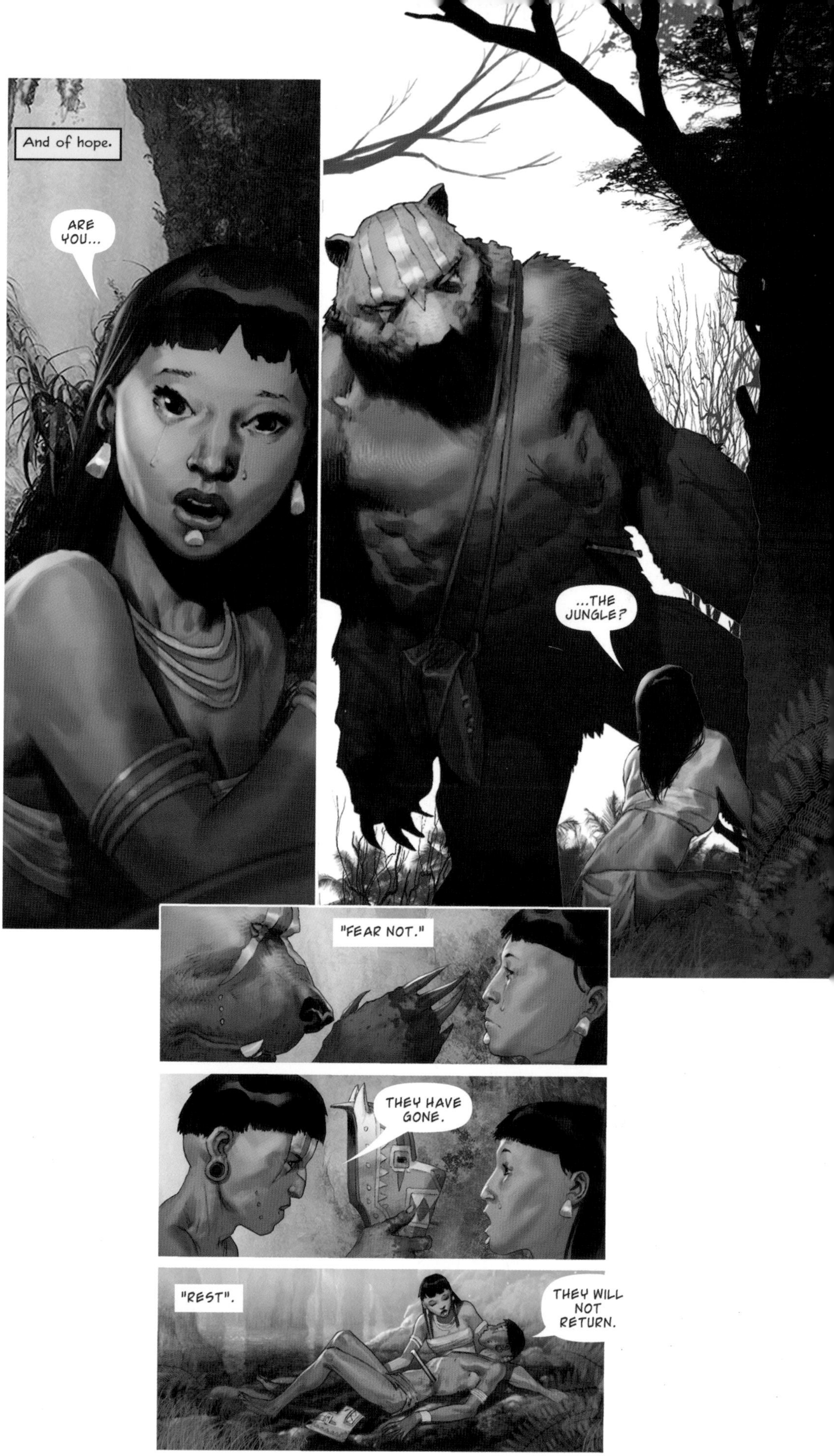
And of hope.
ARE YOU...
...THE JUNGLE?
"FEAR NOT."
THEY HAVE GONE.
"REST".
THEY WILL NOT RETURN.

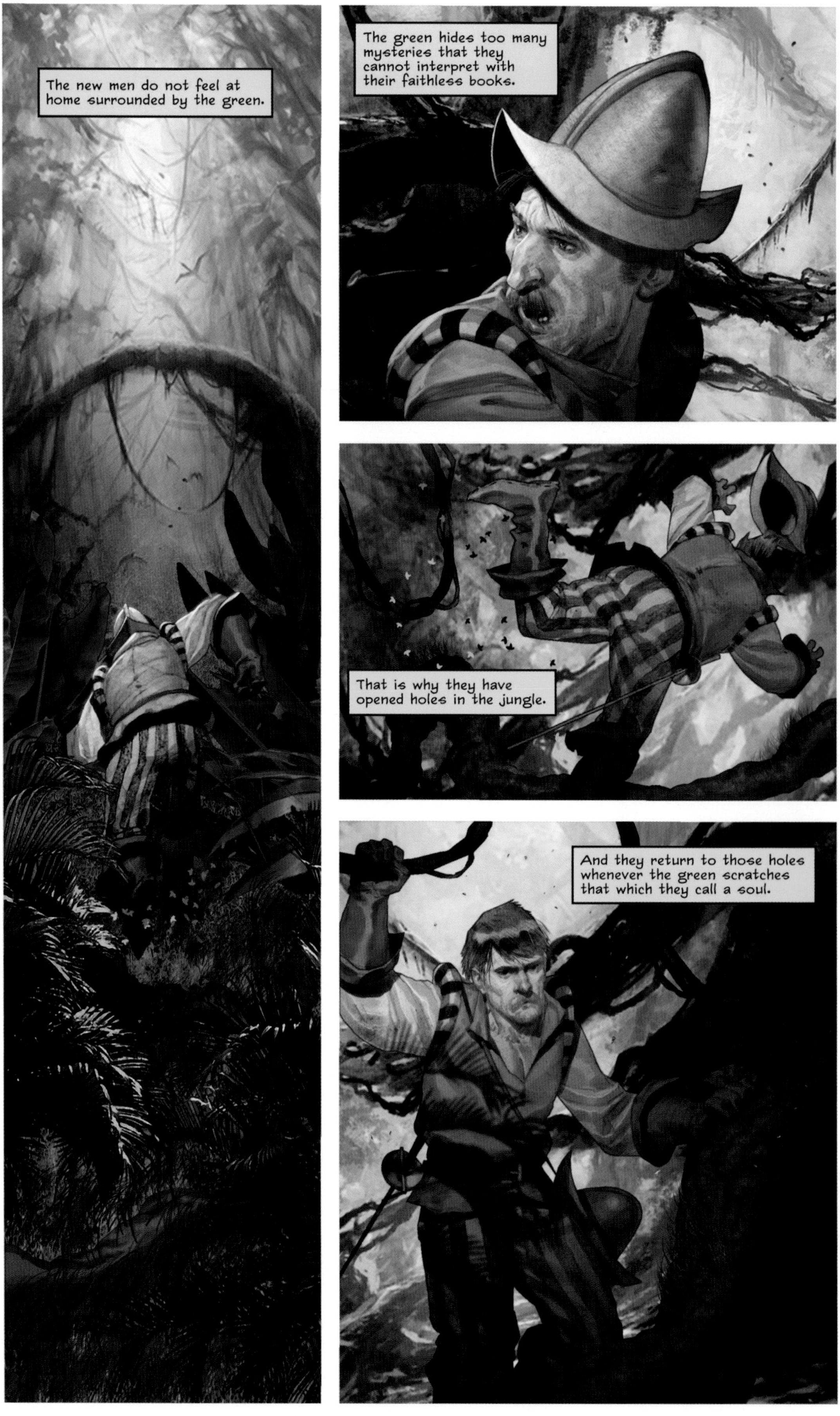
The new men do not feel at home surrounded by the green.
The green hides too many mysteries that they cannot interpret with their faithless books.
That is why they have opened holes in the jungle.
And they return to those holes whenever the green scratches that which they call a soul.

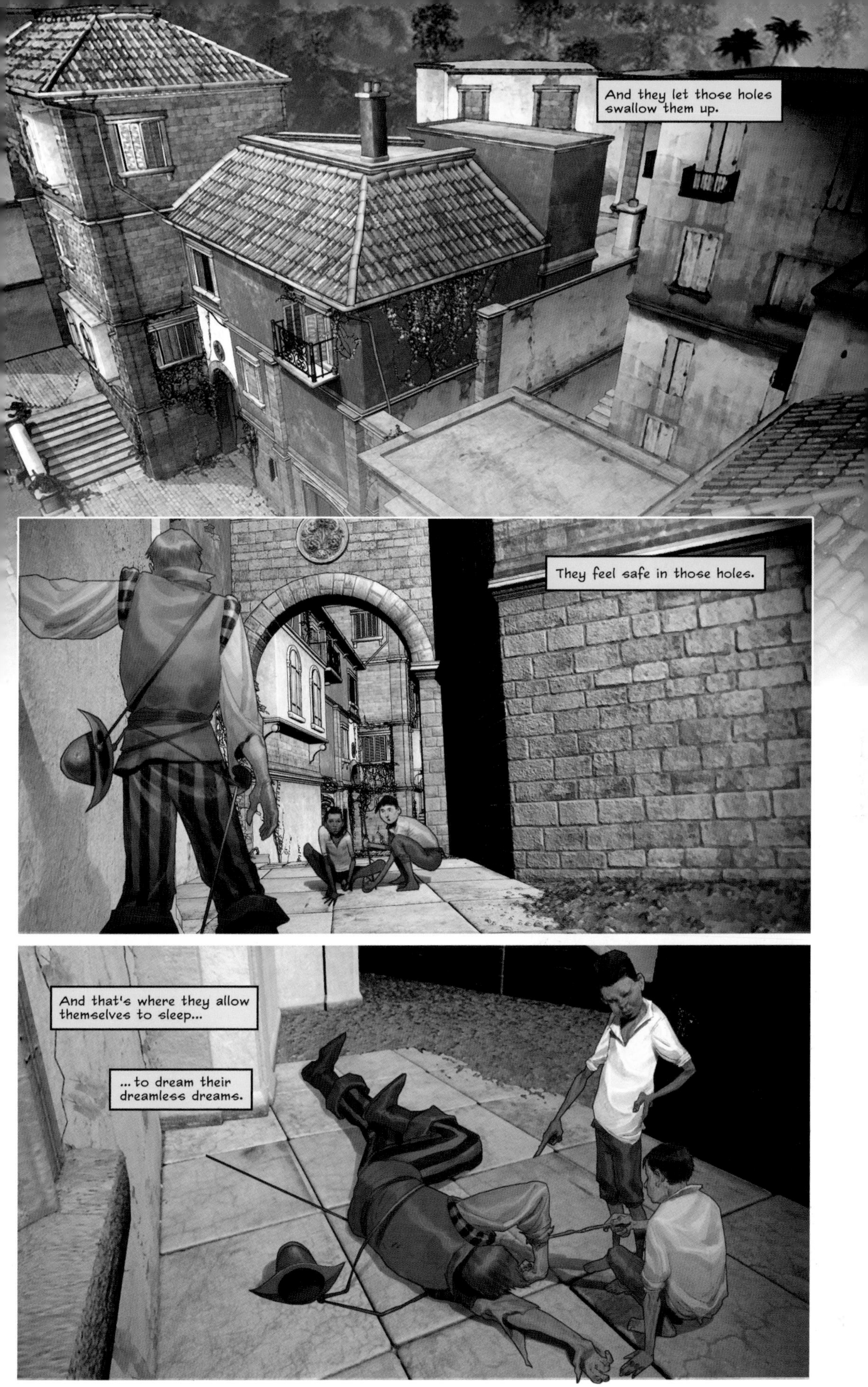

And they let those holes swallow them up.
They feel safe in those holes.
And that's where they allow themselves to sleep...
...to dream their dreamless dreams.

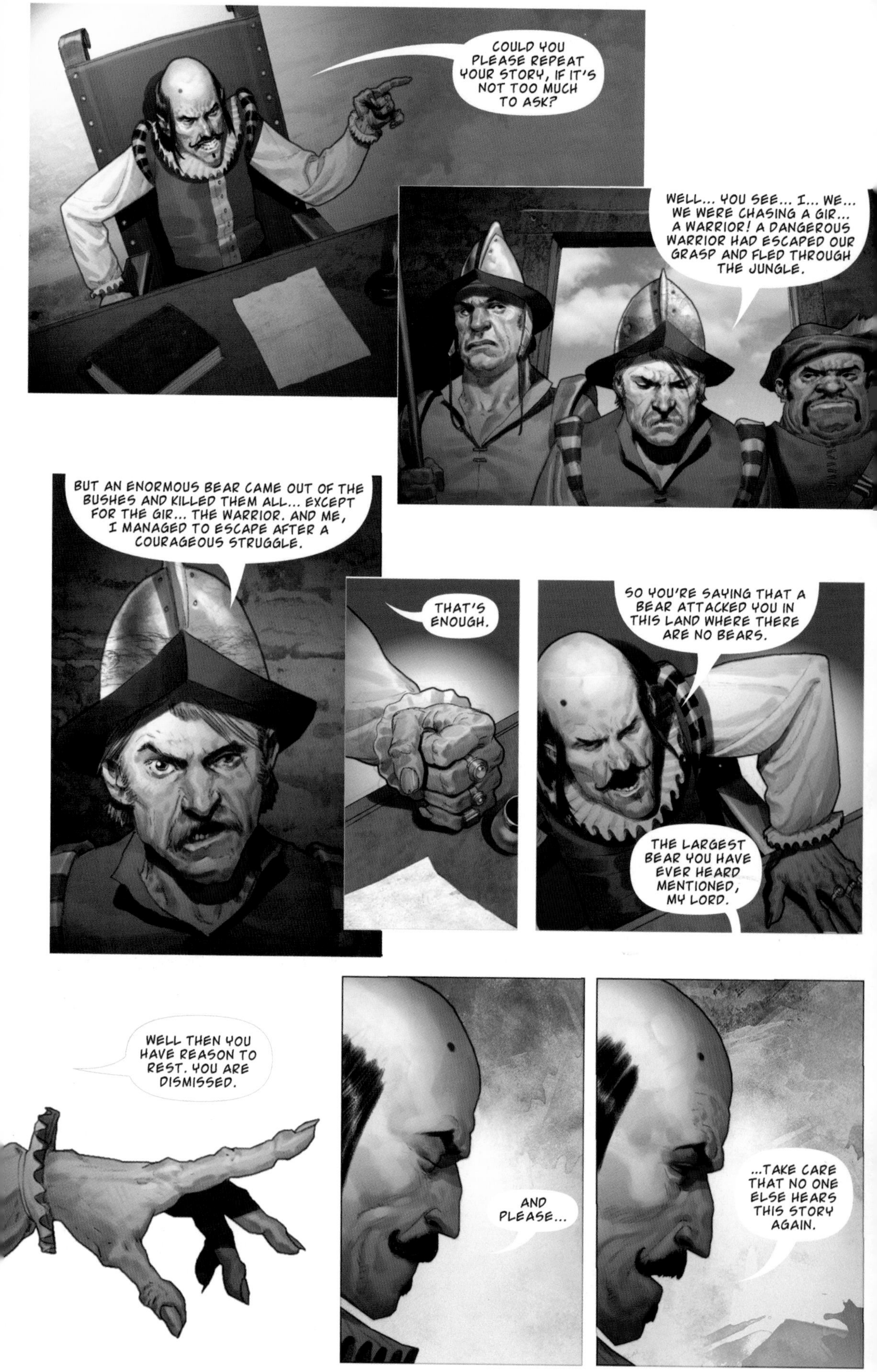
COULD YOU PLEASE REPEAT YOUR STORY, IF IT'S NOT TOO MUCH TO ASK?
WELL... YOU SEE... I... WE... WE WERE CHASING A GIR... A WARRIOR! A DANGEROUS WARRIOR HAD ESCAPED OUR GRASP AND FLED THROUGH THE JUNGLE.
BUT AN ENORMOUS BEAR CAME OUT OF THE BUSHES AND KILLED THEM ALL... EXCEPT FOR THE GIR... THE WARRIOR. AND ME, I MANAGED TO ESCAPE AFTER A COURAGEOUS STRUGGLE.
THAT'S ENOUGH.
SO YOU'RE SAYING THAT A BEAR ATTACKED YOU IN THIS LAND WHERE THERE ARE NO BEARS.
THE LARGEST BEAR YOU HAVE EVER HEARD MENTIONED, MY LORD.
WELL THEN YOU HAVE REASON TO REST. YOU ARE DISMISSED.
AND PLEASE...
...TAKE CARE THAT NO ONE ELSE HEARS THIS STORY AGAIN.

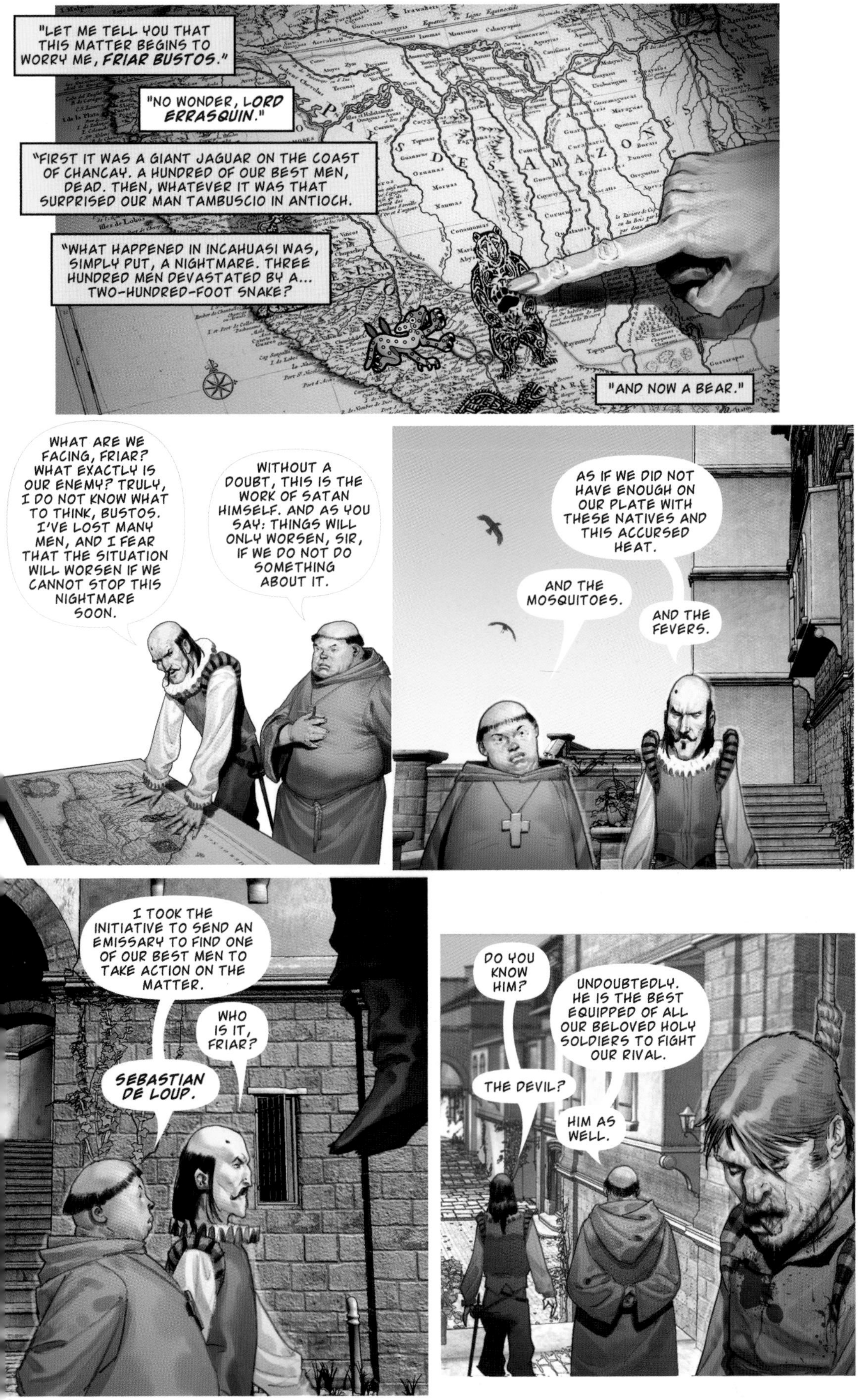
"LET ME TELL YOU THAT THIS MATTER BEGINS TO WORRY ME, FRIAR BUSTOS."
"NO WONDER, LORD ERRASQUIN."
"FIRST IT WAS A GIANT JAGUAR ON THE COAST OF CHANCAY. A HUNDRED OF OUR BEST MEN, DEAD. THEN, WHATEVER IT WAS THAT SURPRISED OUR MAN TAMBUSCIO IN ANTIOCH.
"WHAT HAPPENED IN INCAHUASI WAS, SIMPLY PUT, A NIGHTMARE. THREE HUNDRED MEN DEVASTATED BY A... TWO-HUNDRED-FOOT SNAKE?
"AND NOW A BEAR."
WHAT ARE WE FACING, FRIAR? WHAT EXACTLY IS OUR ENEMY? TRULY, I DO NOT KNOW WHAT TO THINK, BUSTOS. I'VE LOST MANY MEN, AND I FEAR THAT THE SITUATION WILL WORSEN IF WE CANNOT STOP THIS NIGHTMARE SOON.
WITHOUT A DOUBT, THIS IS THE WORK OF SATAN HIMSELF. AND AS YOU SAY: THINGS WILL ONLY WORSEN, SIR, IF WE DO NOT DO SOMETHING ABOUT IT.
AS IF WE DID NOT HAVE ENOUGH ON OUR PLATE WITH THESE NATIVES AND THIS ACCURSED HEAT.
AND THE MOSQUITOES.
AND THE FEVERS.
I TOOK THE INITIATIVE TO SEND AN EMISSARY TO FIND ONE OF OUR BEST MEN TO TAKE ACTION ON THE MATTER.
WHO IS IT, FRIAR?
SEBASTIAN DE LOUP.
DO YOU KNOW HIM?
UNDOUBTEDLY. HE IS THE BEST EQUIPPED OF ALL OUR BELOVED HOLY SOLDIERS TO FIGHT OUR RIVAL.
THE DEVIL?
HIM AS WELL.

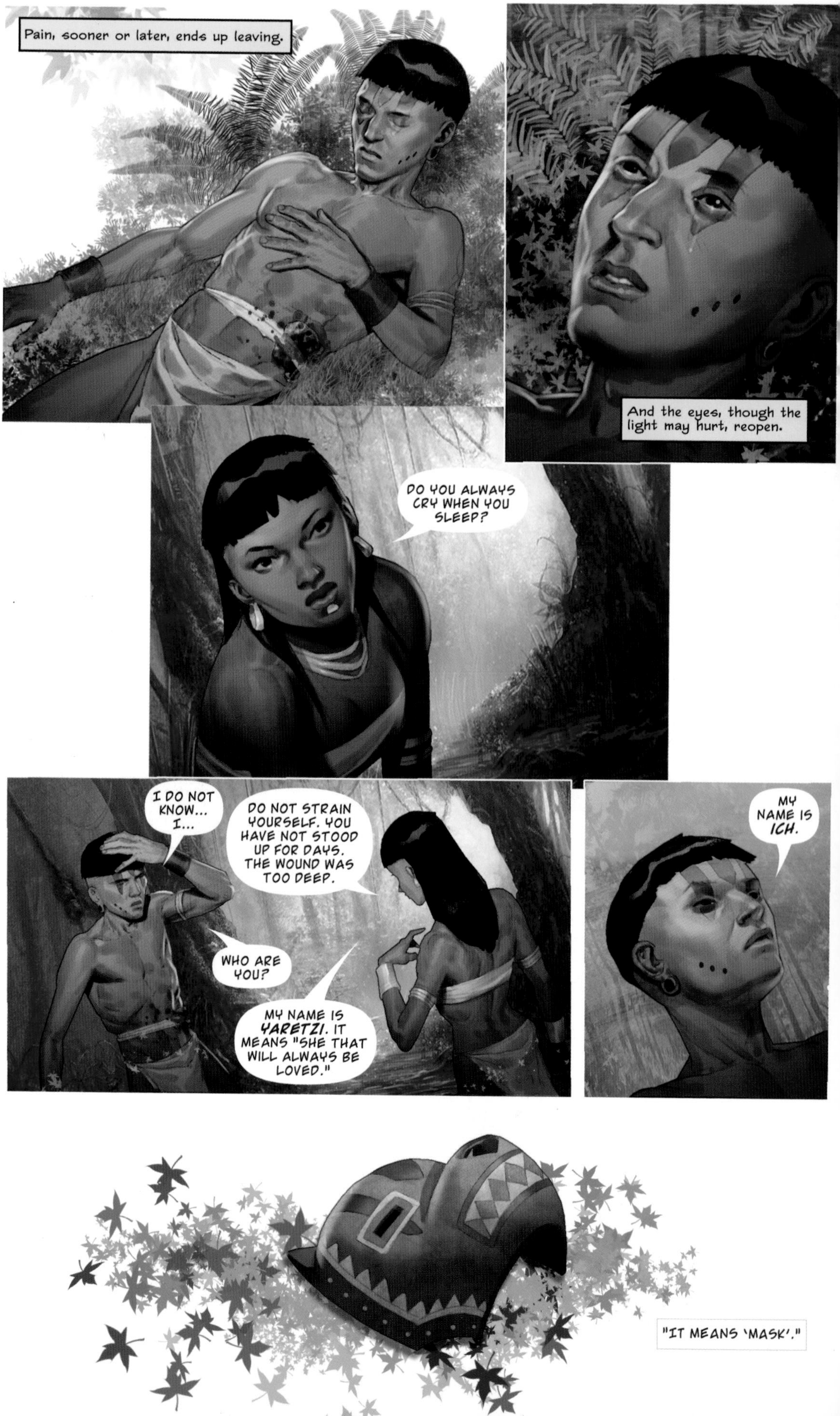
Pain, sooner or later, ends up leaving.
And the eyes, though the light may hurt, reopen.
DO YOU ALWAYS CRY WHEN YOU SLEEP?
I DO NOT KNOW... I...
DO NOT STRAIN YOURSELF. YOU HAVE NOT STOOD UP FOR DAYS. THE WOUND WAS TOO DEEP.
WHO ARE YOU?
MY NAME IS YARETZI. IT MEANS "SHE THAT WILL ALWAYS BE LOVED."
MY NAME IS ICH.
"IT MEANS 'MASK'."

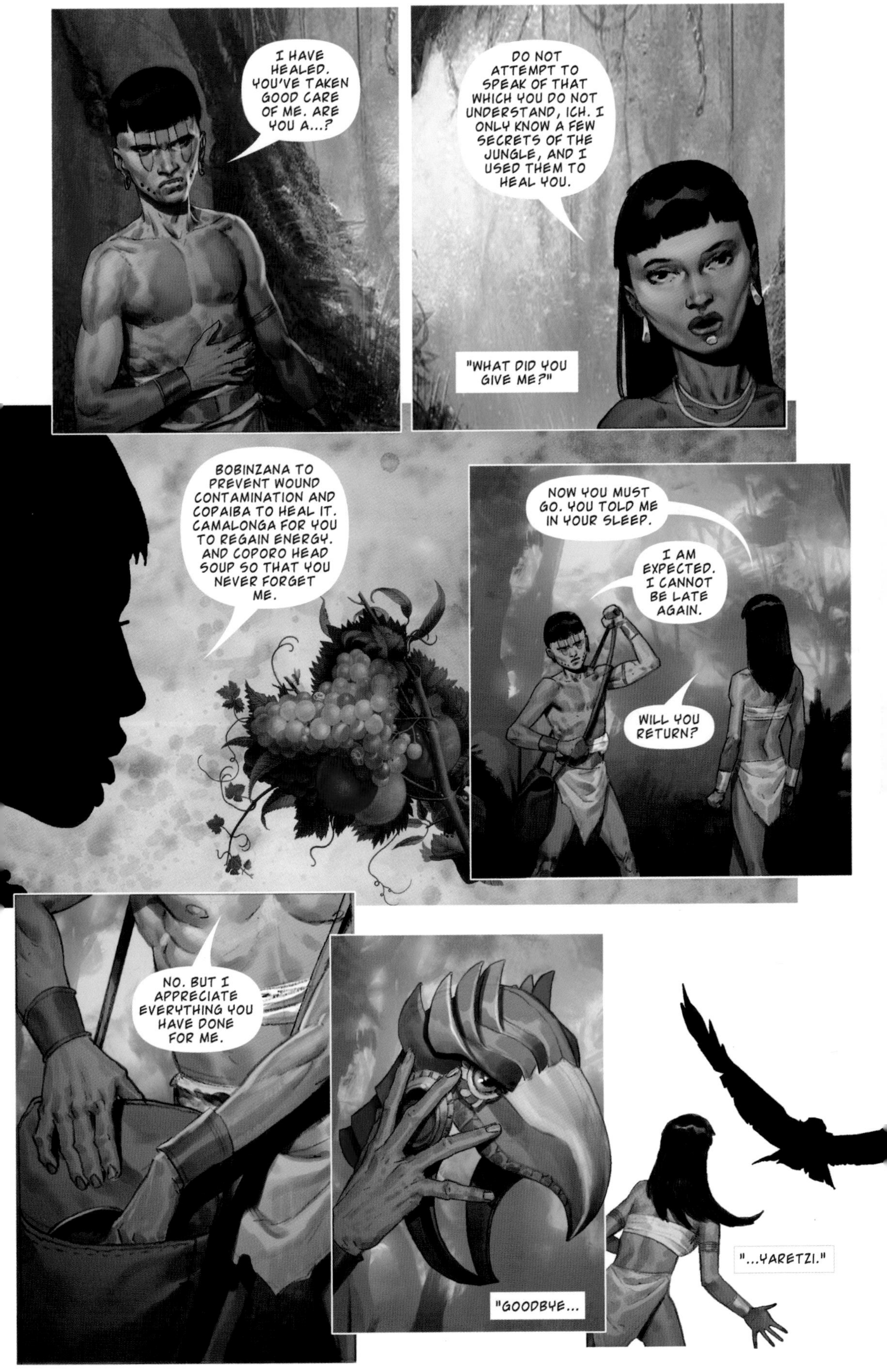

I HAVE HEALED. YOU'VE TAKEN GOOD CARE OF ME. ARE YOU A...?
DO NOT ATTEMPT TO SPEAK OF THAT WHICH YOU DO NOT UNDERSTAND, ICH. I ONLY KNOW A FEW SECRETS OF THE JUNGLE, AND I USED THEM TO HEAL YOU.
"WHAT DID YOU GIVE ME?"
BOBINZANA TO PREVENT WOUND CONTAMINATION AND COPAIBA TO HEAL IT. CAMALONGA FOR YOU TO REGAIN ENERGY. AND COPORO HEAD SOUP SO THAT YOU NEVER FORGET ME.
NOW YOU MUST GO. YOU TOLD ME IN YOUR SLEEP.
I AM EXPECTED. I CANNOT BE LATE AGAIN.
WILL YOU RETURN?
NO. BUT I APPRECIATE EVERYTHING YOU HAVE DONE FOR ME.
"GOODBYE...
"...YARETZI."

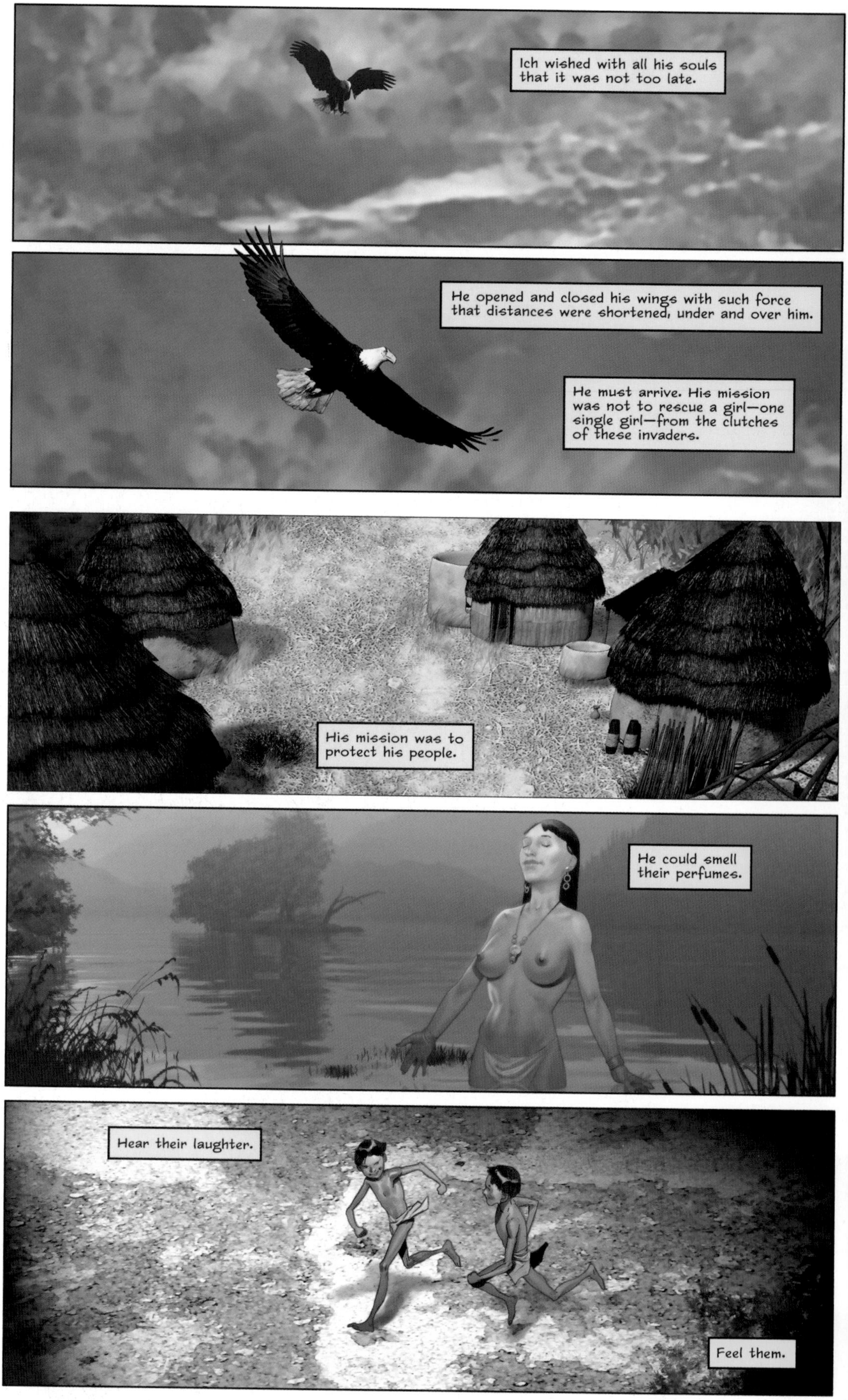
Ich wished with all his souls that it was not too late.
He opened and closed his wings with such force that distances were shortened, under and over him.
He must arrive. His mission was not to rescue a girl—one single girl—from the clutches of these invaders.
His mission was to protect his people.
He could smell their perfumes.
Hear their laughter.
Feel them.

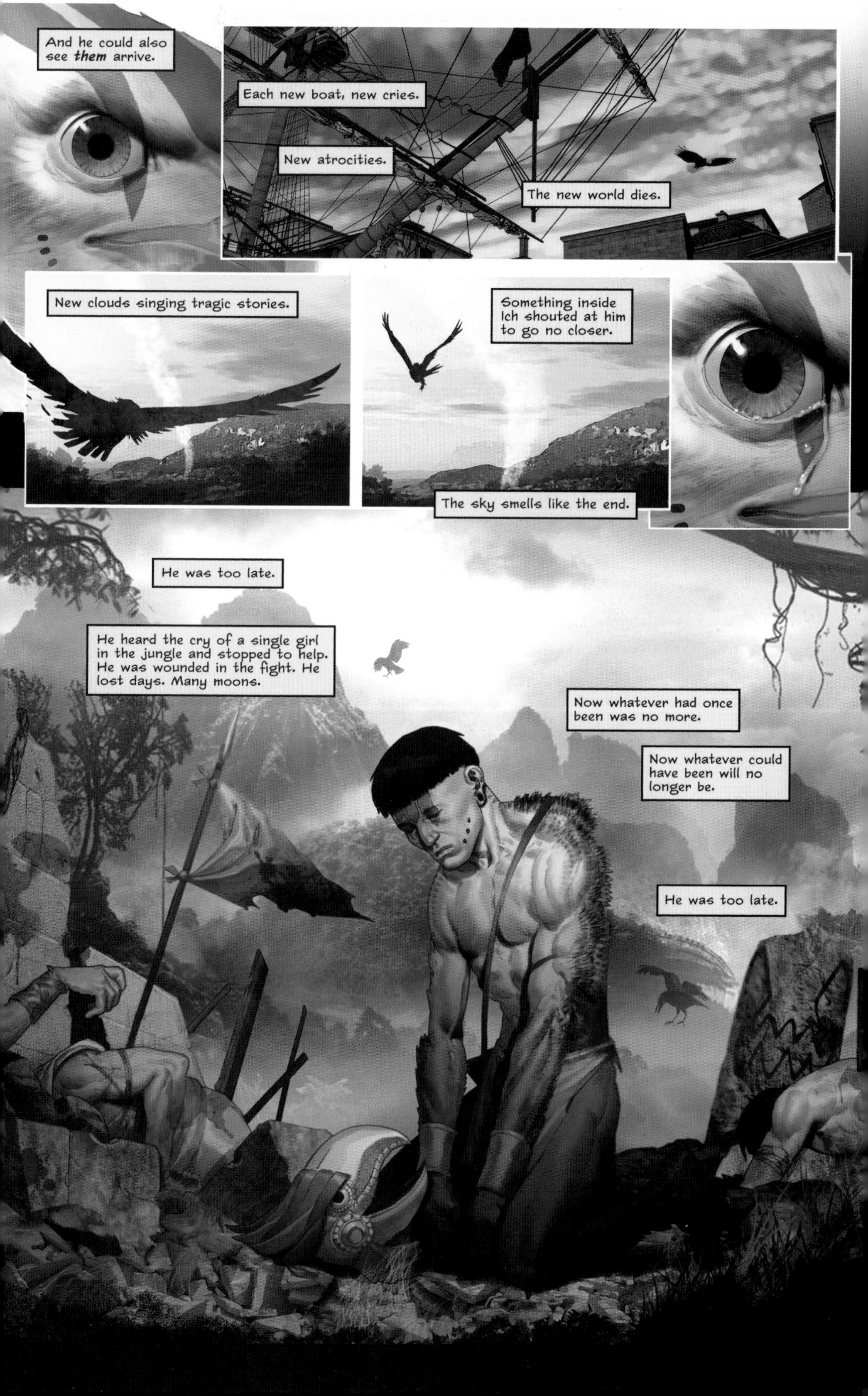
And he could also see *them* arrive.
Each new boat, new cries.
New atrocities.
The new world dies.
New clouds singing tragic stories.
Something inside Ich shouted at him to go no closer.
The sky smells like the end.
He was too late.
He heard the cry of a single girl in the jungle and stopped to help. He was wounded in the fight. He lost days. Many moons.
Now whatever had once been was no more.
Now whatever could have been will no longer be.
He was too late.

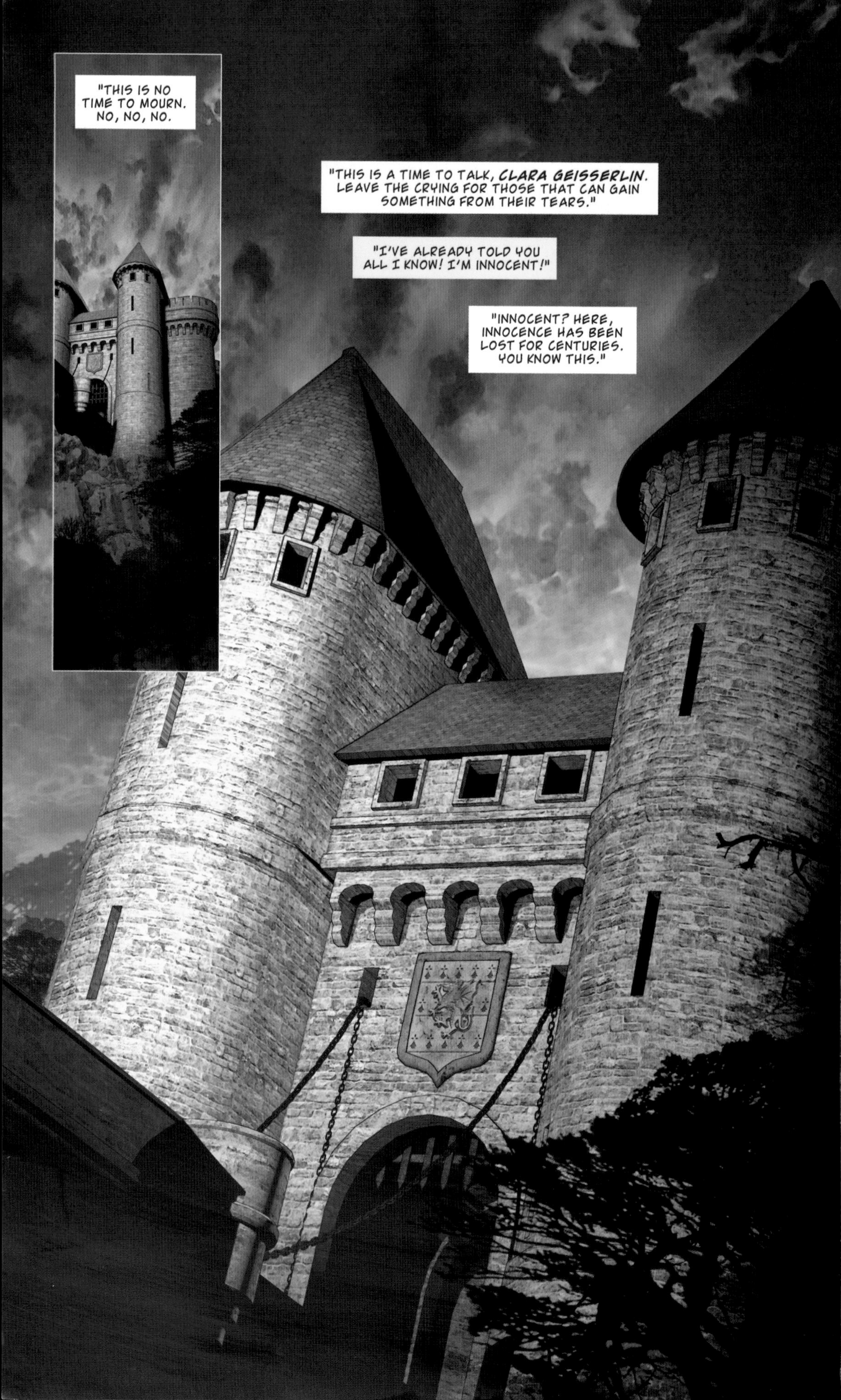
"THIS IS NO TIME TO MOURN. NO, NO, NO.
"THIS IS A TIME TO TALK, CLARA GEISSERLIN. LEAVE THE CRYING FOR THOSE THAT CAN GAIN SOMETHING FROM THEIR TEARS."
"I'VE ALREADY TOLD YOU ALL I KNOW! I'M INNOCENT!"
"INNOCENT? HERE, INNOCENCE HAS BEEN LOST FOR CENTURIES. YOU KNOW THIS."

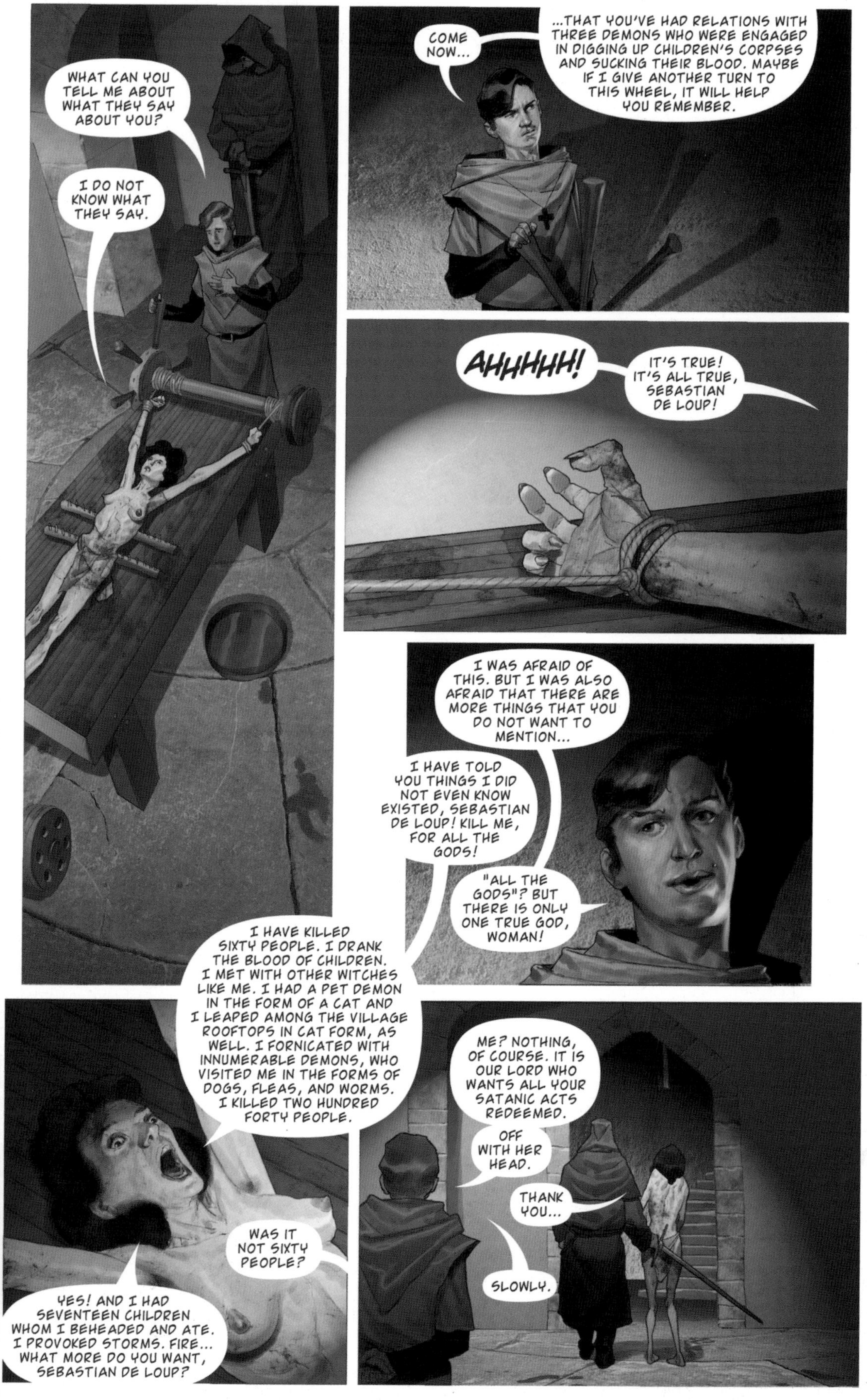
WHAT CAN YOU TELL ME ABOUT WHAT THEY SAY ABOUT YOU?
I DO NOT KNOW WHAT THEY SAY.
COME NOW...
...THAT YOU'VE HAD RELATIONS WITH THREE DEMONS WHO WERE ENGAGED IN DIGGING UP CHILDREN'S CORPSES AND SUCKING THEIR BLOOD. MAYBE IF I GIVE ANOTHER TURN TO THIS WHEEL, IT WILL HELP YOU REMEMBER.
AHHHHH!
IT'S TRUE! IT'S ALL TRUE, SEBASTIAN DE LOUP!
I WAS AFRAID OF THIS. BUT I WAS ALSO AFRAID THAT THERE ARE MORE THINGS THAT YOU DO NOT WANT TO MENTION...
I HAVE TOLD YOU THINGS I DID NOT EVEN KNOW EXISTED, SEBASTIAN DE LOUP! KILL ME, FOR ALL THE GODS!
"ALL THE GODS"? BUT THERE IS ONLY ONE TRUE GOD, WOMAN!
I HAVE KILLED SIXTY PEOPLE. I DRANK THE BLOOD OF CHILDREN. I MET WITH OTHER WITCHES LIKE ME. I HAD A PET DEMON IN THE FORM OF A CAT AND I LEAPED AMONG THE VILLAGE ROOFTOPS IN CAT FORM, AS WELL. I FORNICATED WITH INNUMERABLE DEMONS, WHO VISITED ME IN THE FORMS OF DOGS, FLEAS, AND WORMS. I KILLED TWO HUNDRED FORTY PEOPLE.
WAS IT NOT SIXTY PEOPLE?
YES! AND I HAD SEVENTEEN CHILDREN WHOM I BEHEADED AND ATE. I PROVOKED STORMS. FIRE... WHAT MORE DO YOU WANT, SEBASTIAN DE LOUP?
ME? NOTHING, OF COURSE. IT IS OUR LORD WHO WANTS ALL YOUR SATANIC ACTS REDEEMED.
OFF WITH HER HEAD.
THANK YOU...
SLOWLY.

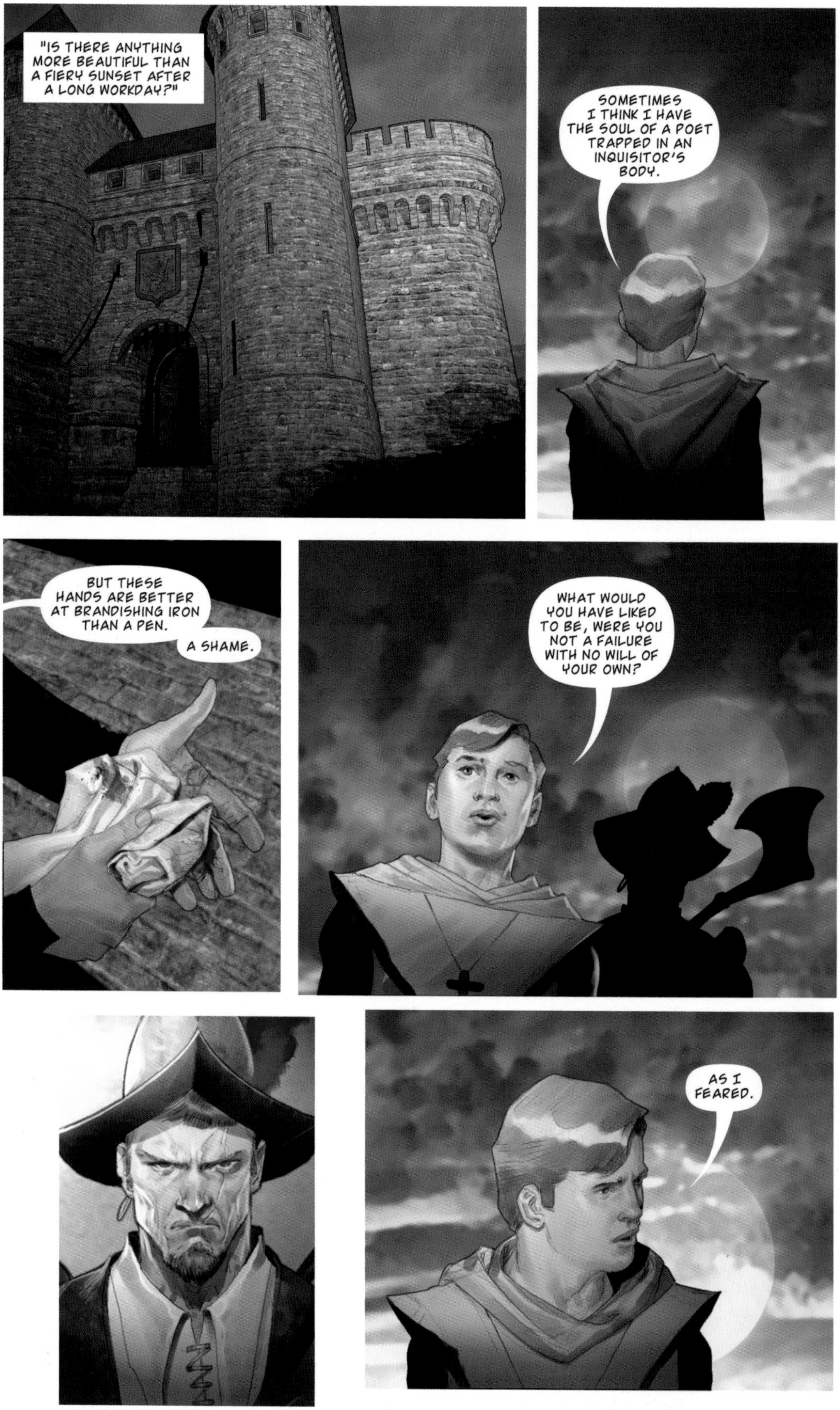
"IS THERE ANYTHING MORE BEAUTIFUL THAN A FIERY SUNSET AFTER A LONG WORKDAY?"
SOMETIMES I THINK I HAVE THE SOUL OF A POET TRAPPED IN AN INQUISITOR'S BODY.
BUT THESE HANDS ARE BETTER AT BRANDISHING IRON THAN A PEN.
A SHAME.
WHAT WOULD YOU HAVE LIKED TO BE, WERE YOU NOT A FAILURE WITH NO WILL OF YOUR OWN?
AS I FEARED.

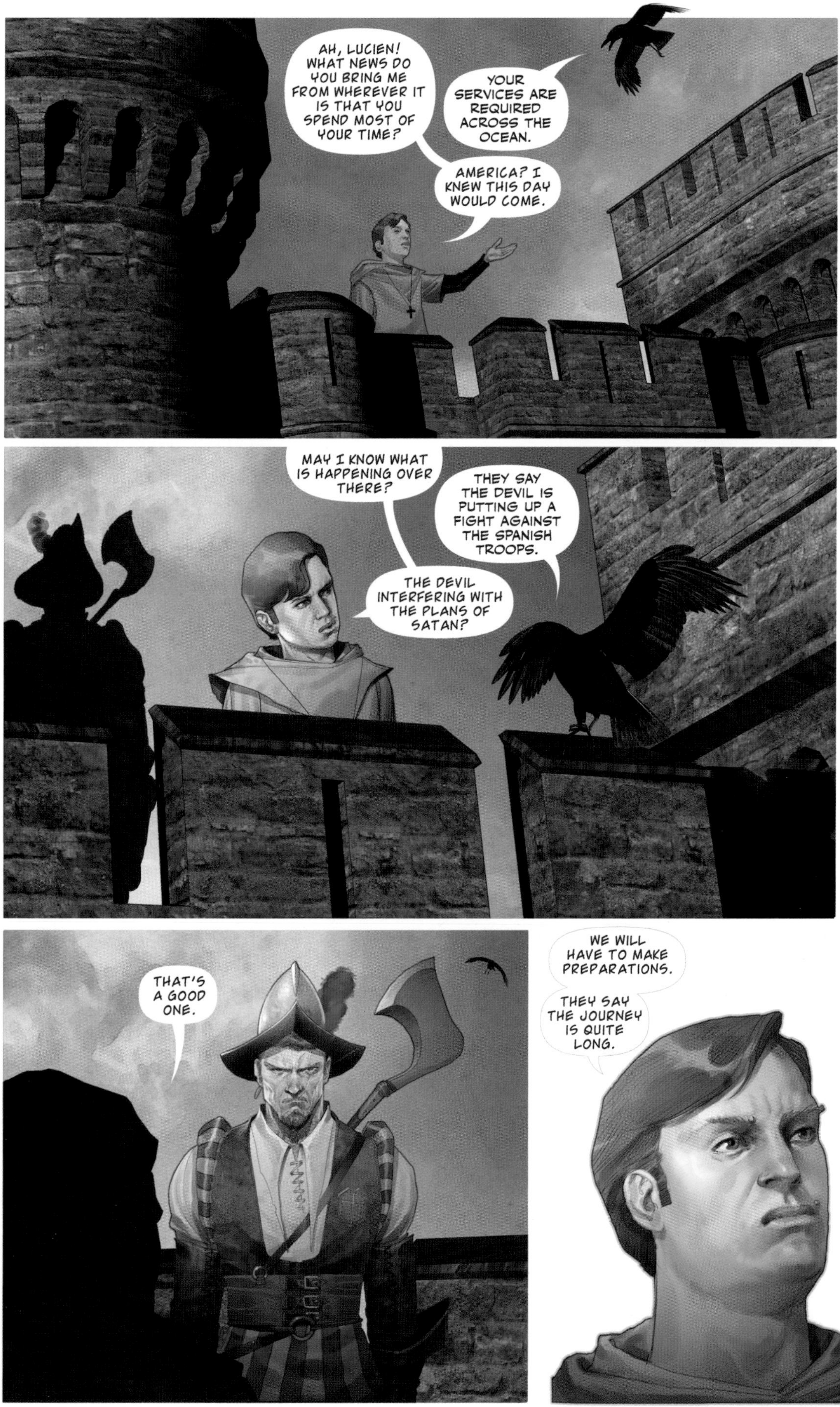
AH, LUCIEN! WHAT NEWS DO YOU BRING ME FROM WHEREVER IT IS THAT YOU SPEND MOST OF YOUR TIME?
YOUR SERVICES ARE REQUIRED ACROSS THE OCEAN.
AMERICA? I KNEW THIS DAY WOULD COME.
MAY I KNOW WHAT IS HAPPENING OVER THERE?
THEY SAY THE DEVIL IS PUTTING UP A FIGHT AGAINST THE SPANISH TROOPS.
THE DEVIL INTERFERING WITH THE PLANS OF SATAN?
THAT'S A GOOD ONE.
WE WILL HAVE TO MAKE PREPARATIONS.
THEY SAY THE JOURNEY IS QUITE LONG.

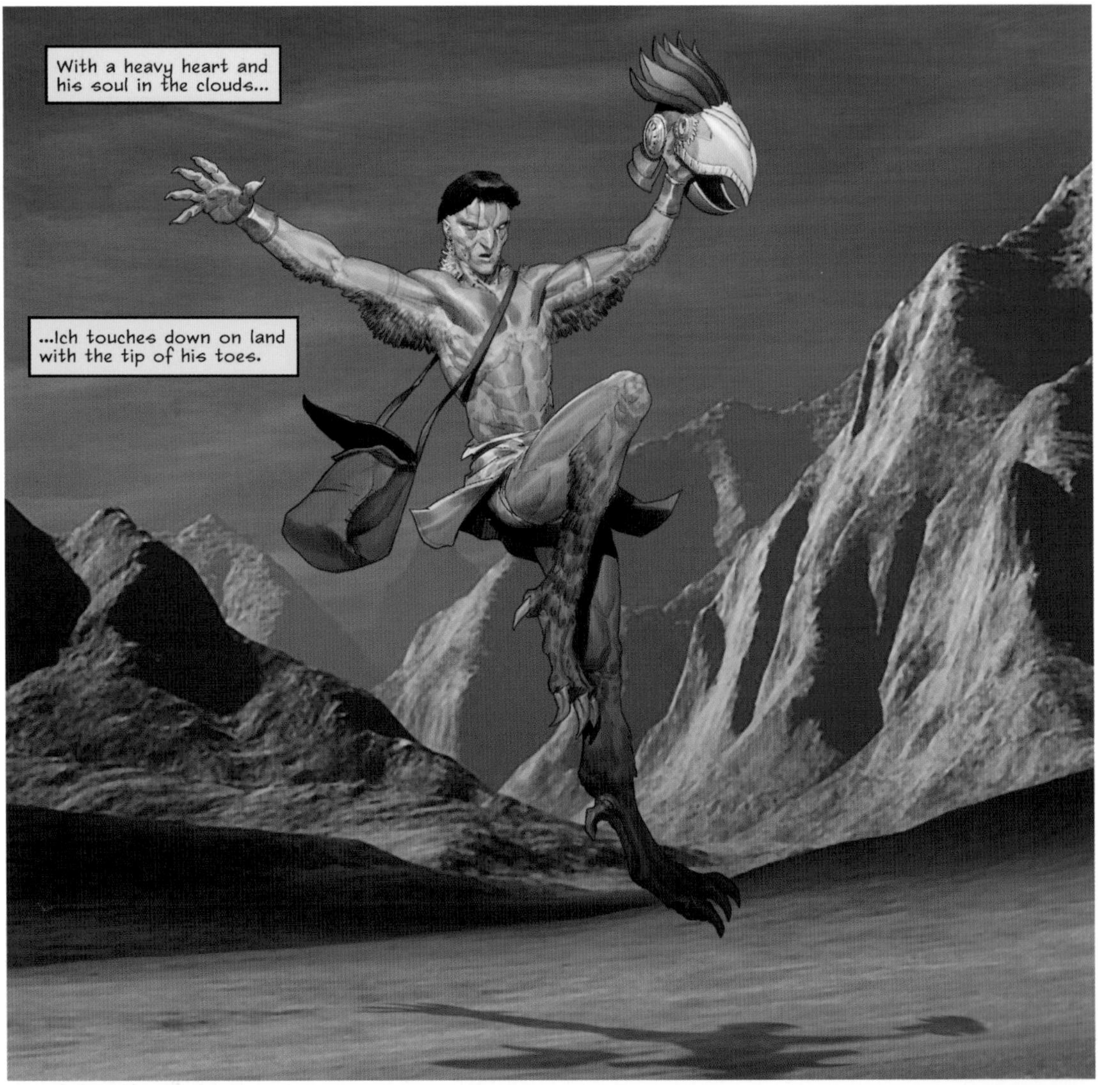
With a heavy heart and his soul in the clouds...
...Ich touches down on land with the tip of his toes.

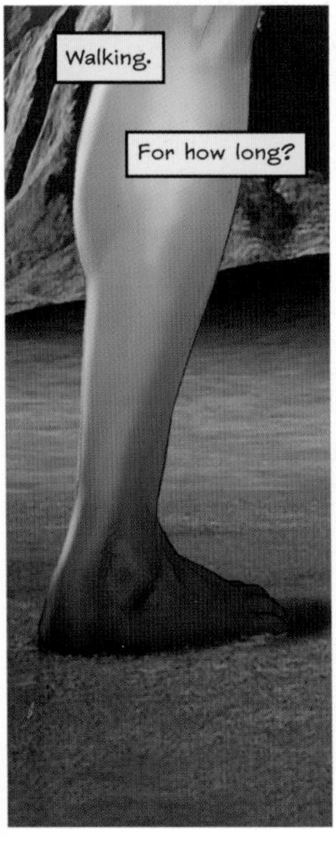
Walking.
For how long?

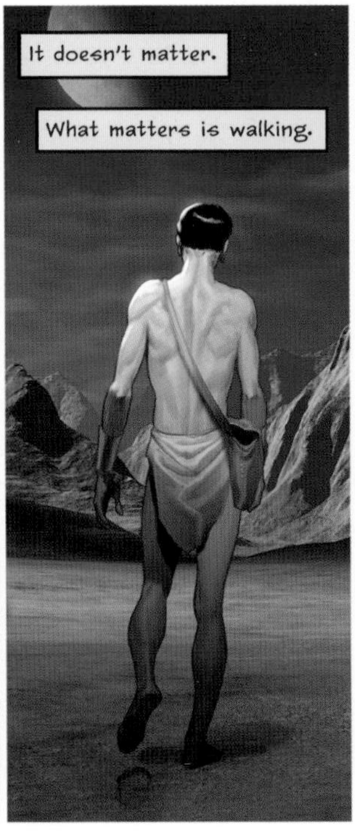
It doesn't matter.
What matters is walking.

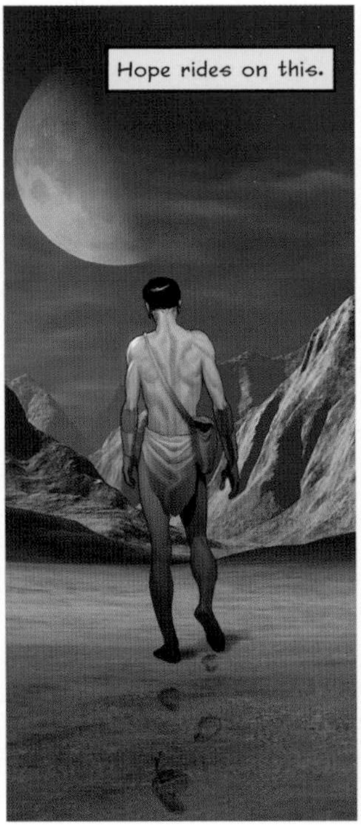
Hope rides on this.

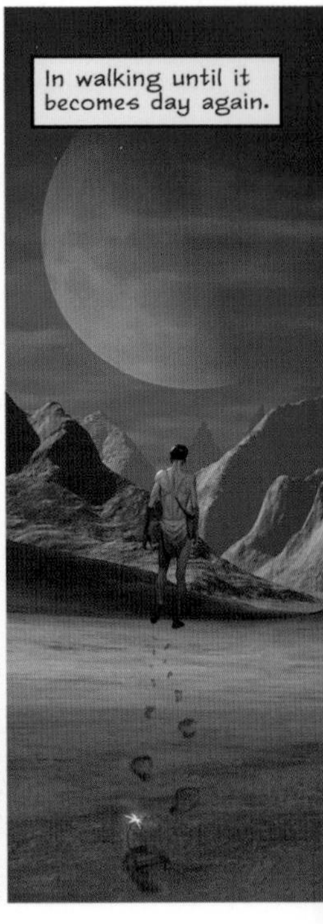
In walking until it becomes day again.

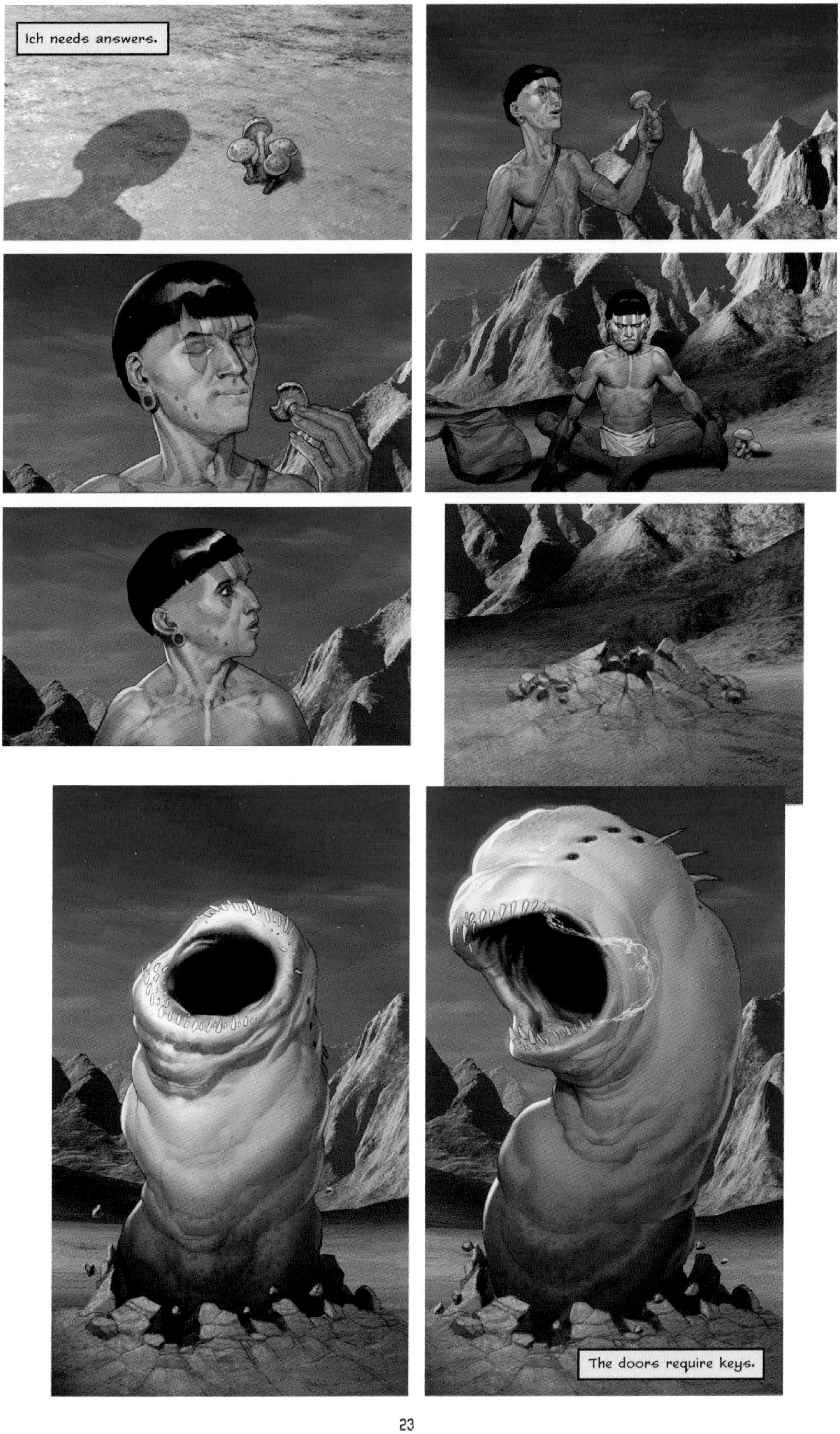
Ich needs answers.
The doors require keys.

The answers always appear...
...when the keys find their door.

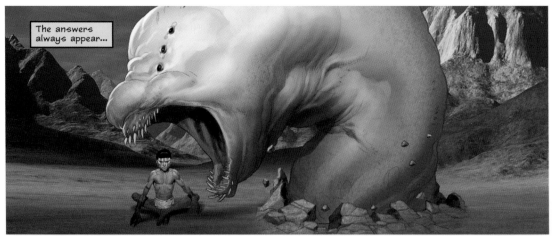

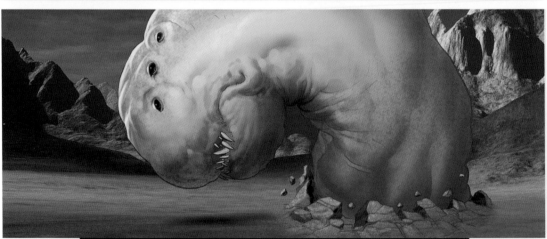

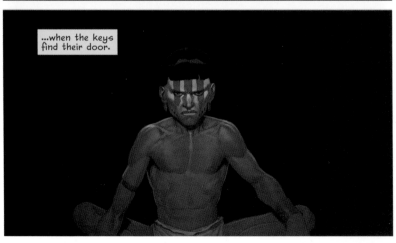

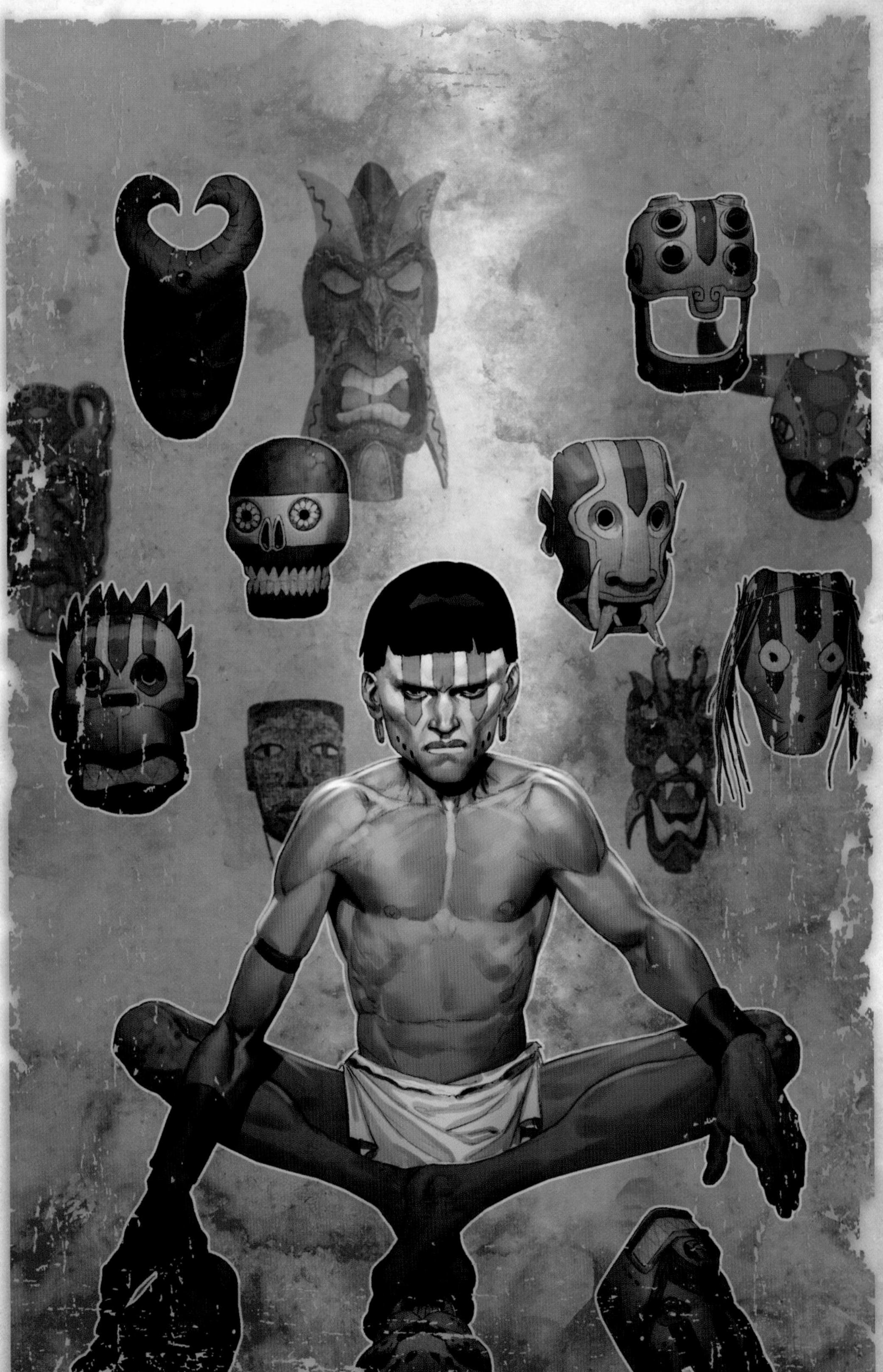

II

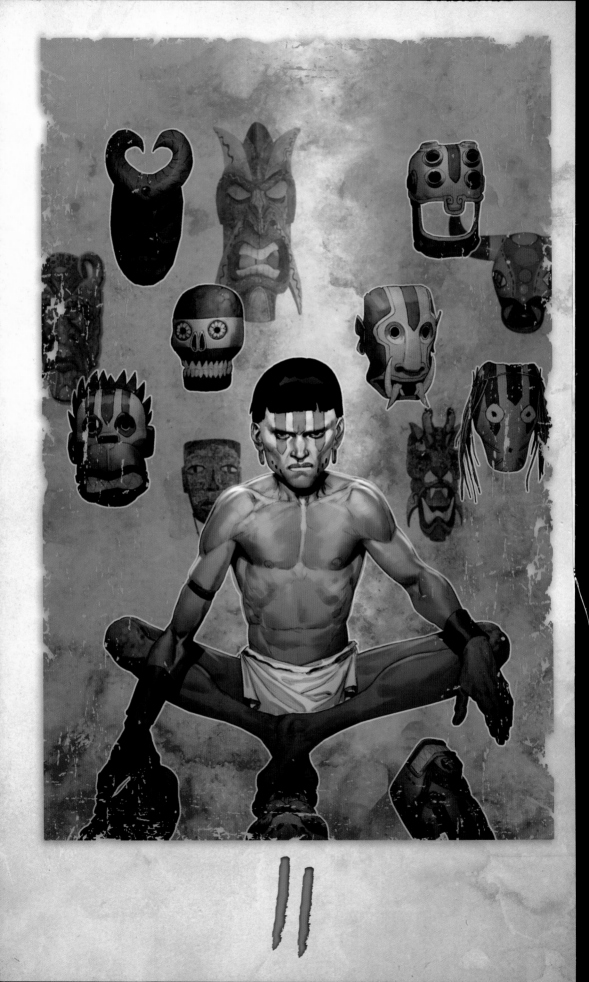

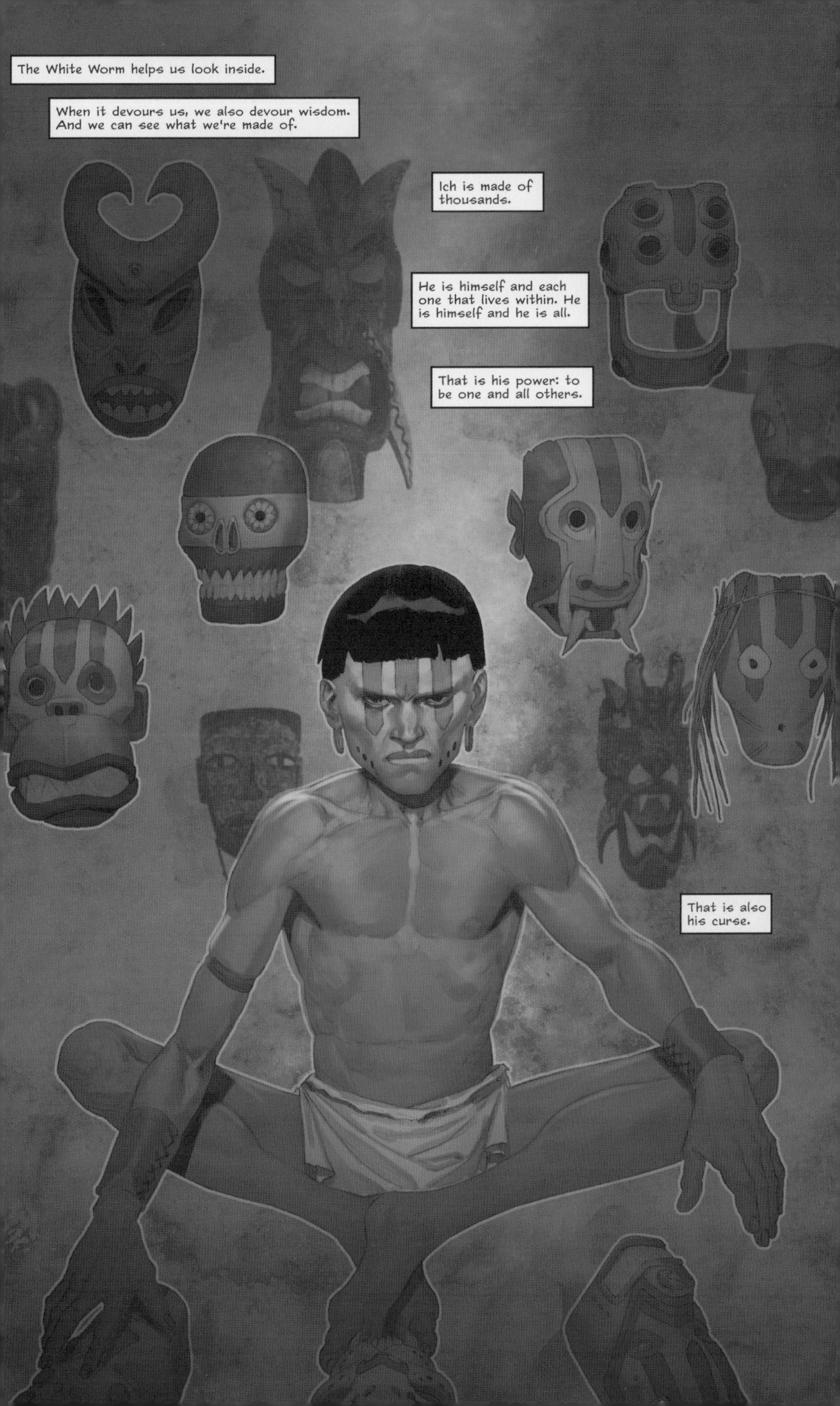
The White Worm helps us look inside.
When it devours us, we also devour wisdom. And we can see what we're made of.
Ich is made of thousands.
He is himself and each one that lives within. He is himself and he is all.
That is his power: to be one and all others.
That is also his curse.

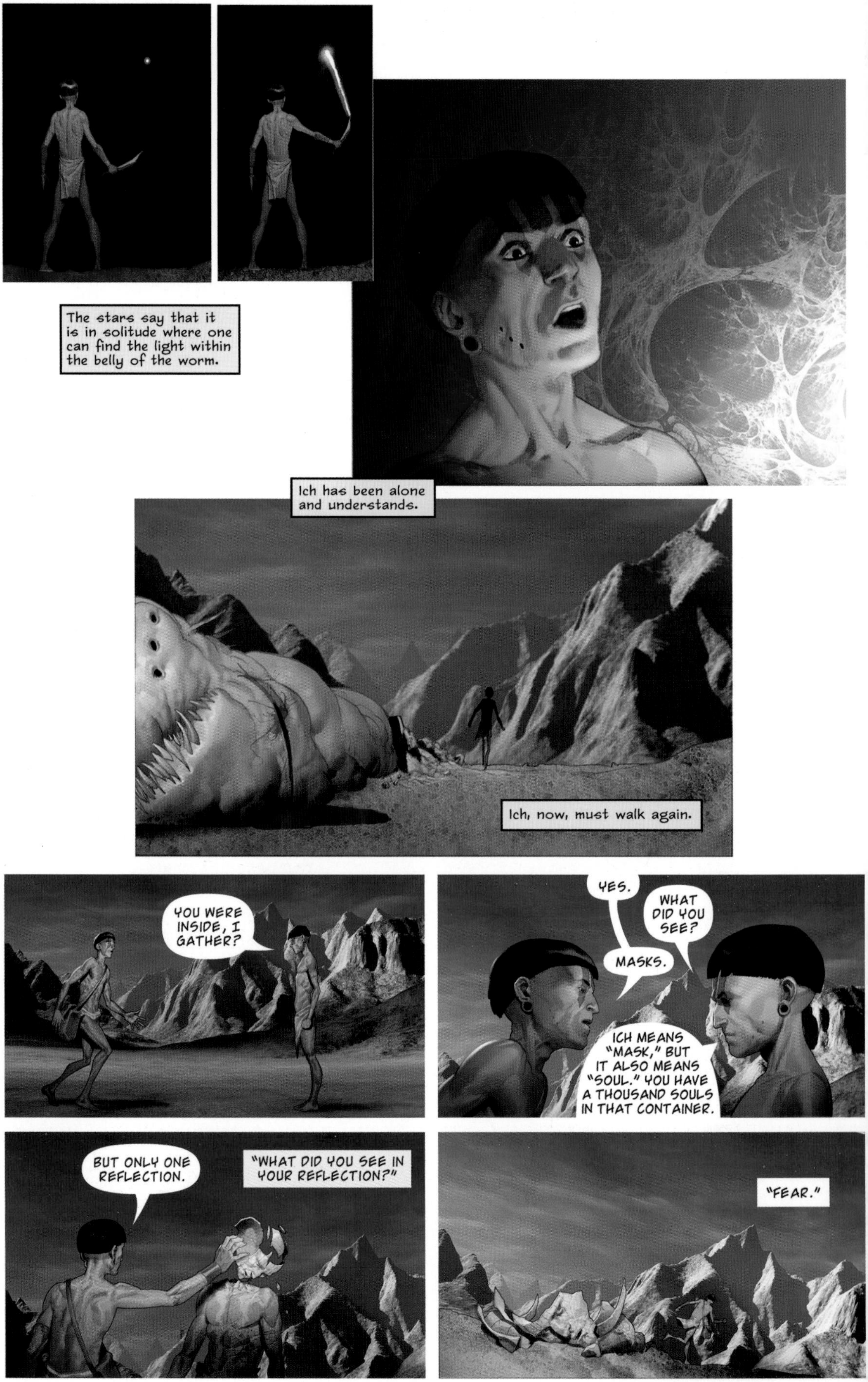

The stars say that it is in solitude where one can find the light within the belly of the worm.
Ich has been alone and understands.
Ich, now, must walk again.
YOU WERE INSIDE, I GATHER?
YES.
WHAT DID YOU SEE?
MASKS.
ICH MEANS "MASK," BUT IT ALSO MEANS "SOUL." YOU HAVE A THOUSAND SOULS IN THAT CONTAINER.
BUT ONLY ONE REFLECTION.
"WHAT DID YOU SEE IN YOUR REFLECTION?"
"FEAR."

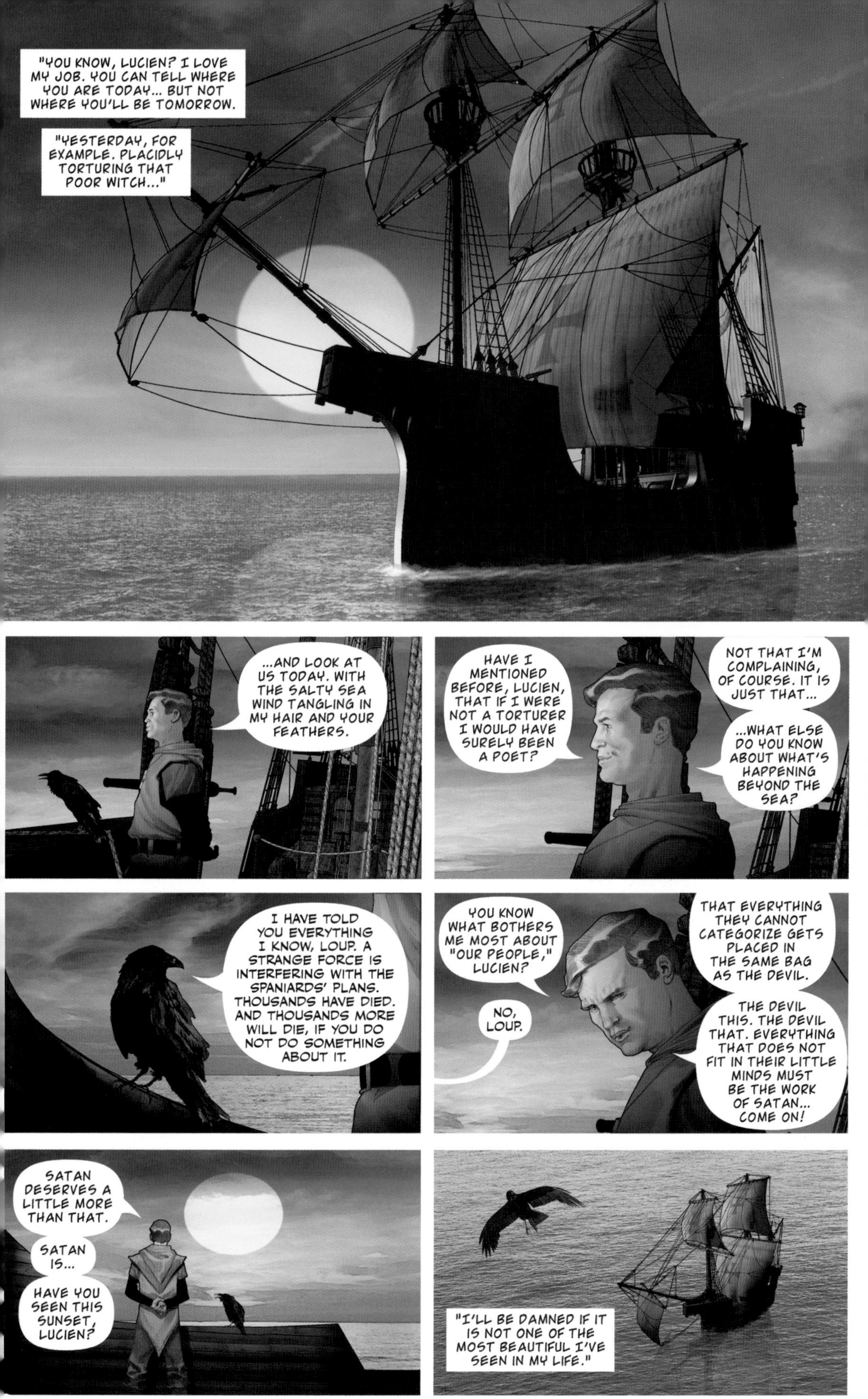
"YOU KNOW, LUCIEN? I LOVE MY JOB. YOU CAN TELL WHERE YOU ARE TODAY... BUT NOT WHERE YOU'LL BE TOMORROW.
"YESTERDAY, FOR EXAMPLE. PLACIDLY TORTURING THAT POOR WITCH..."
...AND LOOK AT US TODAY. WITH THE SALTY SEA WIND TANGLING IN MY HAIR AND YOUR FEATHERS.
HAVE I MENTIONED BEFORE, LUCIEN, THAT IF I WERE NOT A TORTURER I WOULD HAVE SURELY BEEN A POET?
NOT THAT I'M COMPLAINING, OF COURSE. IT IS JUST THAT...
...WHAT ELSE DO YOU KNOW ABOUT WHAT'S HAPPENING BEYOND THE SEA?
I HAVE TOLD YOU EVERYTHING I KNOW, LOUP. A STRANGE FORCE IS INTERFERING WITH THE SPANIARDS' PLANS. THOUSANDS HAVE DIED. AND THOUSANDS MORE WILL DIE, IF YOU DO NOT DO SOMETHING ABOUT IT.
YOU KNOW WHAT BOTHERS ME MOST ABOUT "OUR PEOPLE," LUCIEN?
NO, LOUP.
THAT EVERYTHING THEY CANNOT CATEGORIZE GETS PLACED IN THE SAME BAG AS THE DEVIL.
THE DEVIL THIS. THE DEVIL THAT. EVERYTHING THAT DOES NOT FIT IN THEIR LITTLE MINDS MUST BE THE WORK OF SATAN... COME ON!
SATAN DESERVES A LITTLE MORE THAN THAT.
SATAN IS...
HAVE YOU SEEN THIS SUNSET, LUCIEN?
"I'LL BE DAMNED IF IT IS NOT ONE OF THE MOST BEAUTIFUL I'VE SEEN IN MY LIFE."

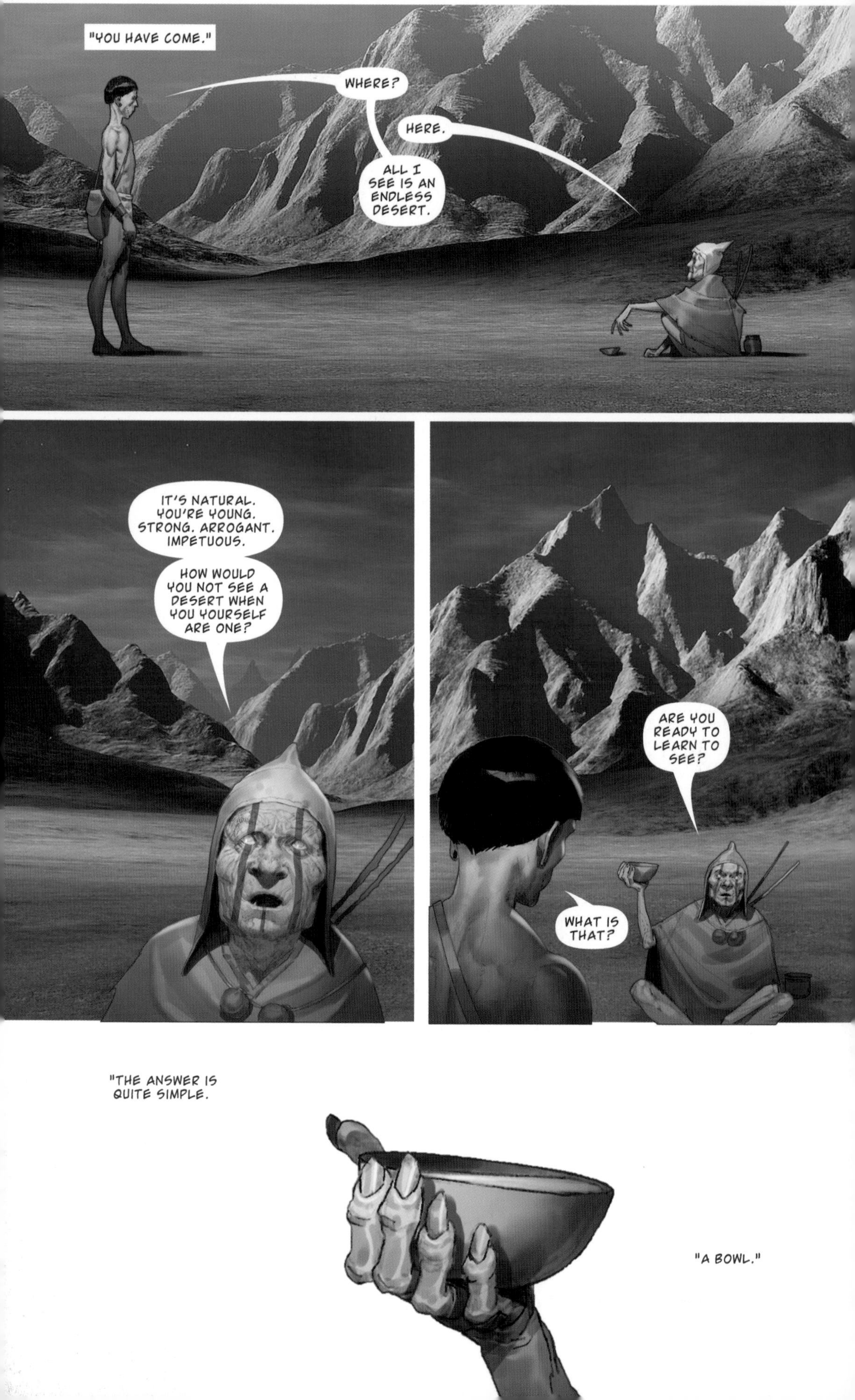
"YOU HAVE COME."
WHERE?
HERE.
ALL I SEE IS AN ENDLESS DESERT.
IT'S NATURAL. YOU'RE YOUNG. STRONG. ARROGANT. IMPETUOUS.
HOW WOULD YOU NOT SEE A DESERT WHEN YOU YOURSELF ARE ONE?
ARE YOU READY TO LEARN TO SEE?
WHAT IS THAT?
"THE ANSWER IS QUITE SIMPLE.
"A BOWL."

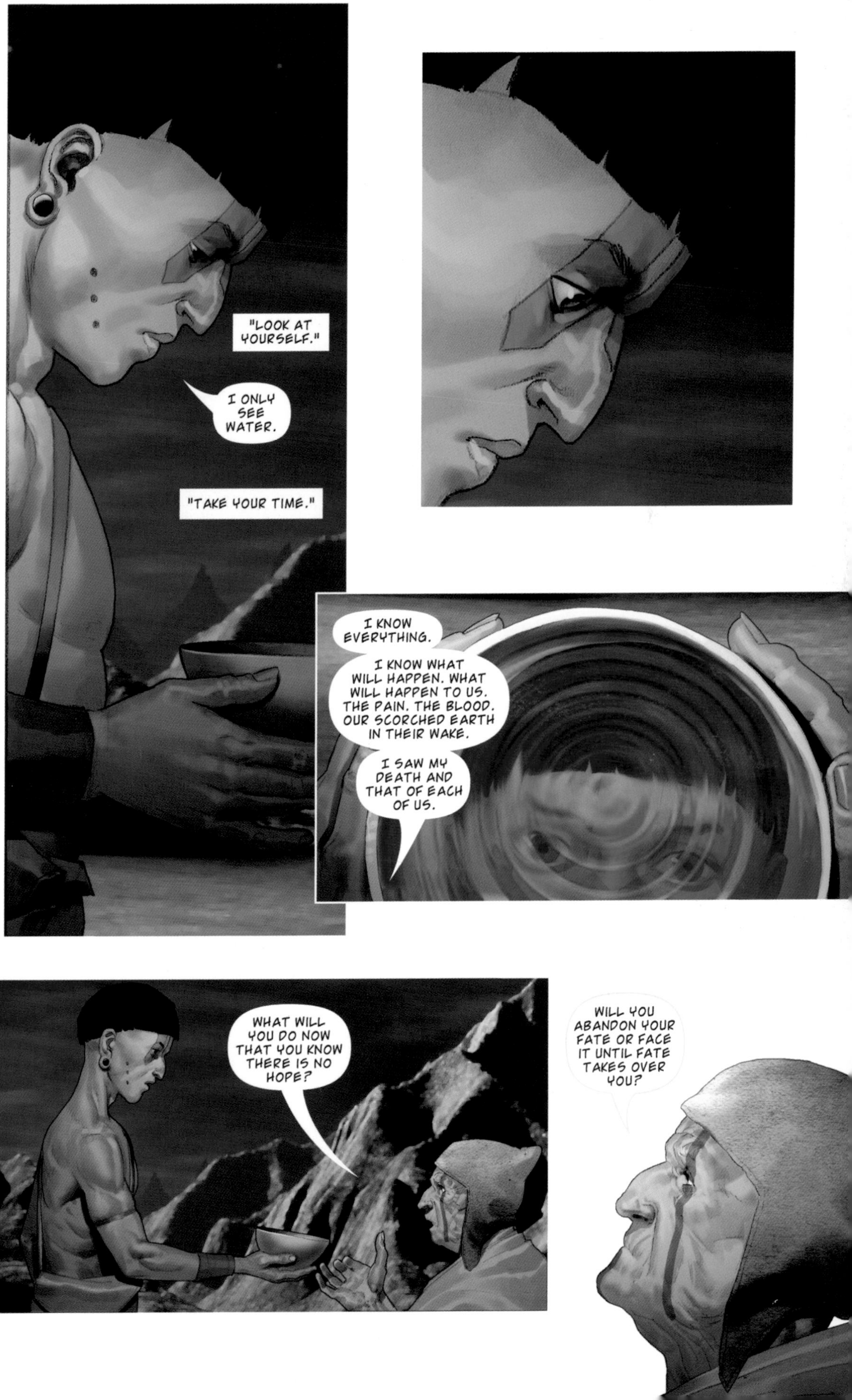
"LOOK AT YOURSELF."
I ONLY SEE WATER.
"TAKE YOUR TIME."
I KNOW EVERYTHING.
I KNOW WHAT WILL HAPPEN. WHAT WILL HAPPEN TO US. THE PAIN. THE BLOOD. OUR SCORCHED EARTH IN THEIR WAKE.
I SAW MY DEATH AND THAT OF EACH OF US.
WHAT WILL YOU DO NOW THAT YOU KNOW THERE IS NO HOPE?
WILL YOU ABANDON YOUR FATE OR FACE IT UNTIL FATE TAKES OVER YOU?

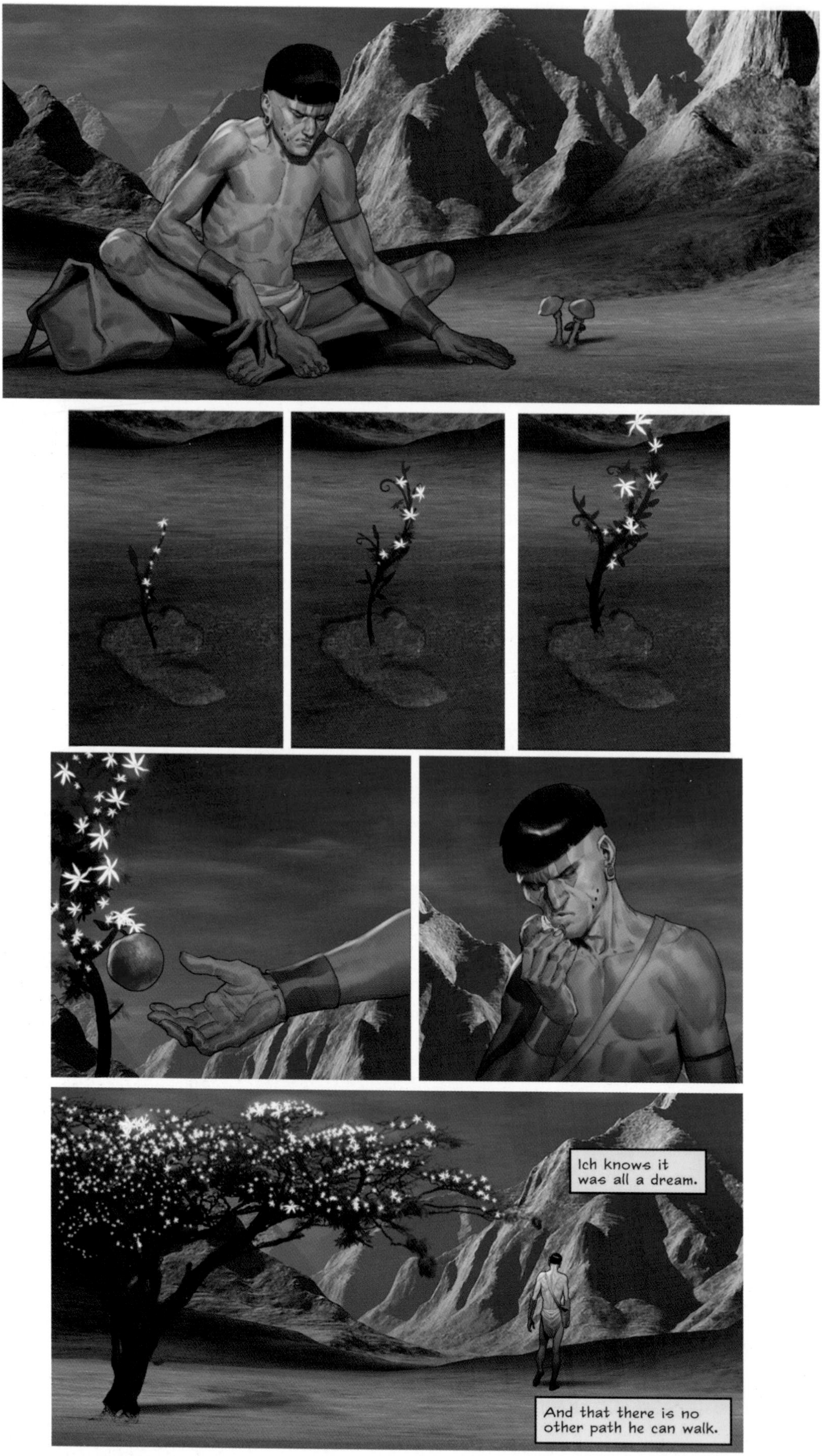
Ich knows it
was all a dream.
And that there is no
other path he can walk.

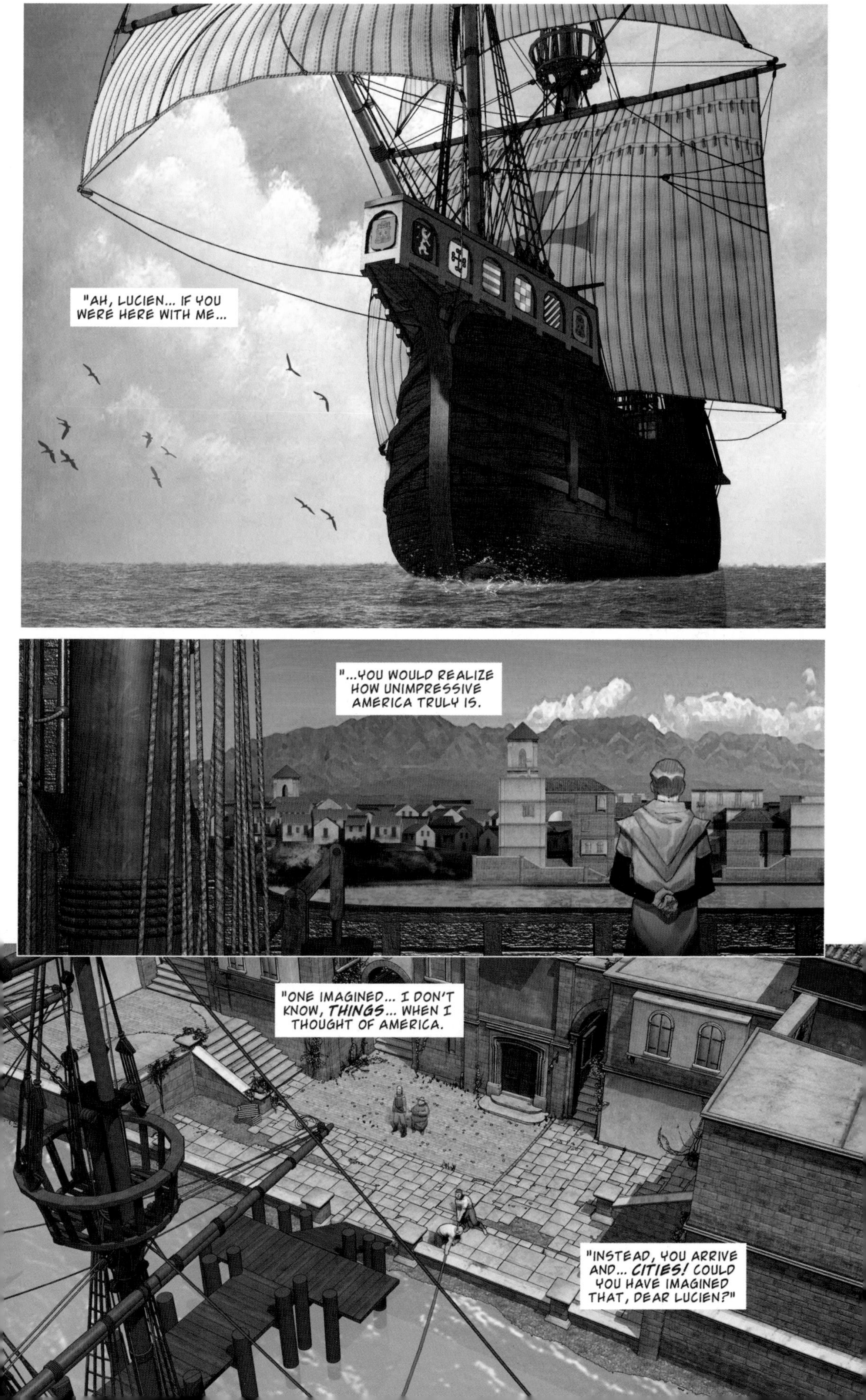
"AH, LUCIEN... IF YOU WERE HERE WITH ME...
"...YOU WOULD REALIZE HOW UNIMPRESSIVE AMERICA TRULY IS.
"ONE IMAGINED... I DON'T KNOW, THINGS... WHEN I THOUGHT OF AMERICA.
"INSTEAD, YOU ARRIVE AND... CITIES! COULD YOU HAVE IMAGINED THAT, DEAR LUCIEN?"

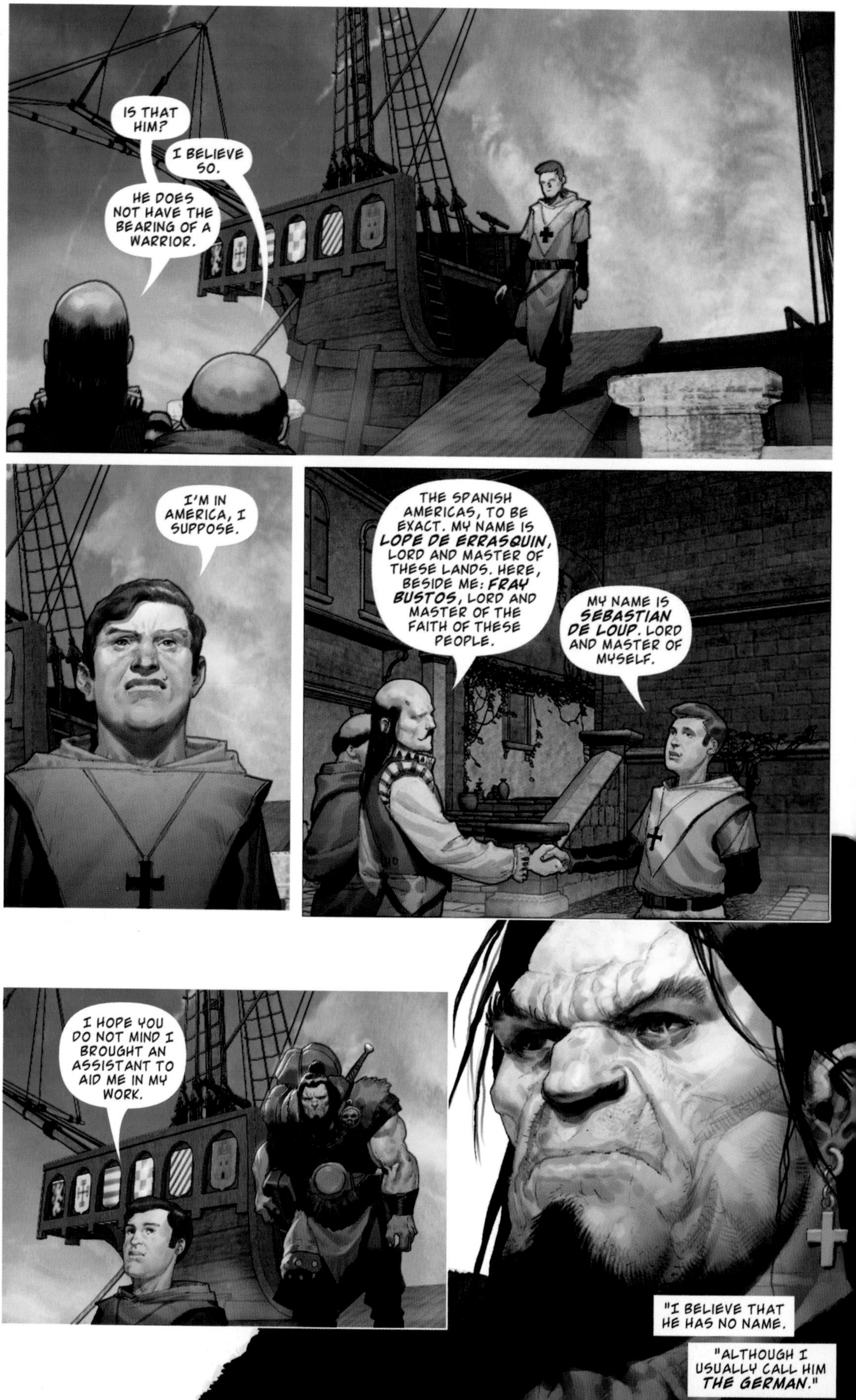
IS THAT HIM?
I BELIEVE SO.
HE DOES NOT HAVE THE BEARING OF A WARRIOR.
I'M IN AMERICA, I SUPPOSE.
THE SPANISH AMERICAS, TO BE EXACT. MY NAME IS LOPE DE ERRASQUIN, LORD AND MASTER OF THESE LANDS. HERE, BESIDE ME: FRAY BUSTOS, LORD AND MASTER OF THE FAITH OF THESE PEOPLE.
MY NAME IS SEBASTIAN DE LOUP. LORD AND MASTER OF MYSELF.
I HOPE YOU DO NOT MIND I BROUGHT AN ASSISTANT TO AID ME IN MY WORK.
"I BELIEVE THAT HE HAS NO NAME.
"ALTHOUGH I USUALLY CALL HIM THE GERMAN."

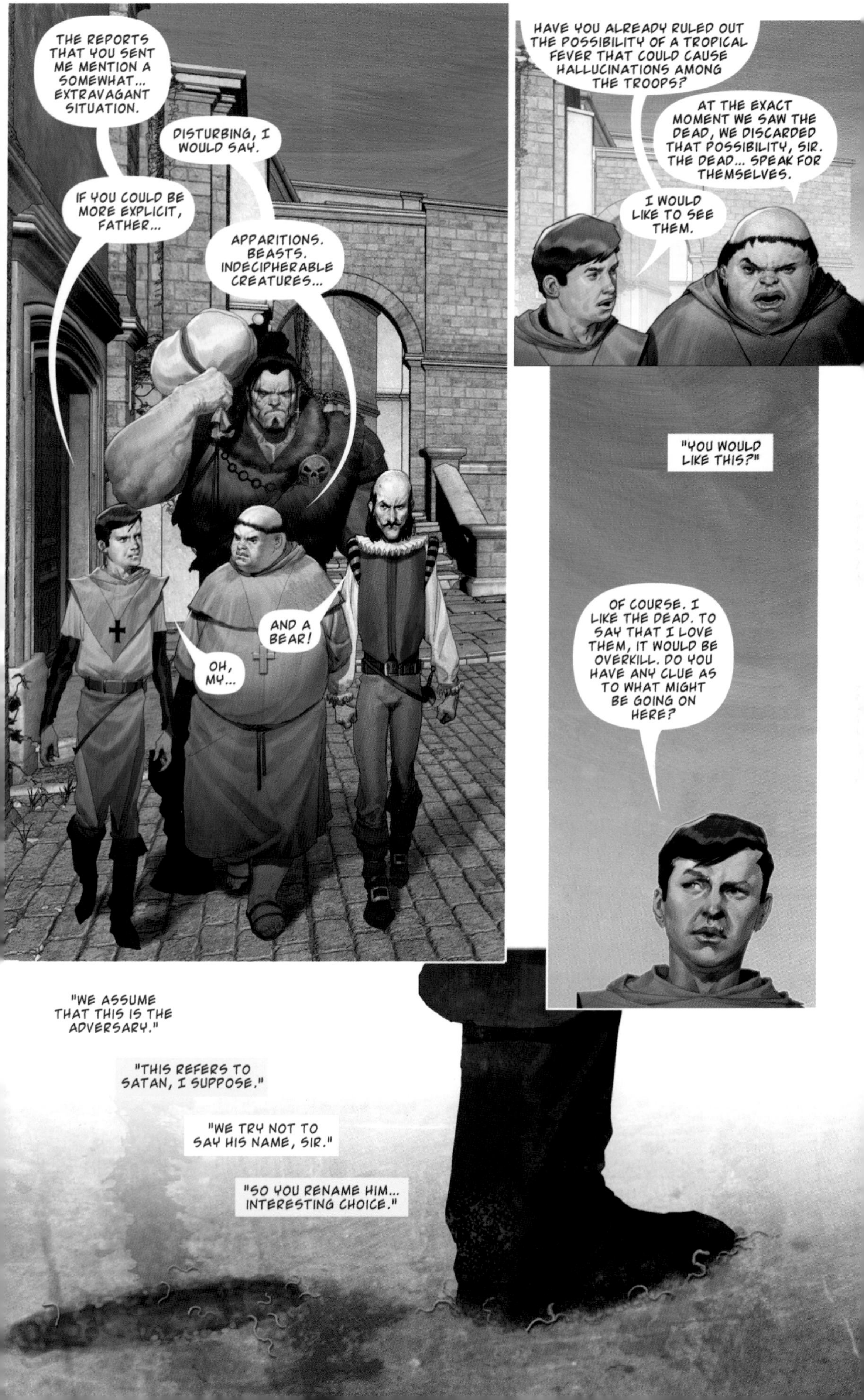
THE REPORTS THAT YOU SENT ME MENTION A SOMEWHAT... EXTRAVAGANT SITUATION.
DISTURBING, I WOULD SAY.
IF YOU COULD BE MORE EXPLICIT, FATHER...
APPARITIONS. BEASTS. INDECIPHERABLE CREATURES...
AND A BEAR!
OH, MY...
HAVE YOU ALREADY RULED OUT THE POSSIBILITY OF A TROPICAL FEVER THAT COULD CAUSE HALLUCINATIONS AMONG THE TROOPS?
AT THE EXACT MOMENT WE SAW THE DEAD, WE DISCARDED THAT POSSIBILITY, SIR. THE DEAD... SPEAK FOR THEMSELVES.
I WOULD LIKE TO SEE THEM.
"YOU WOULD LIKE THIS?"
OF COURSE. I LIKE THE DEAD. TO SAY THAT I LOVE THEM, IT WOULD BE OVERKILL. DO YOU HAVE ANY CLUE AS TO WHAT MIGHT BE GOING ON HERE?
"WE ASSUME THAT THIS IS THE ADVERSARY."
"THIS REFERS TO SATAN, I SUPPOSE."
"WE TRY NOT TO SAY HIS NAME, SIR."
"SO YOU RENAME HIM... INTERESTING CHOICE."

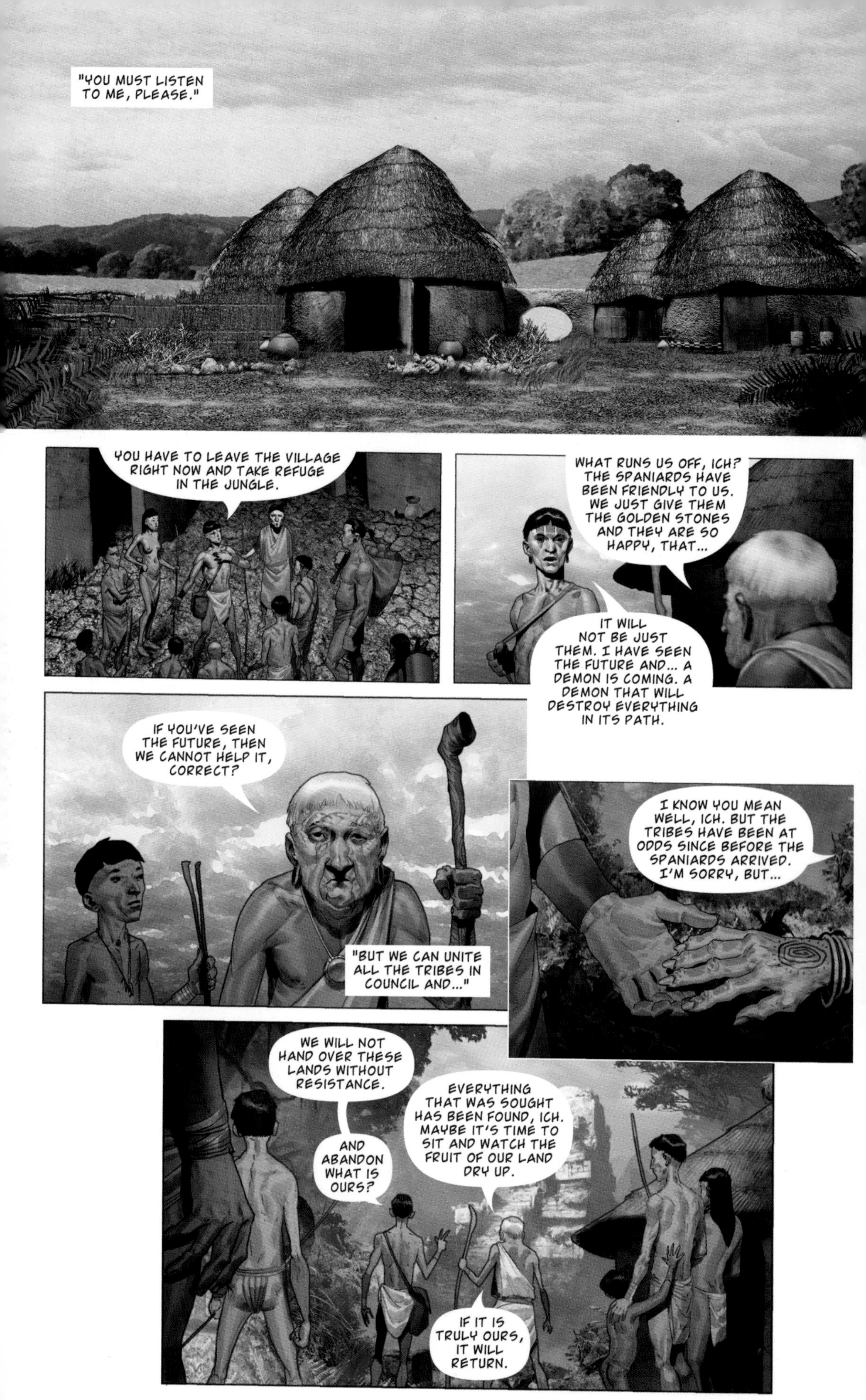
"YOU MUST LISTEN TO ME, PLEASE."
YOU HAVE TO LEAVE THE VILLAGE RIGHT NOW AND TAKE REFUGE IN THE JUNGLE.
WHAT RUNS US OFF, ICH? THE SPANIARDS HAVE BEEN FRIENDLY TO US. WE JUST GIVE THEM THE GOLDEN STONES AND THEY ARE SO HAPPY, THAT...
IT WILL NOT BE JUST THEM. I HAVE SEEN THE FUTURE AND... A DEMON IS COMING. A DEMON THAT WILL DESTROY EVERYTHING IN ITS PATH.
IF YOU'VE SEEN THE FUTURE, THEN WE CANNOT HELP IT, CORRECT?
"BUT WE CAN UNITE ALL THE TRIBES IN COUNCIL AND..."
I KNOW YOU MEAN WELL, ICH. BUT THE TRIBES HAVE BEEN AT ODDS SINCE BEFORE THE SPANIARDS ARRIVED. I'M SORRY, BUT...
WE WILL NOT HAND OVER THESE LANDS WITHOUT RESISTANCE.
AND ABANDON WHAT IS OURS?
EVERYTHING THAT WAS SOUGHT HAS BEEN FOUND, ICH. MAYBE IT'S TIME TO SIT AND WATCH THE FRUIT OF OUR LAND DRY UP.
IF IT IS TRULY OURS, IT WILL RETURN.

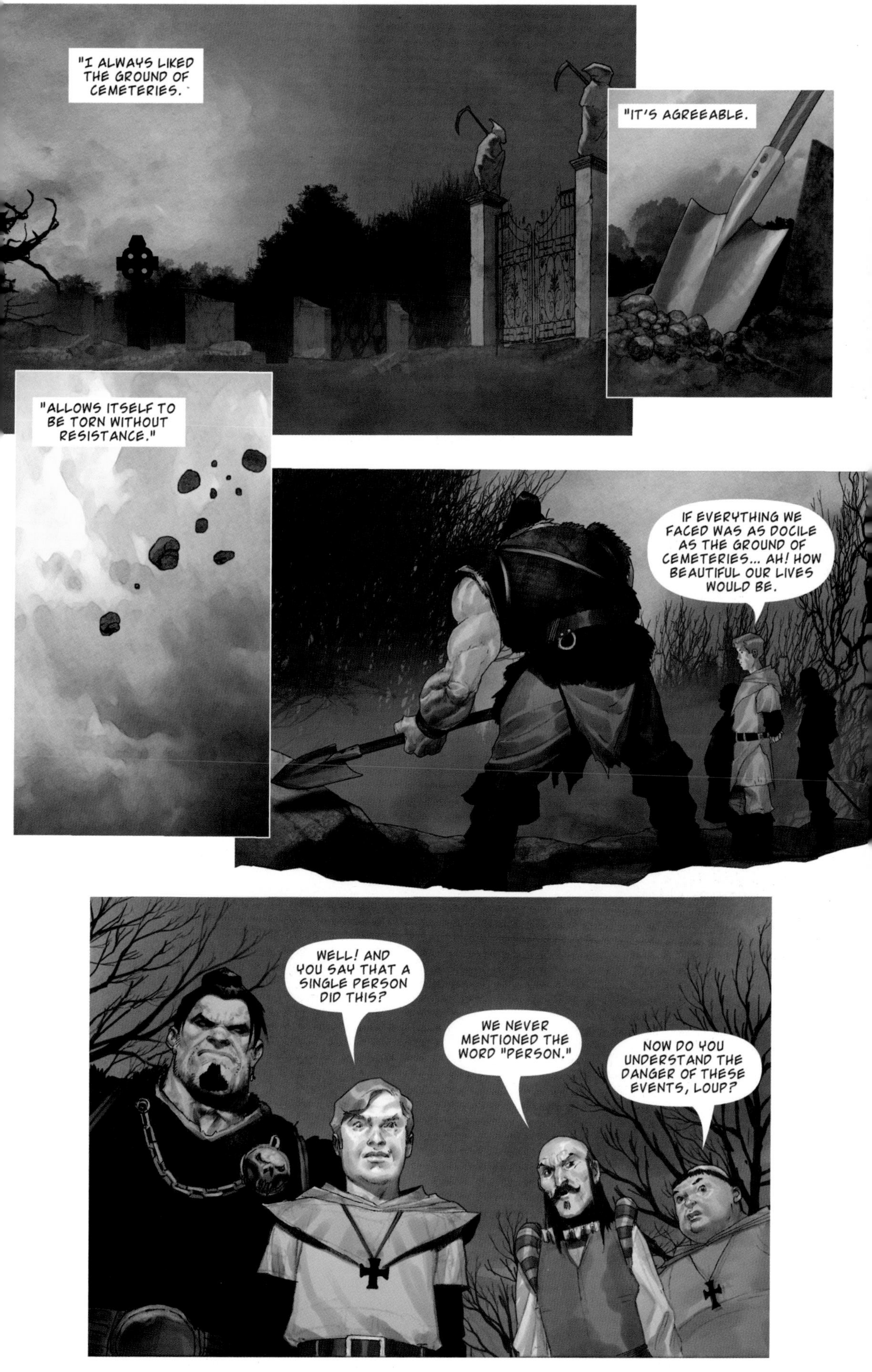
"I ALWAYS LIKED THE GROUND OF CEMETERIES.
"IT'S AGREEABLE.
"ALLOWS ITSELF TO BE TORN WITHOUT RESISTANCE."
IF EVERYTHING WE FACED WAS AS DOCILE AS THE GROUND OF CEMETERIES... AH! HOW BEAUTIFUL OUR LIVES WOULD BE.
WELL! AND YOU SAY THAT A SINGLE PERSON DID THIS?
WE NEVER MENTIONED THE WORD "PERSON."
NOW DO YOU UNDERSTAND THE DANGER OF THESE EVENTS, LOUP?

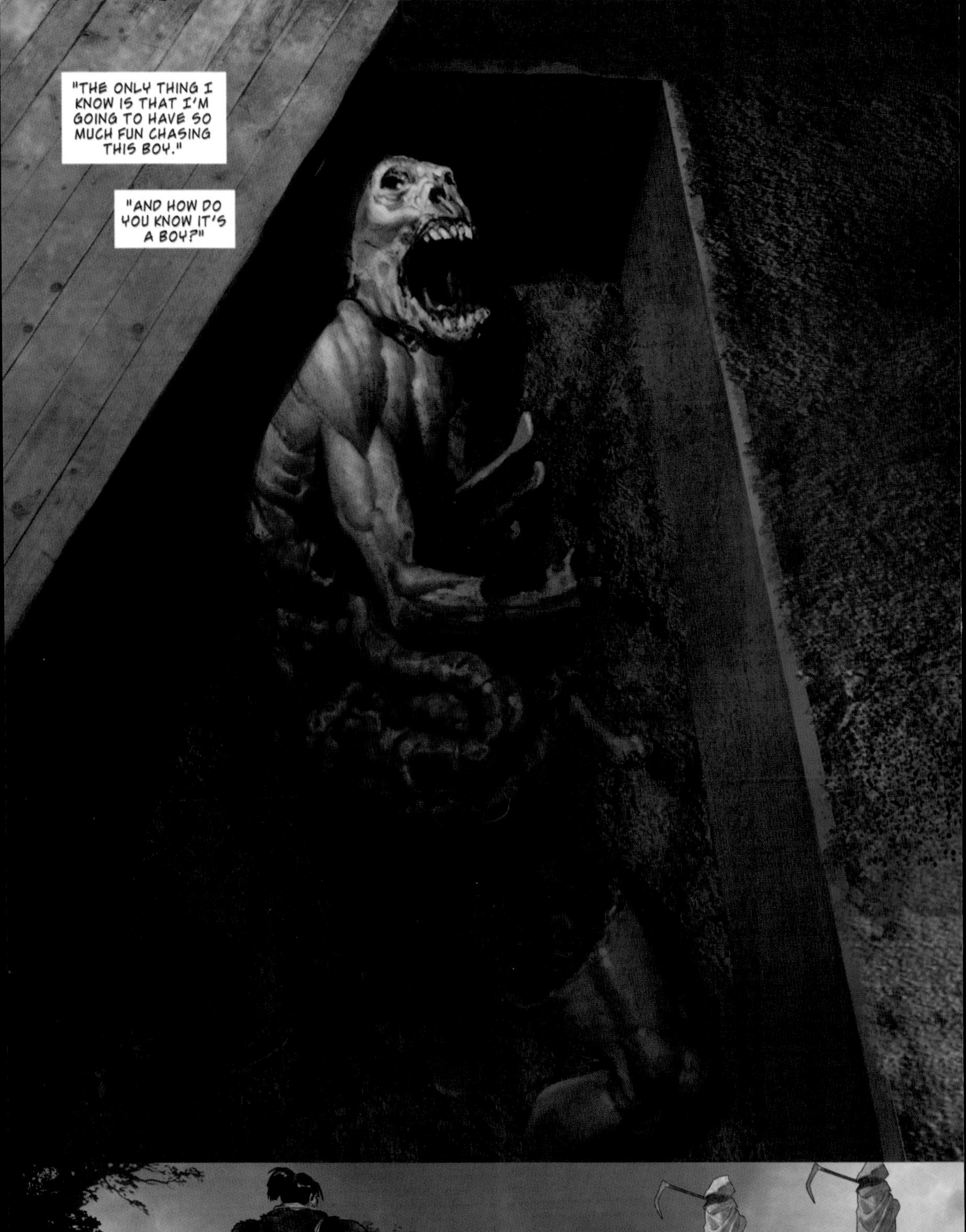
"THE ONLY THING I KNOW IS THAT I'M GOING TO HAVE SO MUCH FUN CHASING THIS BOY."
"AND HOW DO YOU KNOW IT'S A BOY?"

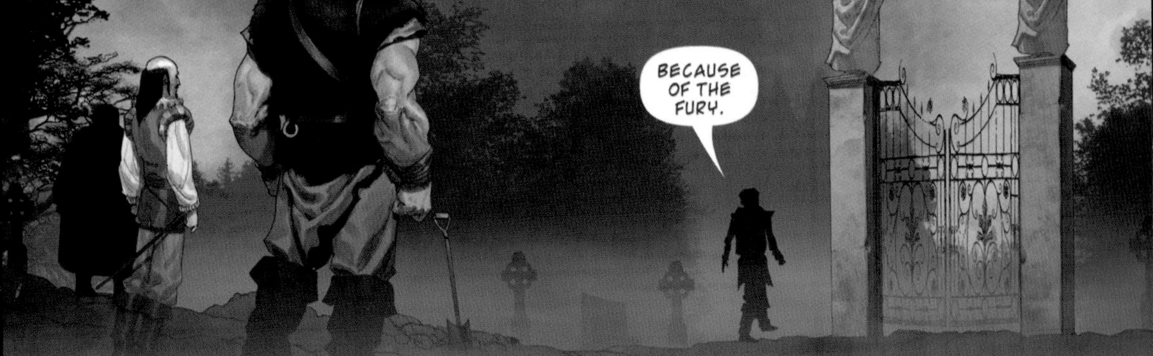
BECAUSE OF THE FURY.

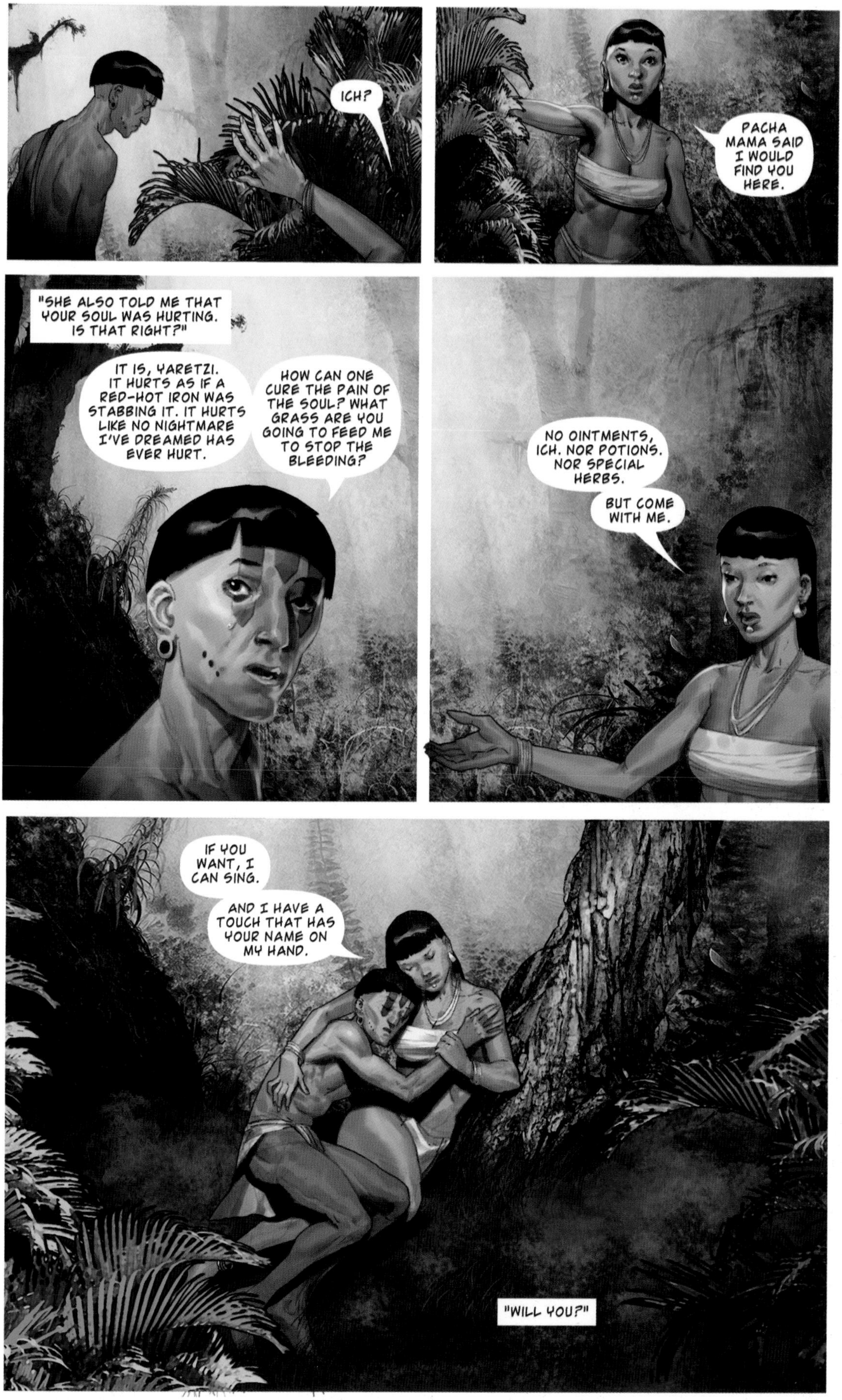
ICH?
PACHA MAMA SAID I WOULD FIND YOU HERE.
"SHE ALSO TOLD ME THAT YOUR SOUL WAS HURTING. IS THAT RIGHT?"
IT IS, YARETZI. IT HURTS AS IF A RED-HOT IRON WAS STABBING IT. IT HURTS LIKE NO NIGHTMARE I'VE DREAMED HAS EVER HURT.
HOW CAN ONE CURE THE PAIN OF THE SOUL? WHAT GRASS ARE YOU GOING TO FEED ME TO STOP THE BLEEDING?
NO OINTMENTS, ICH. NOR POTIONS. NOR SPECIAL HERBS.
BUT COME WITH ME.
IF YOU WANT, I CAN SING.
AND I HAVE A TOUCH THAT HAS YOUR NAME ON MY HAND.
"WILL YOU?"

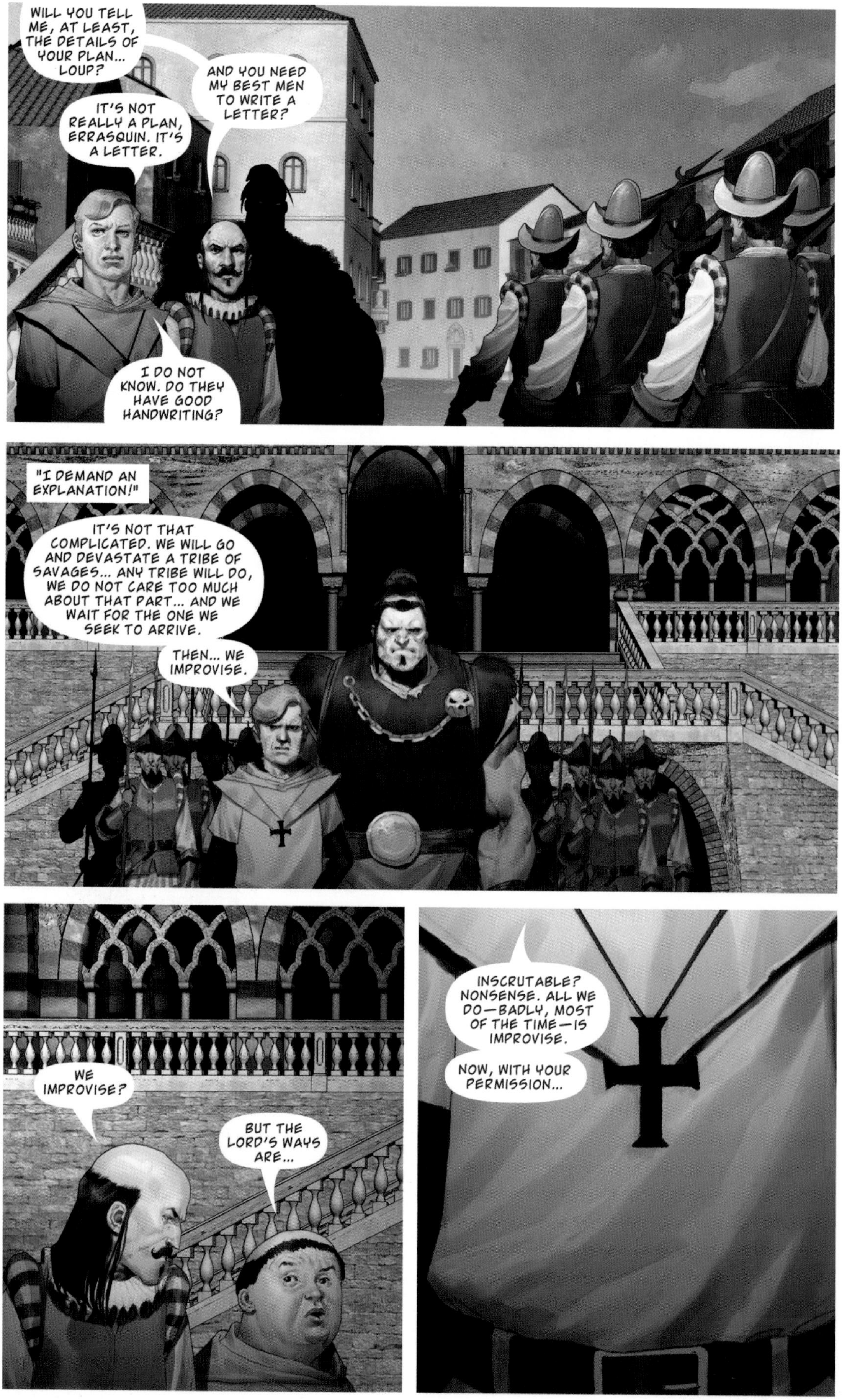
WILL YOU TELL ME, AT LEAST, THE DETAILS OF YOUR PLAN... LOUP?
IT'S NOT REALLY A PLAN, ERRASQUIN. IT'S A LETTER.
AND YOU NEED MY BEST MEN TO WRITE A LETTER?
I DO NOT KNOW. DO THEY HAVE GOOD HANDWRITING?
"I DEMAND AN EXPLANATION!"
IT'S NOT THAT COMPLICATED. WE WILL GO AND DEVASTATE A TRIBE OF SAVAGES... ANY TRIBE WILL DO, WE DO NOT CARE TOO MUCH ABOUT THAT PART... AND WE WAIT FOR THE ONE WE SEEK TO ARRIVE.
THEN... WE IMPROVISE.
WE IMPROVISE?
BUT THE LORD'S WAYS ARE...
INSCRUTABLE? NONSENSE. ALL WE DO—BADLY, MOST OF THE TIME—IS IMPROVISE.
NOW, WITH YOUR PERMISSION...

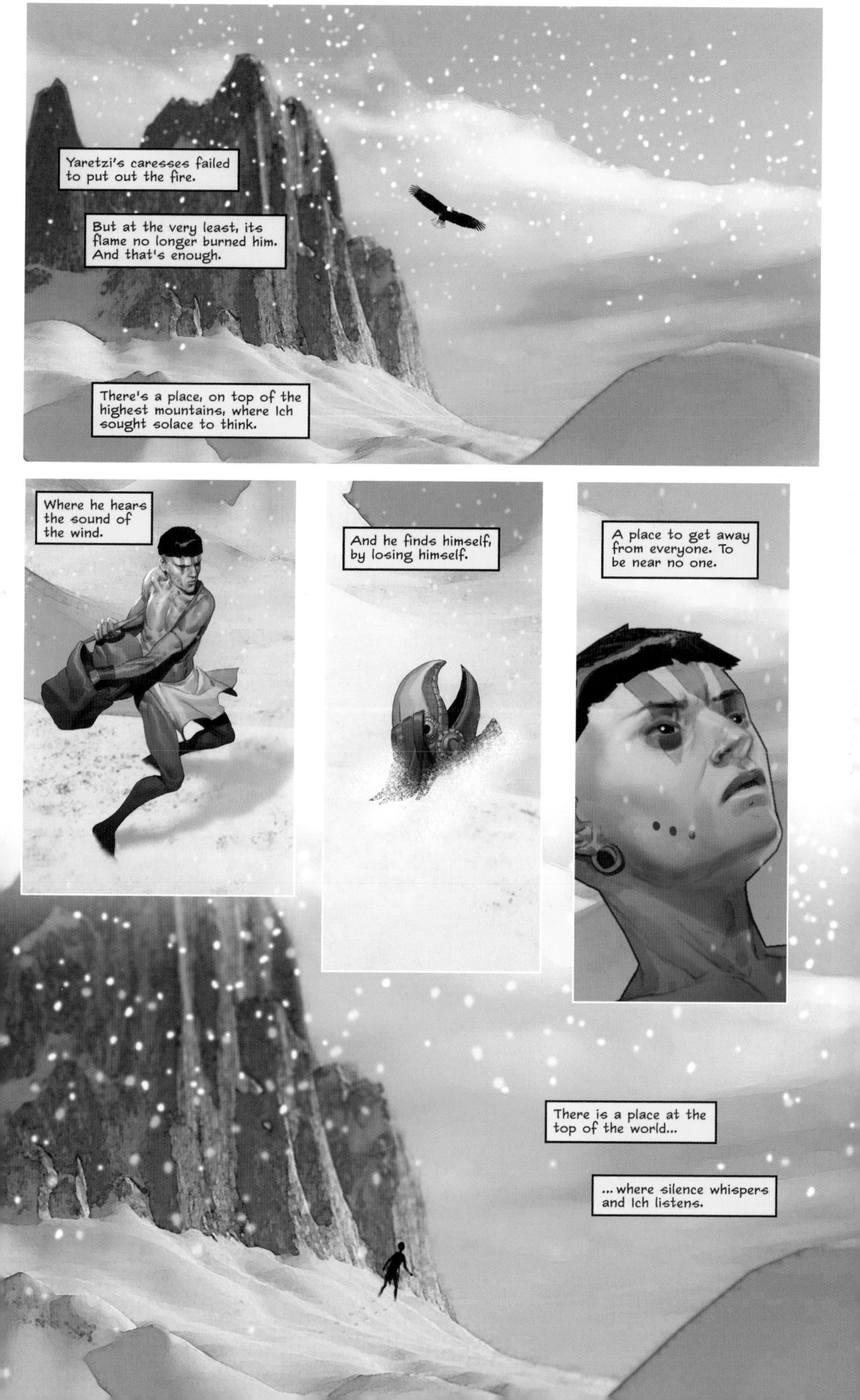
Yaretzi's caresses failed to put out the fire.
But at the very least, its flame no longer burned him. And that's enough.
There's a place, on top of the highest mountains, where Ich sought solace to think.
Where he hears the sound of the wind.
And he finds himself, by losing himself.
A place to get away from everyone. To be near no one.
There is a place at the top of the world...
... where silence whispers and Ich listens.

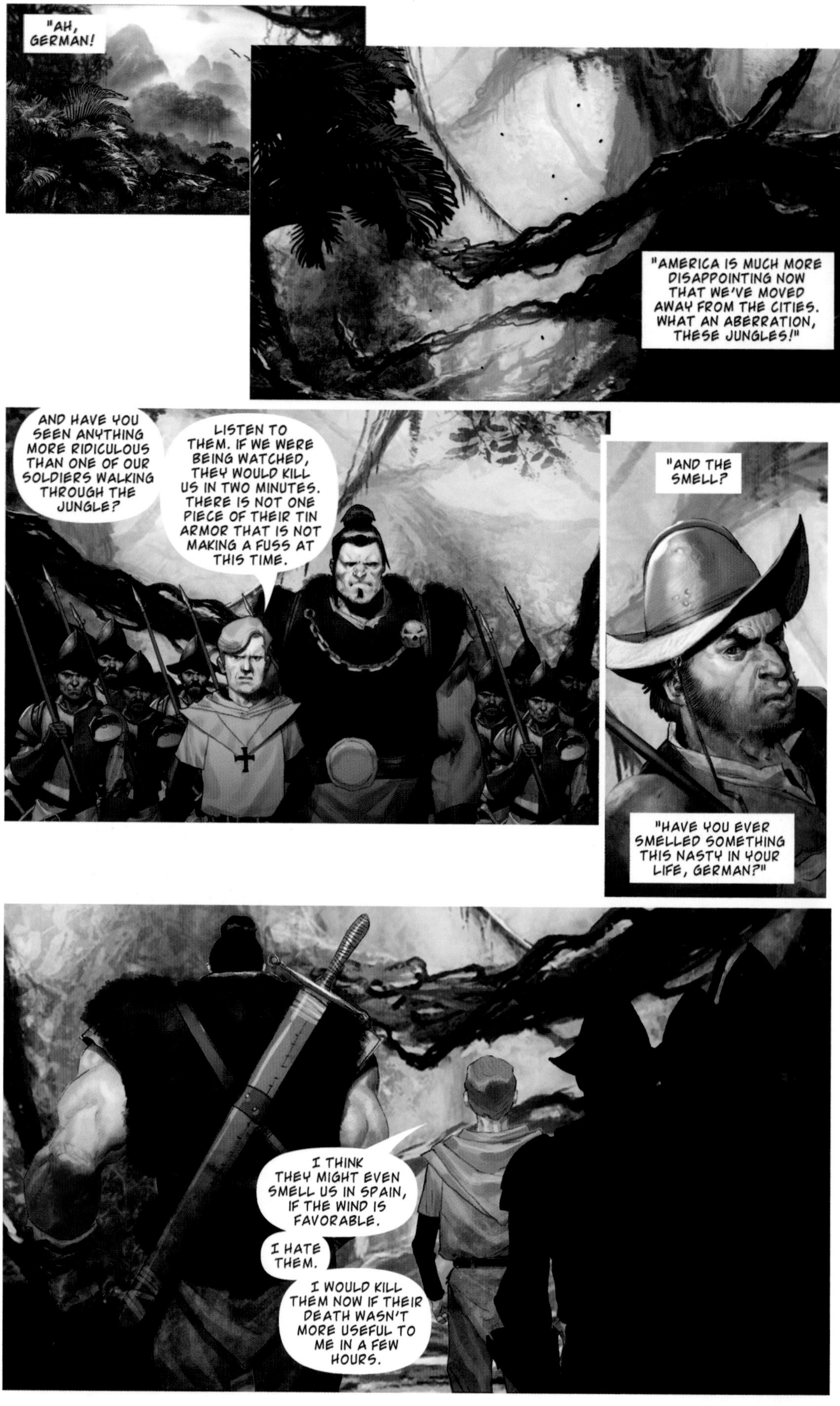
"AH, GERMAN!
"AMERICA IS MUCH MORE DISAPPOINTING NOW THAT WE'VE MOVED AWAY FROM THE CITIES. WHAT AN ABERRATION, THESE JUNGLES!"
AND HAVE YOU SEEN ANYTHING MORE RIDICULOUS THAN ONE OF OUR SOLDIERS WALKING THROUGH THE JUNGLE?
LISTEN TO THEM. IF WE WERE BEING WATCHED, THEY WOULD KILL US IN TWO MINUTES. THERE IS NOT ONE PIECE OF THEIR TIN ARMOR THAT IS NOT MAKING A FUSS AT THIS TIME.
"AND THE SMELL?
"HAVE YOU EVER SMELLED SOMETHING THIS NASTY IN YOUR LIFE, GERMAN?"
I THINK THEY MIGHT EVEN SMELL US IN SPAIN, IF THE WIND IS FAVORABLE.
I HATE THEM.
I WOULD KILL THEM NOW IF THEIR DEATH WASN'T MORE USEFUL TO ME IN A FEW HOURS.

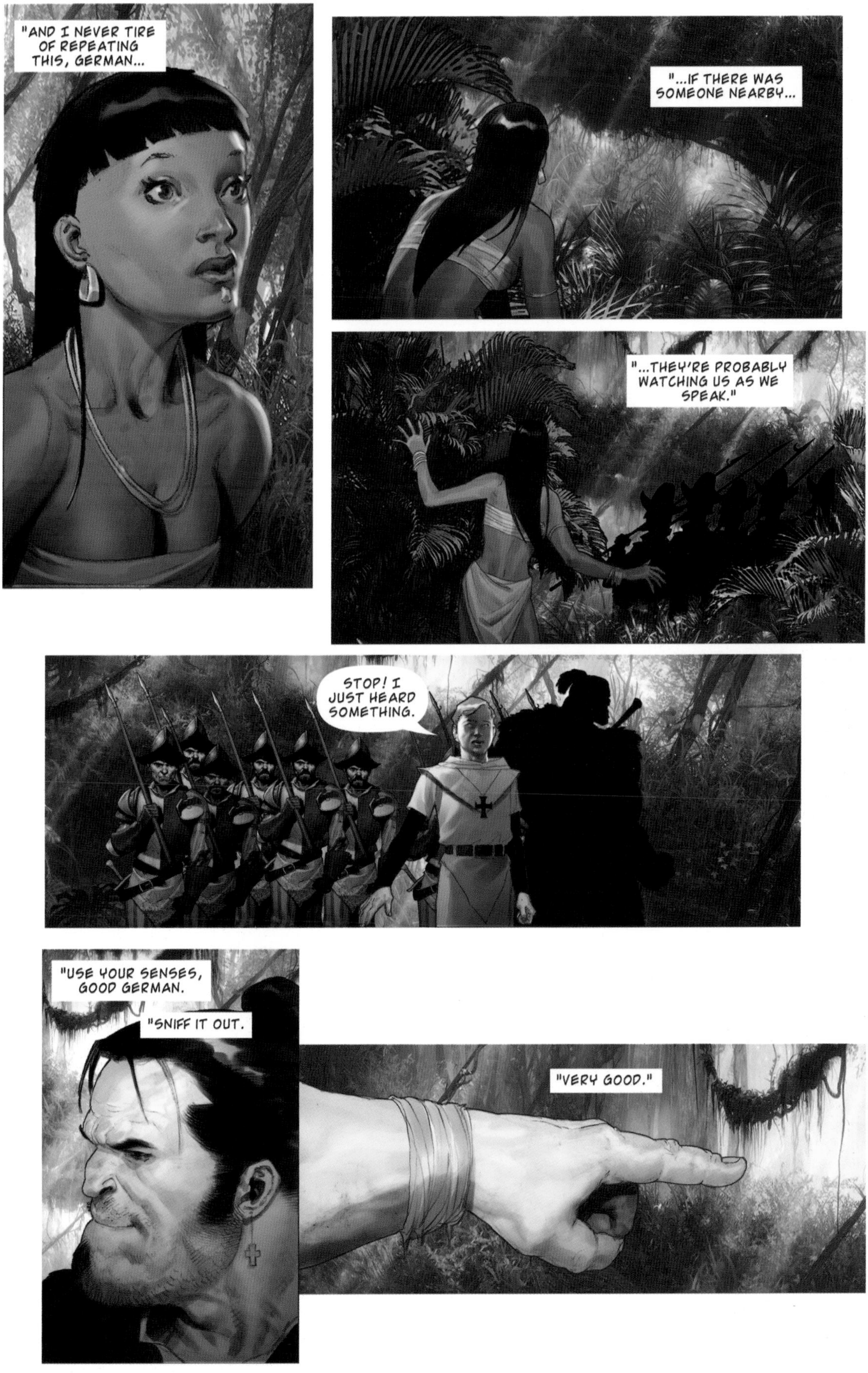
"AND I NEVER TIRE OF REPEATING THIS, GERMAN...
"...IF THERE WAS SOMEONE NEARBY...
"...THEY'RE PROBABLY WATCHING US AS WE SPEAK."
STOP! I JUST HEARD SOMETHING.
"USE YOUR SENSES, GOOD GERMAN.
"SNIFF IT OUT.
"VERY GOOD."

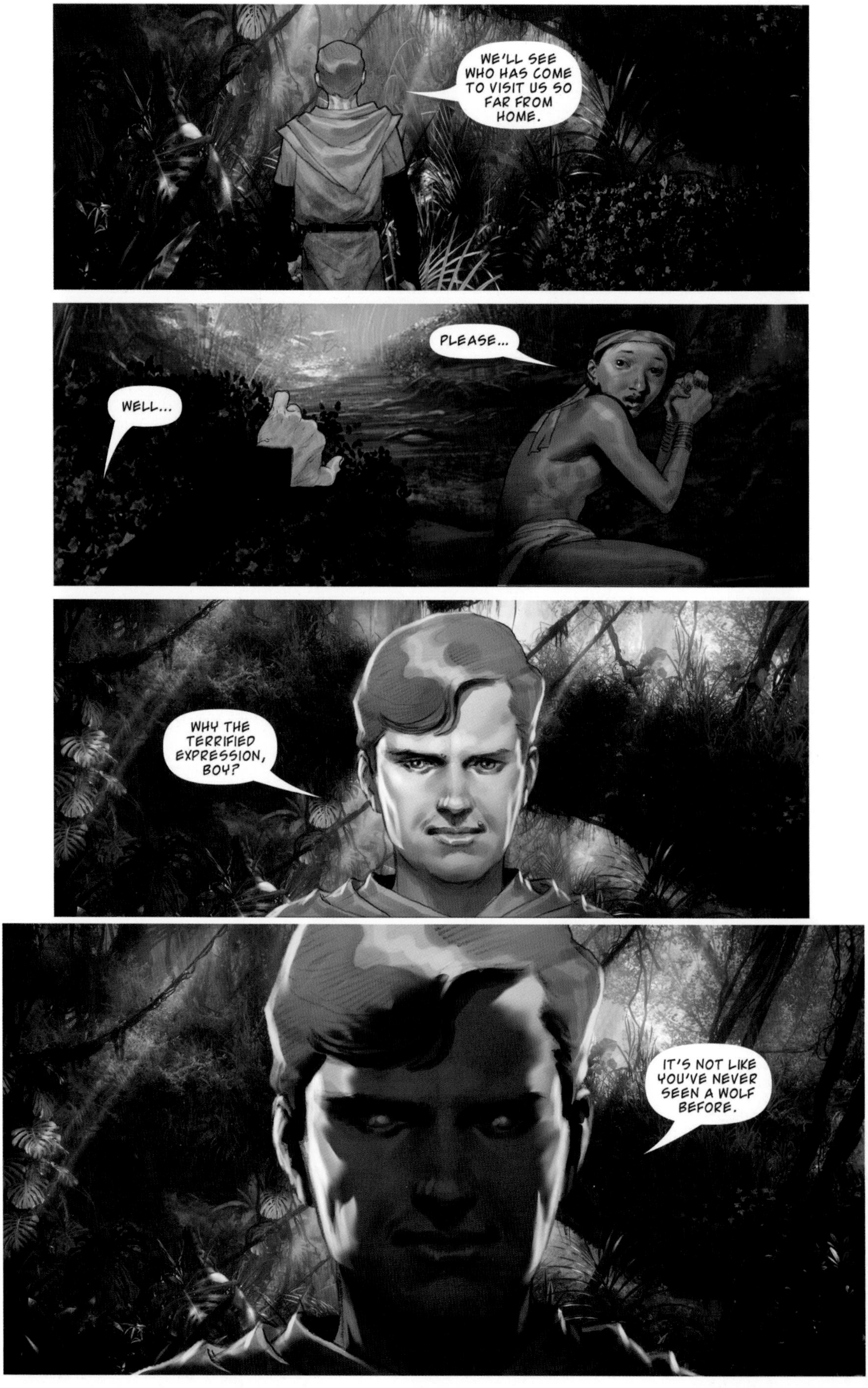
WE'LL SEE WHO HAS COME TO VISIT US SO FAR FROM HOME.
PLEASE...
WELL...
WHY THE TERRIFIED EXPRESSION, BOY?
IT'S NOT LIKE YOU'VE NEVER SEEN A WOLF BEFORE.

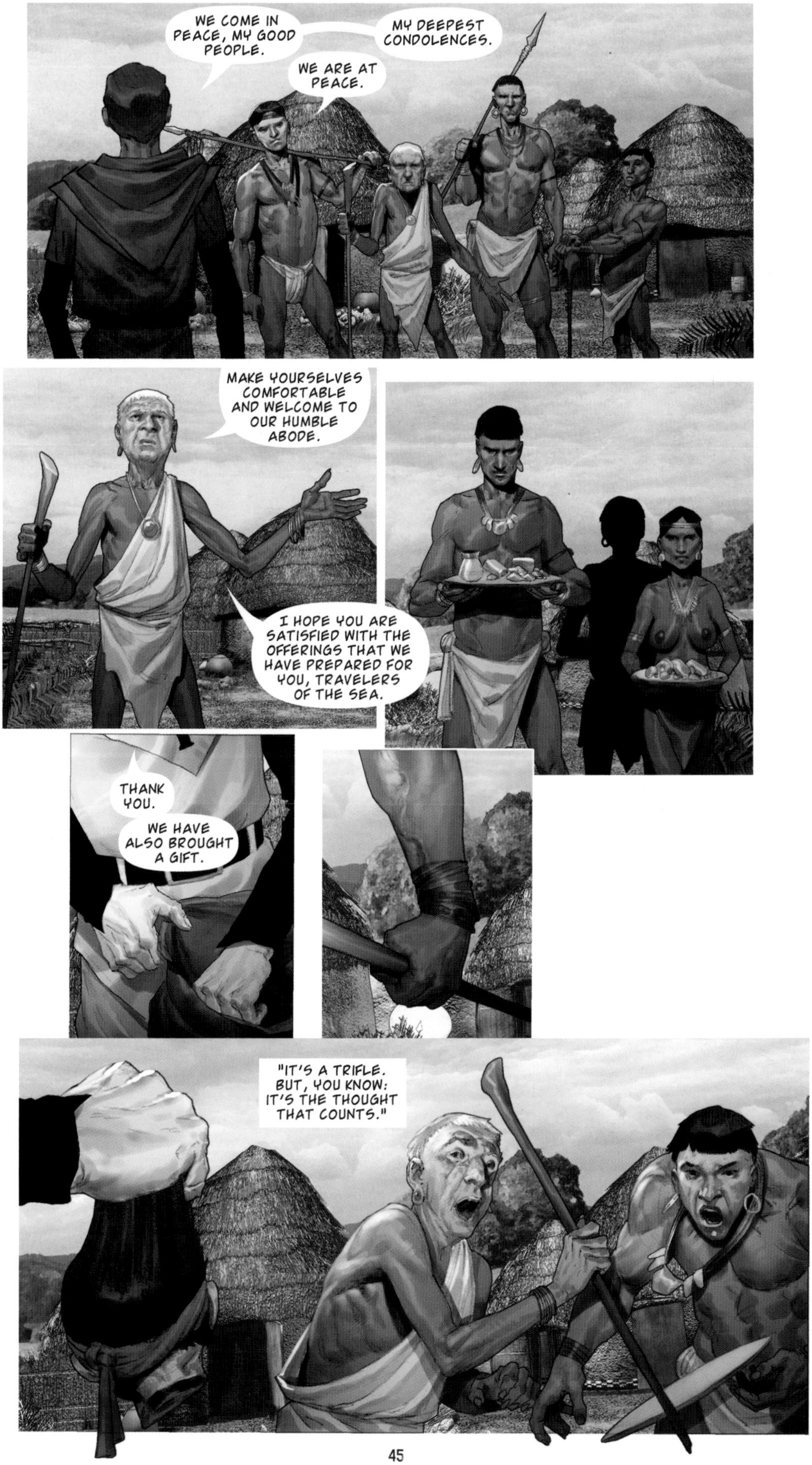
WE COME IN PEACE, MY GOOD PEOPLE.
MY DEEPEST CONDOLENCES.
WE ARE AT PEACE.
MAKE YOURSELVES COMFORTABLE AND WELCOME TO OUR HUMBLE ABODE.
I HOPE YOU ARE SATISFIED WITH THE OFFERINGS THAT WE HAVE PREPARED FOR YOU, TRAVELERS OF THE SEA.
THANK YOU.
WE HAVE ALSO BROUGHT A GIFT.
"IT'S A TRIFLE. BUT, YOU KNOW: IT'S THE THOUGHT THAT COUNTS."

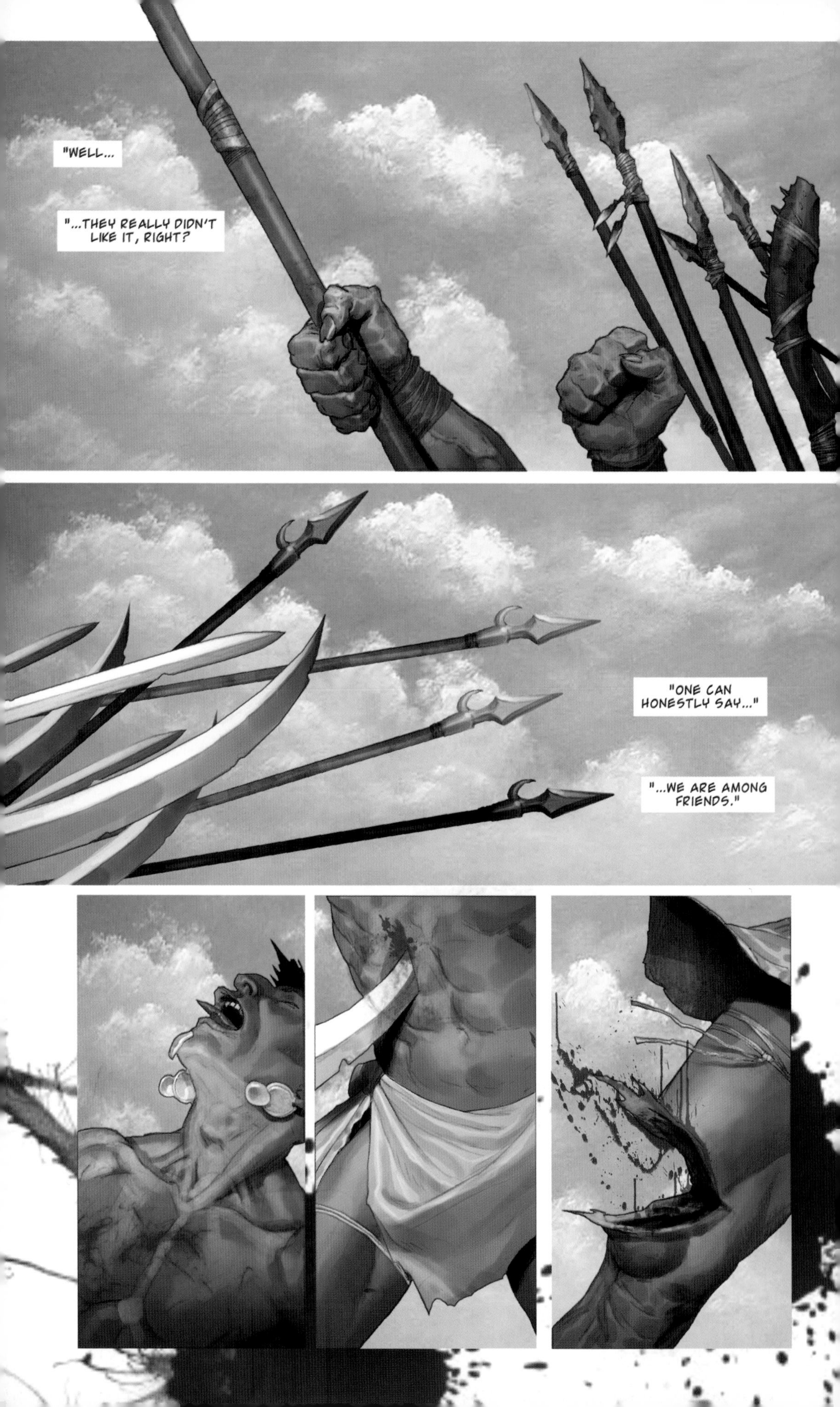
"WELL...
"...THEY REALLY DIDN'T LIKE IT, RIGHT?
"ONE CAN HONESTLY SAY..."
"...WE ARE AMONG FRIENDS."

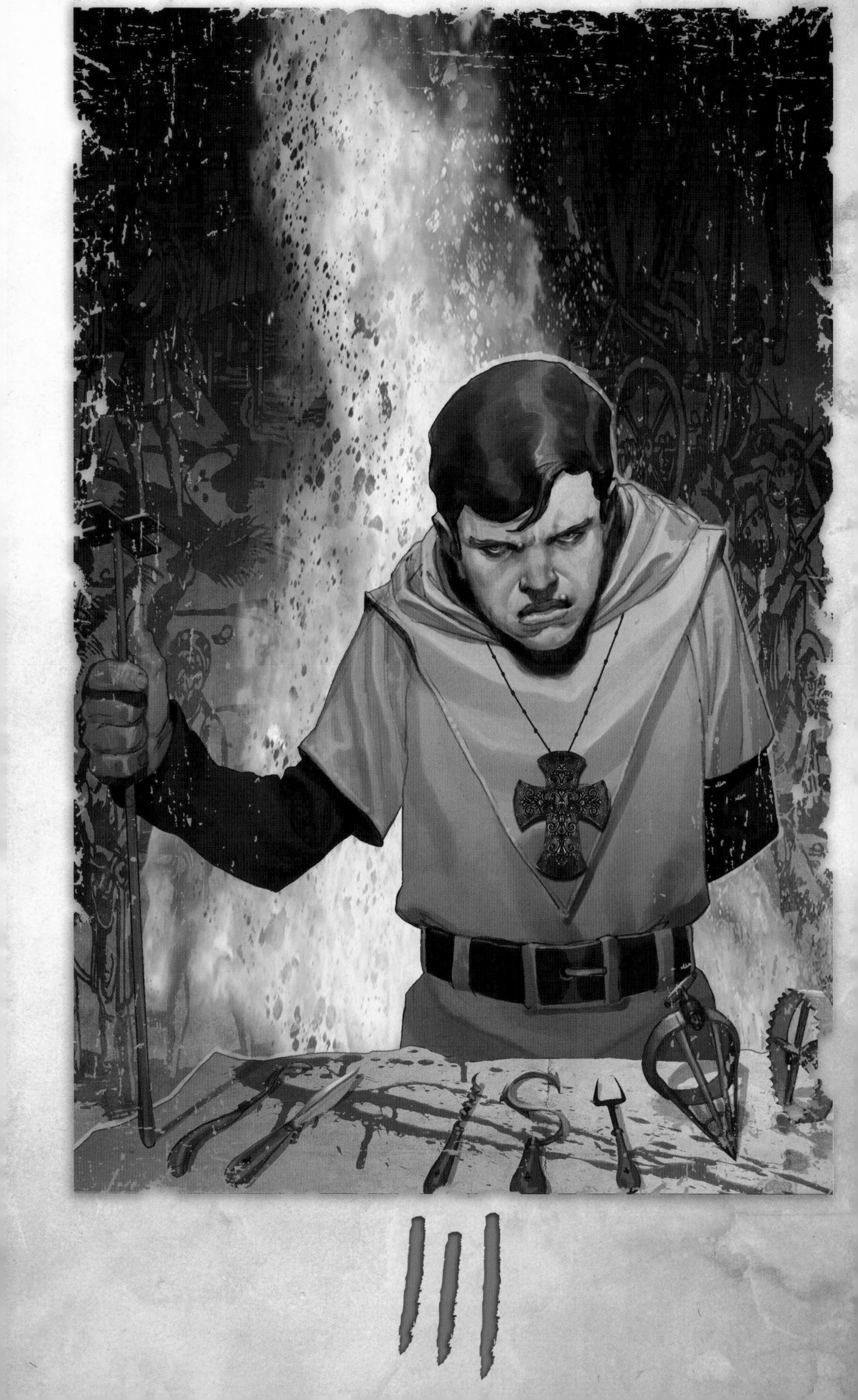

III

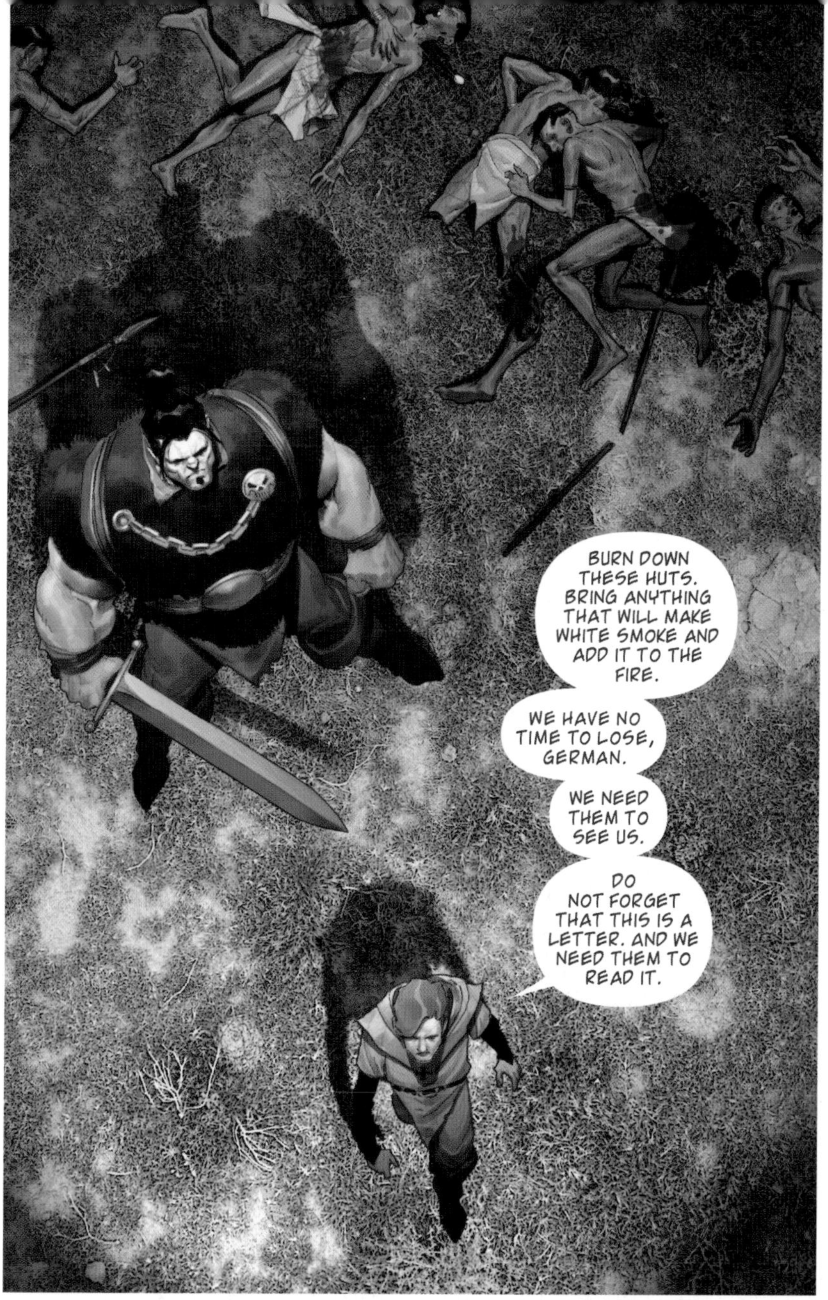
BURN DOWN THESE HUTS. BRING ANYTHING THAT WILL MAKE WHITE SMOKE AND ADD IT TO THE FIRE.
WE HAVE NO TIME TO LOSE, GERMAN.
WE NEED THEM TO SEE US.
DO NOT FORGET THAT THIS IS A LETTER. AND WE NEED THEM TO READ IT.

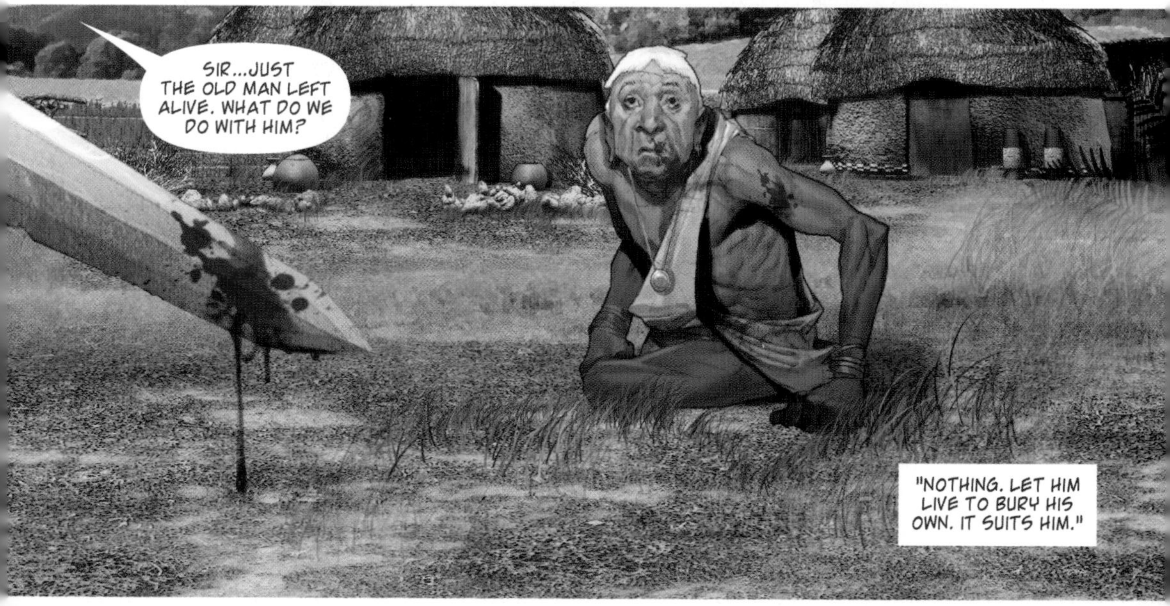
SIR...JUST THE OLD MAN LEFT ALIVE. WHAT DO WE DO WITH HIM?
"NOTHING. LET HIM LIVE TO BURY HIS OWN. IT SUITS HIM."

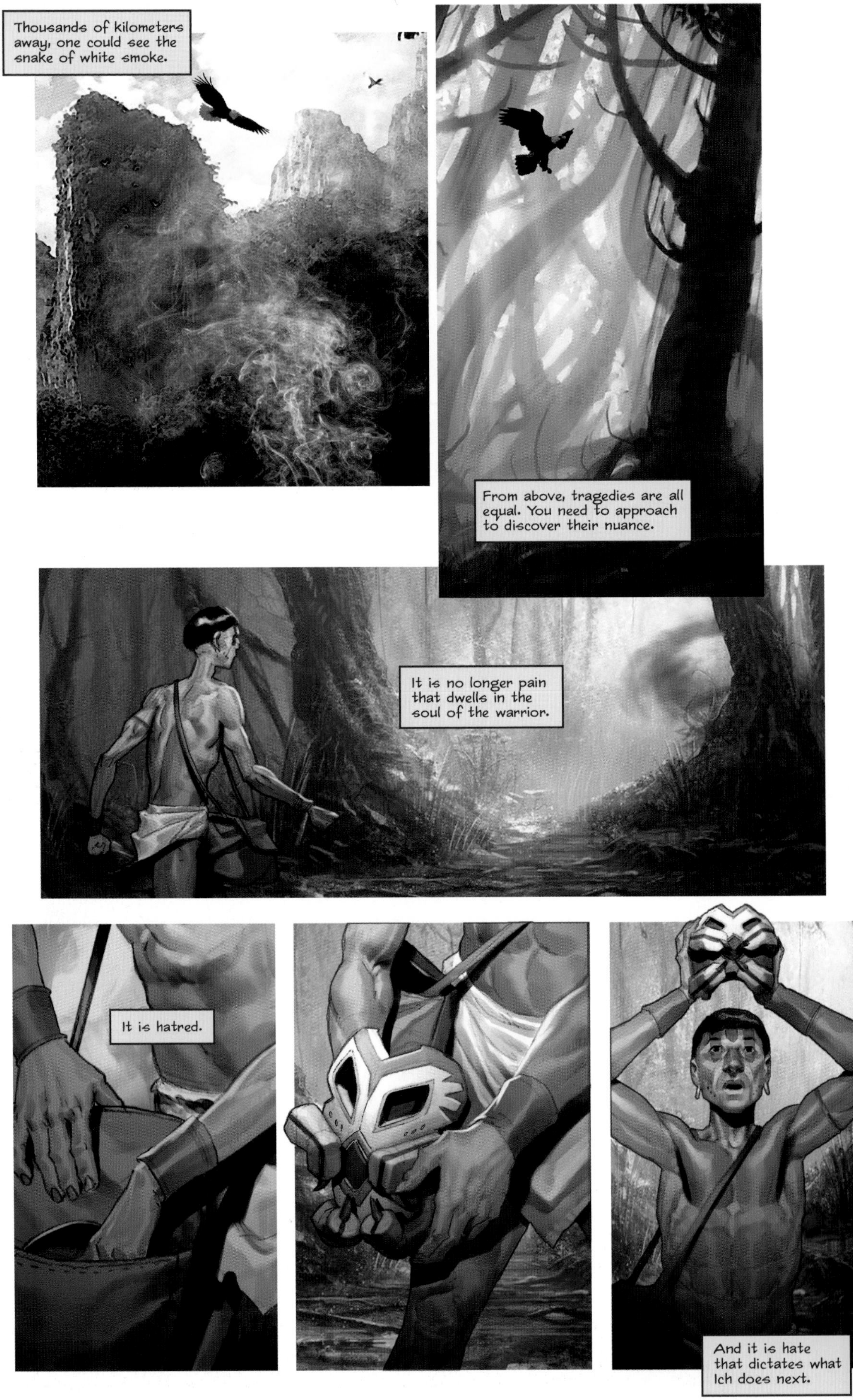
Thousands of kilometers away, one could see the snake of white smoke.
From above, tragedies are all equal. You need to approach to discover their nuance.
It is no longer pain that dwells in the soul of the warrior.
It is hatred.
And it is hate that dictates what Ich does next.

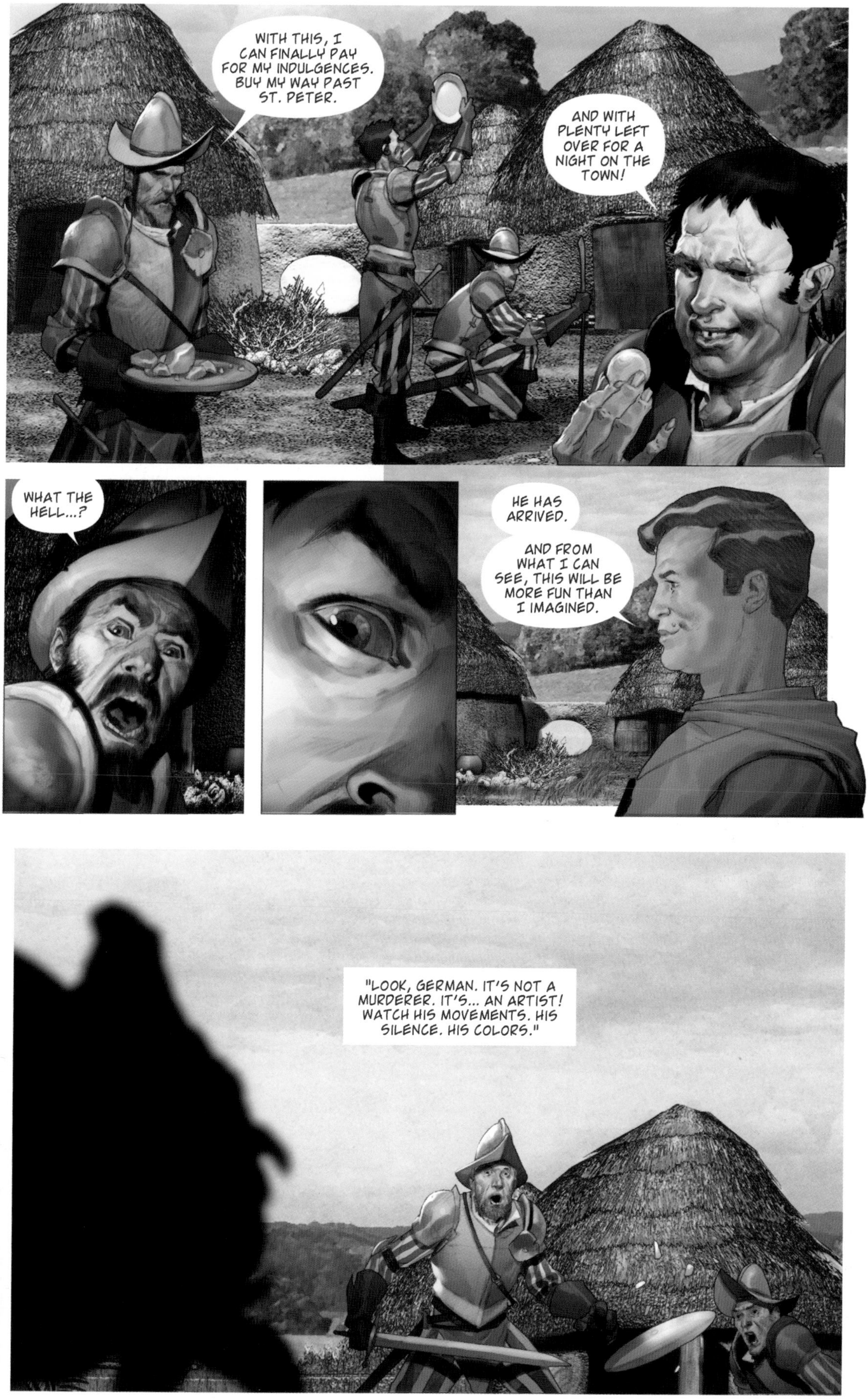
WITH THIS, I CAN FINALLY PAY FOR MY INDULGENCES. BUY MY WAY PAST ST. PETER.
AND WITH PLENTY LEFT OVER FOR A NIGHT ON THE TOWN!
WHAT THE HELL...?
HE HAS ARRIVED.
AND FROM WHAT I CAN SEE, THIS WILL BE MORE FUN THAN I IMAGINED.
"LOOK, GERMAN. IT'S NOT A MURDERER. IT'S... AN ARTIST! WATCH HIS MOVEMENTS. HIS SILENCE. HIS COLORS."

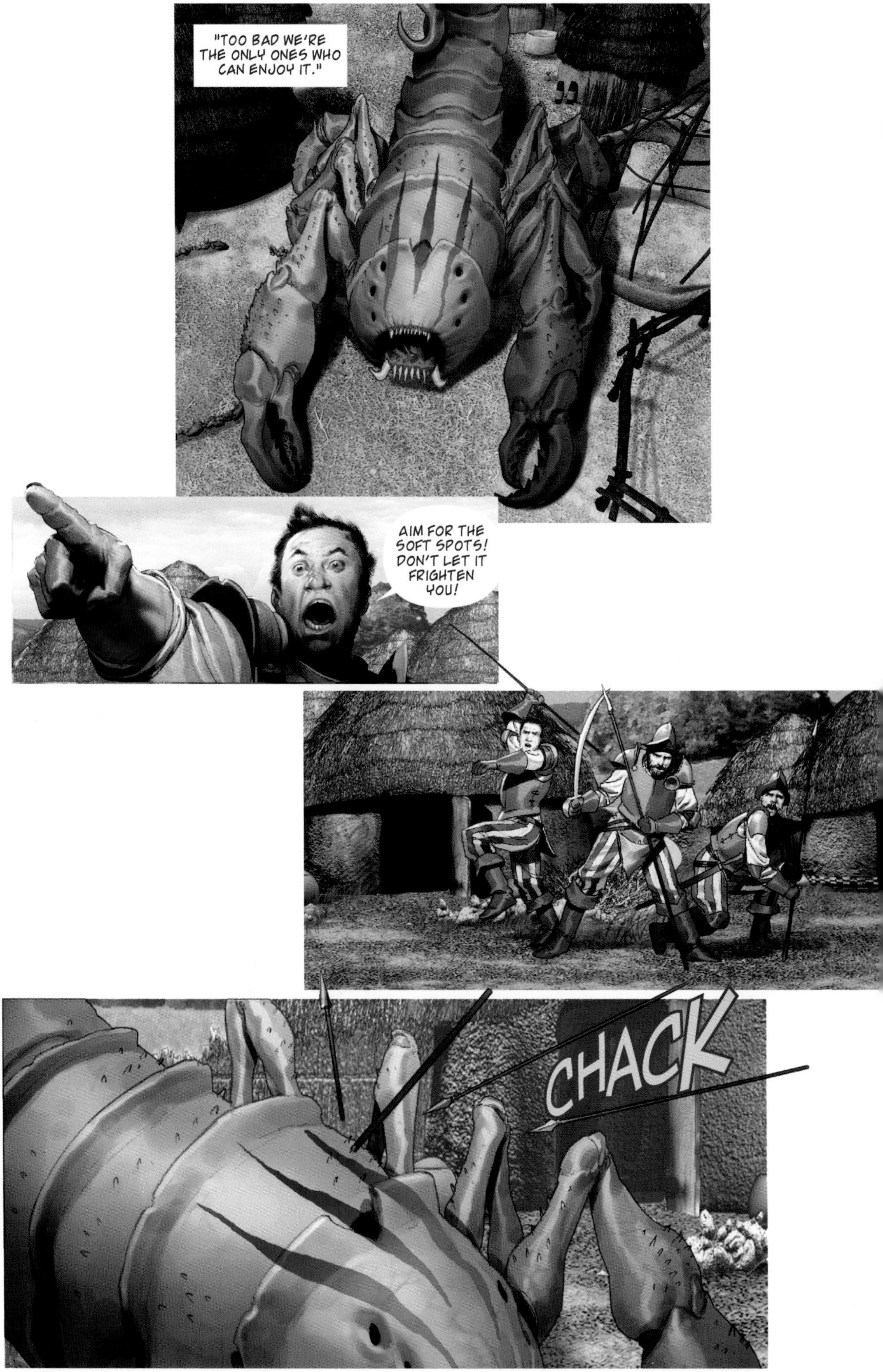
"TOO BAD WE'RE THE ONLY ONES WHO CAN ENJOY IT."
AIM FOR THE SOFT SPOTS! DON'T LET IT FRIGHTEN YOU!
CHACK

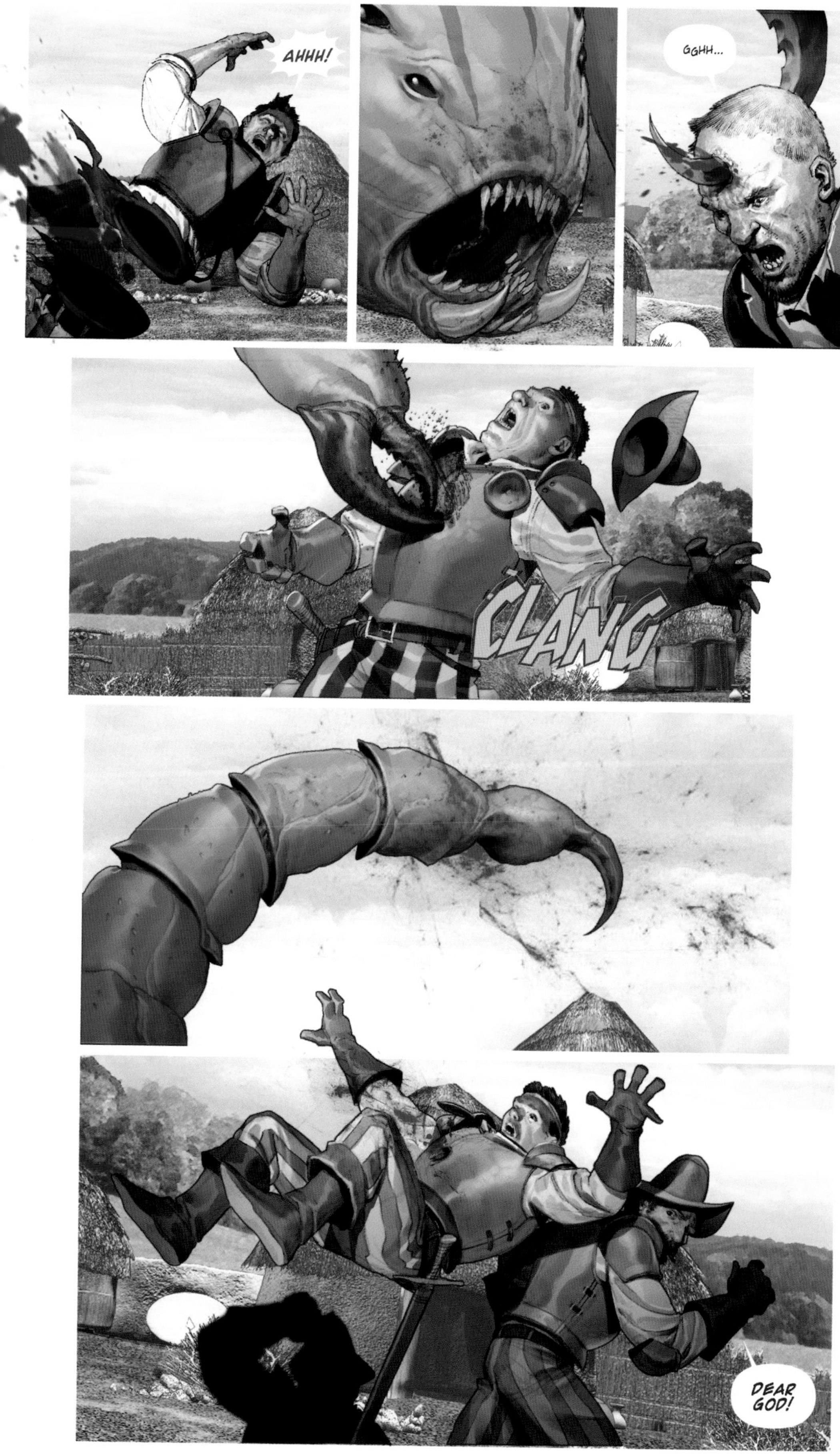
AHHH!
GGHH...
CLANG
DEAR GOD!

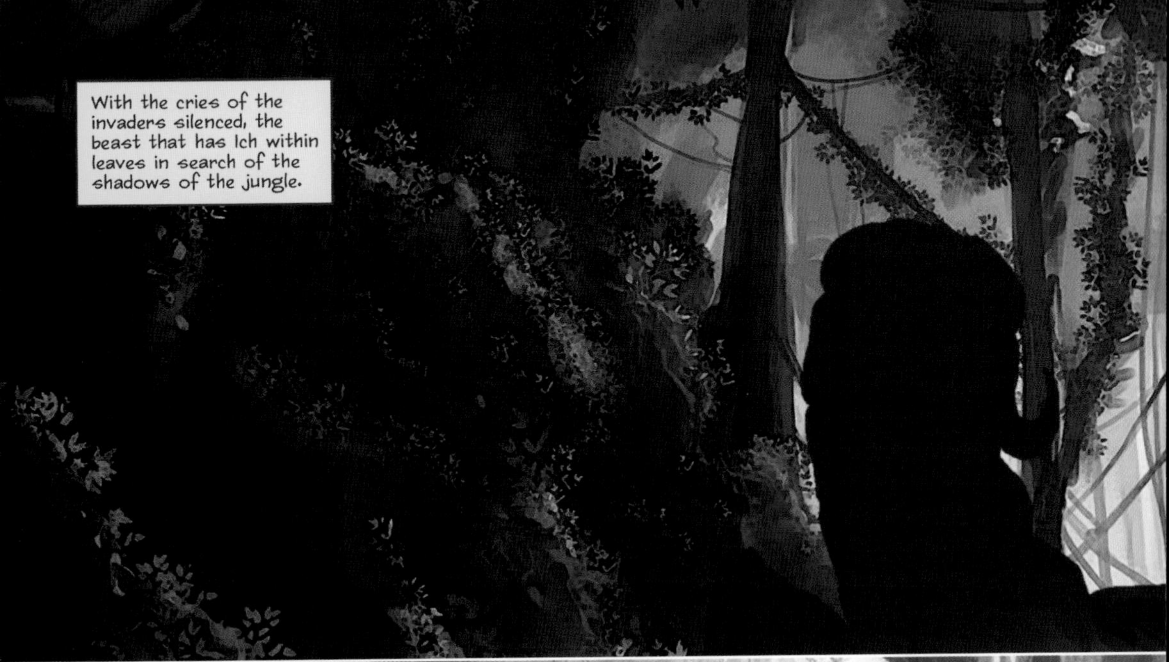
With the cries of the invaders silenced, the beast that has Ich within leaves in search of the shadows of the jungle.

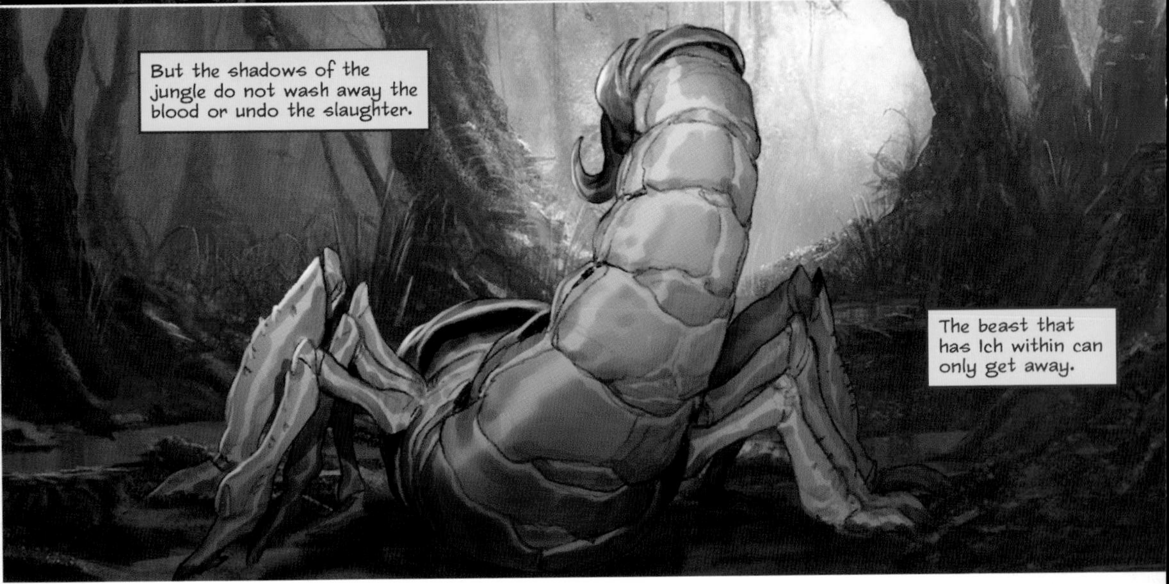
But the shadows of the jungle do not wash away the blood or undo the slaughter.
The beast that has Ich within can only get away.

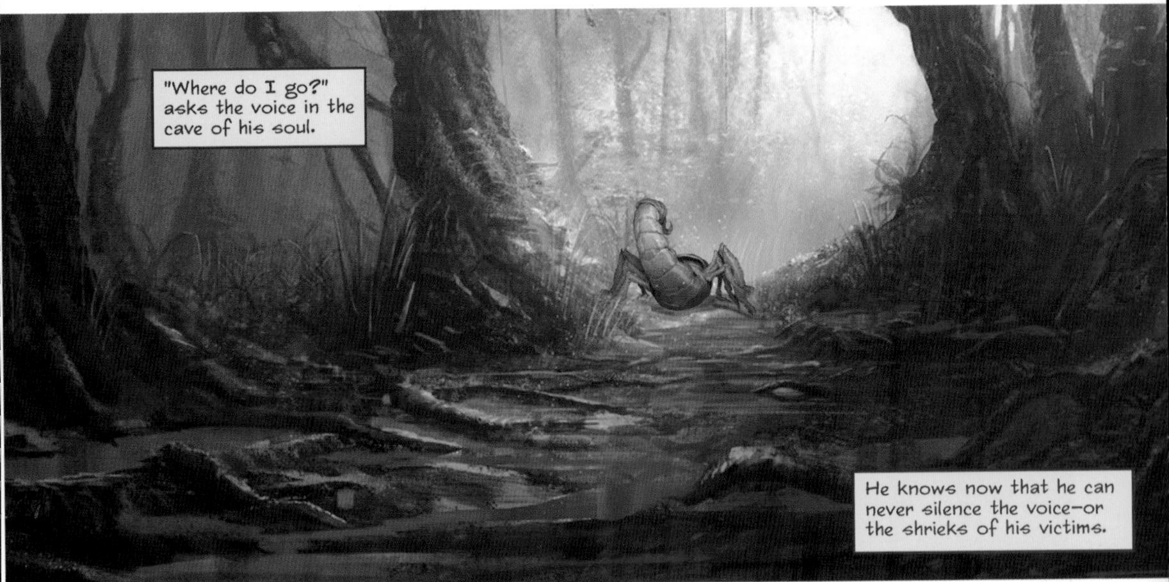
"Where do I go?" asks the voice in the cave of his soul.
He knows now that he can never silence the voice—or the shrieks of his victims.

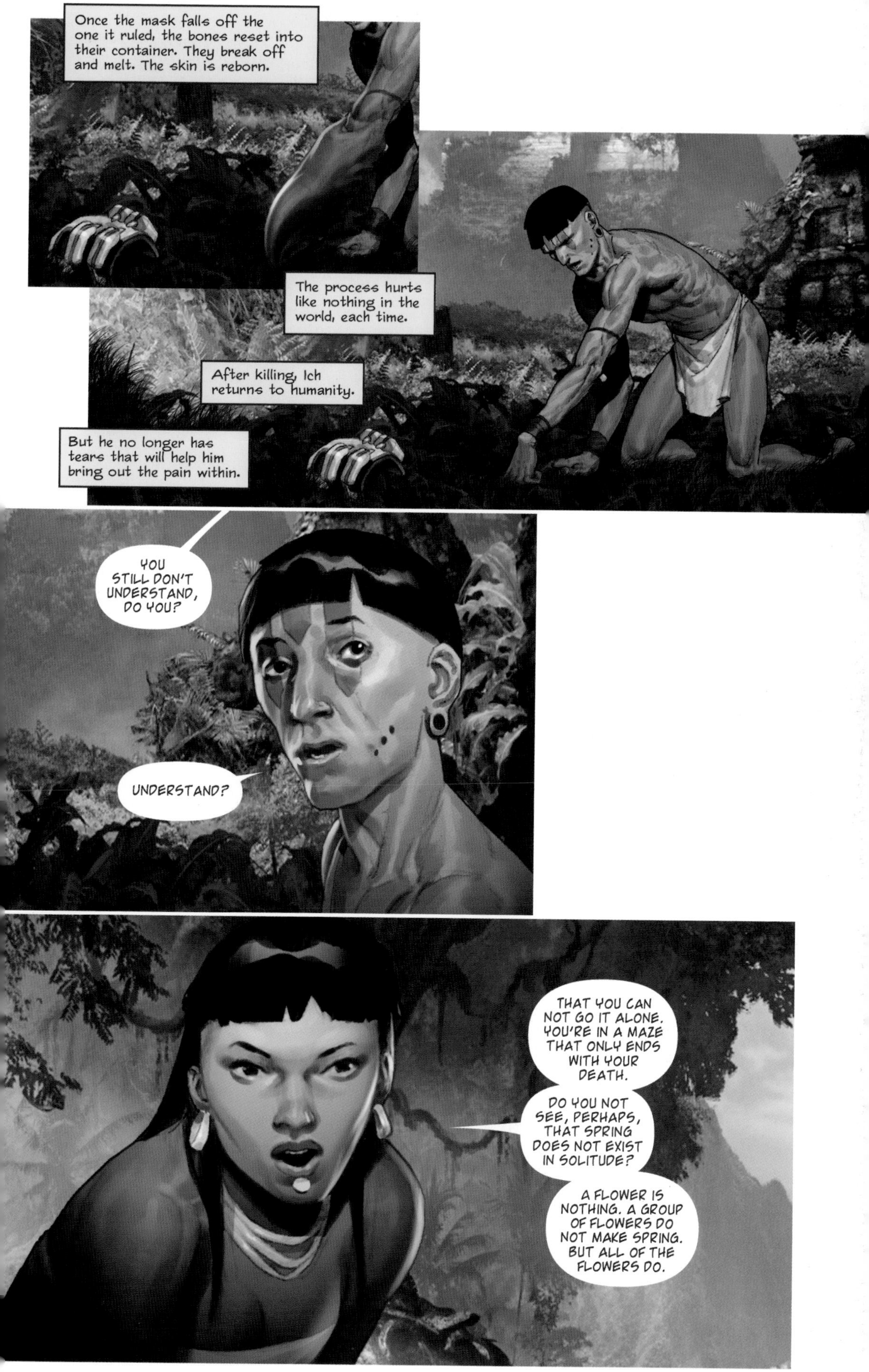
Once the mask falls off the one it ruled, the bones reset into their container. They break off and melt. The skin is reborn.
The process hurts like nothing in the world, each time.
After killing, Ich returns to humanity.
But he no longer has tears that will help him bring out the pain within.
YOU STILL DON'T UNDERSTAND, DO YOU?
UNDERSTAND?
THAT YOU CAN NOT GO IT ALONE. YOU'RE IN A MAZE THAT ONLY ENDS WITH YOUR DEATH.
DO YOU NOT SEE, PERHAPS, THAT SPRING DOES NOT EXIST IN SOLITUDE?
A FLOWER IS NOTHING. A GROUP OF FLOWERS DO NOT MAKE SPRING. BUT ALL OF THE FLOWERS DO.

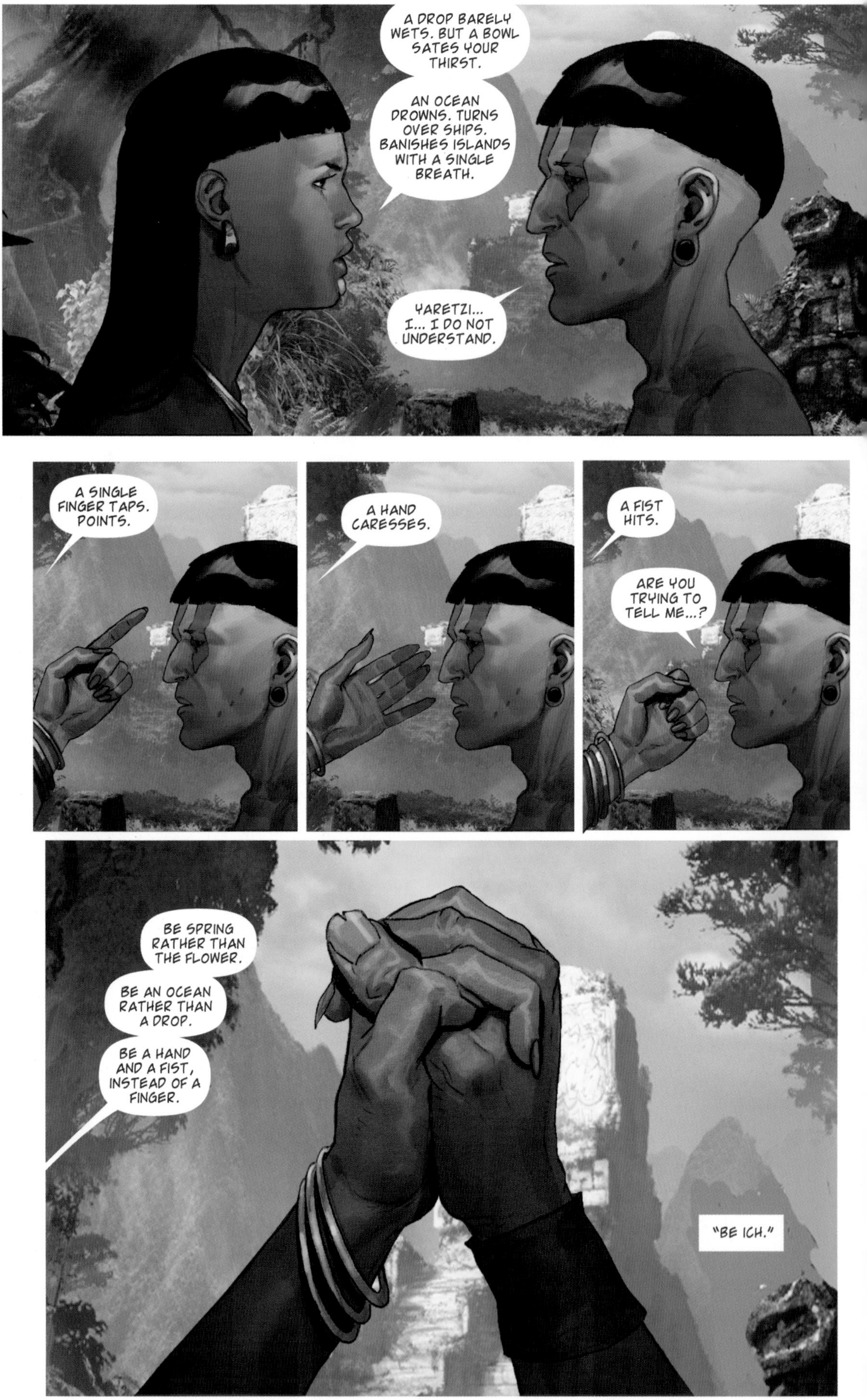
A DROP BARELY WETS. BUT A BOWL SATES YOUR THIRST.
AN OCEAN DROWNS. TURNS OVER SHIPS. BANISHES ISLANDS WITH A SINGLE BREATH.
YARETZI... I... I DO NOT UNDERSTAND.
A SINGLE FINGER TAPS. POINTS.
A HAND CARESSES.
A FIST HITS.
ARE YOU TRYING TO TELL ME...?
BE SPRING RATHER THAN THE FLOWER.
BE AN OCEAN RATHER THAN A DROP.
BE A HAND AND A FIST, INSTEAD OF A FINGER.
"BE ICH."

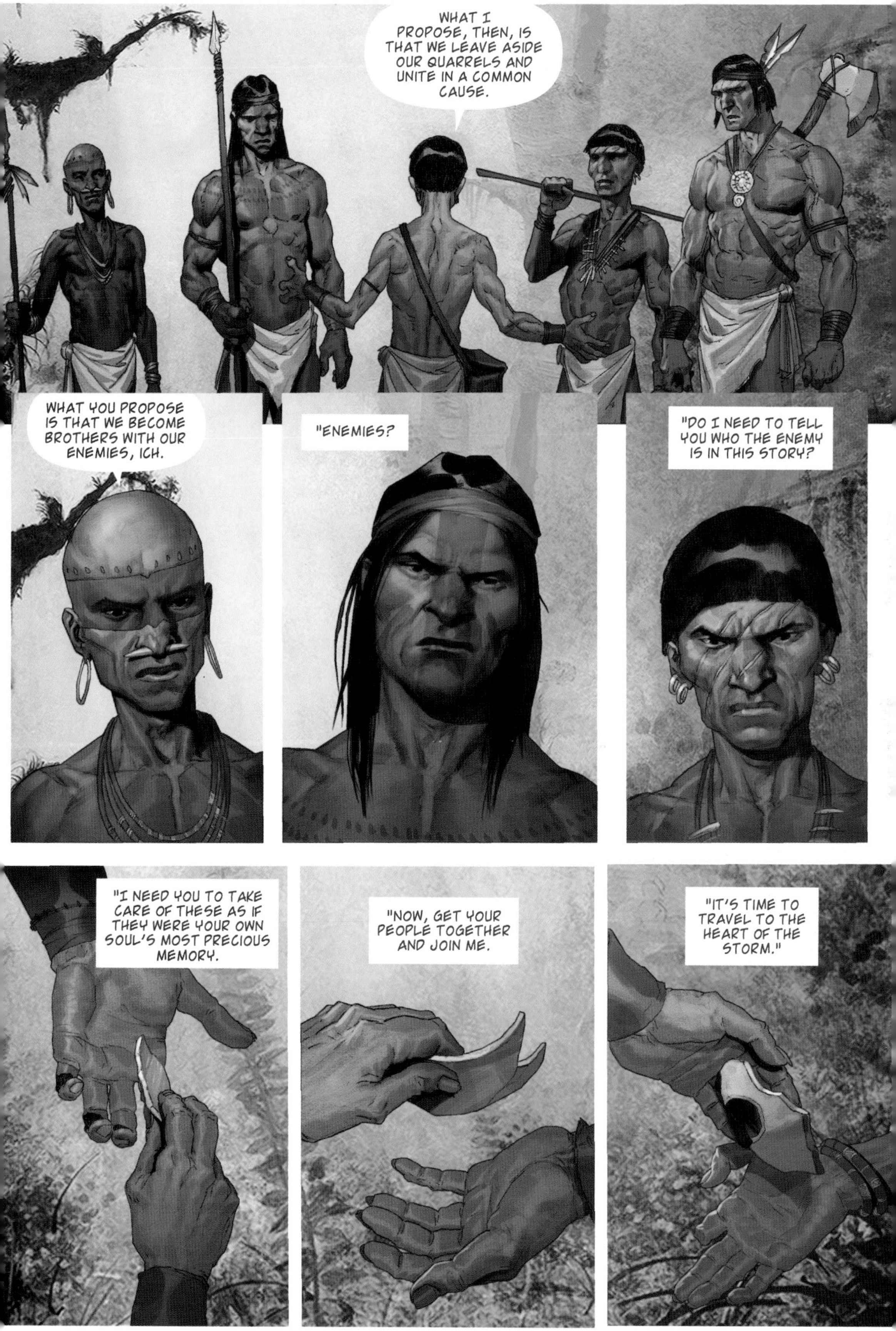
WHAT I PROPOSE, THEN, IS THAT WE LEAVE ASIDE OUR QUARRELS AND UNITE IN A COMMON CAUSE.
WHAT YOU PROPOSE IS THAT WE BECOME BROTHERS WITH OUR ENEMIES, ICH.
"ENEMIES?
"DO I NEED TO TELL YOU WHO THE ENEMY IS IN THIS STORY?
"I NEED YOU TO TAKE CARE OF THESE AS IF THEY WERE YOUR OWN SOUL'S MOST PRECIOUS MEMORY.
"NOW, GET YOUR PEOPLE TOGETHER AND JOIN ME.
"IT'S TIME TO TRAVEL TO THE HEART OF THE STORM."

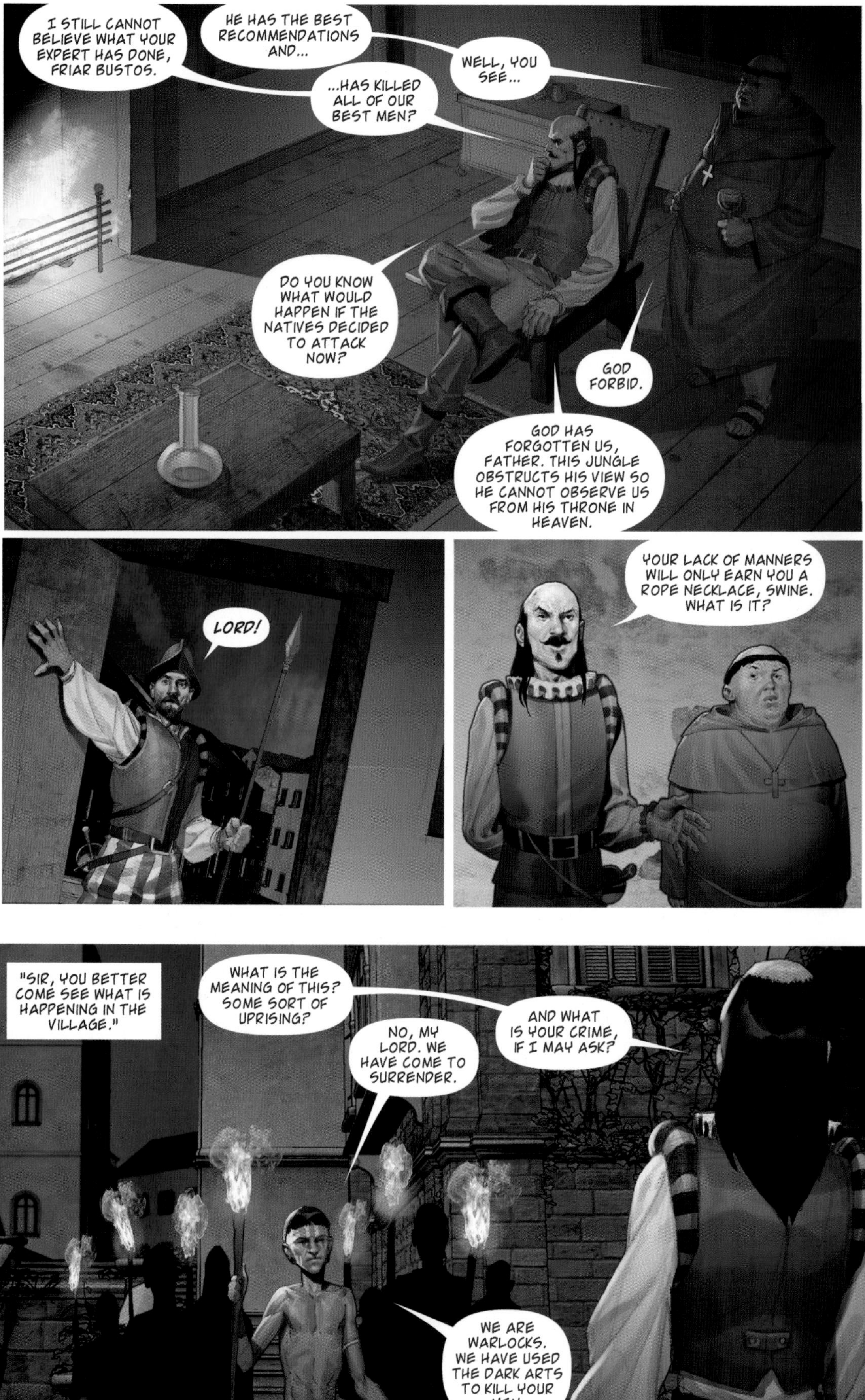
I STILL CANNOT BELIEVE WHAT YOUR EXPERT HAS DONE, FRIAR BUSTOS.
HE HAS THE BEST RECOMMENDATIONS AND...
...HAS KILLED ALL OF OUR BEST MEN?
WELL, YOU SEE...
DO YOU KNOW WHAT WOULD HAPPEN IF THE NATIVES DECIDED TO ATTACK NOW?
GOD FORBID.
GOD HAS FORGOTTEN US, FATHER. THIS JUNGLE OBSTRUCTS HIS VIEW SO HE CANNOT OBSERVE US FROM HIS THRONE IN HEAVEN.
LORD!
YOUR LACK OF MANNERS WILL ONLY EARN YOU A ROPE NECKLACE, SWINE. WHAT IS IT?
"SIR, YOU BETTER COME SEE WHAT IS HAPPENING IN THE VILLAGE."
WHAT IS THE MEANING OF THIS? SOME SORT OF UPRISING?
NO, MY LORD. WE HAVE COME TO SURRENDER.
AND WHAT IS YOUR CRIME, IF I MAY ASK?
WE ARE WARLOCKS. WE HAVE USED THE DARK ARTS TO KILL YOUR MEN.

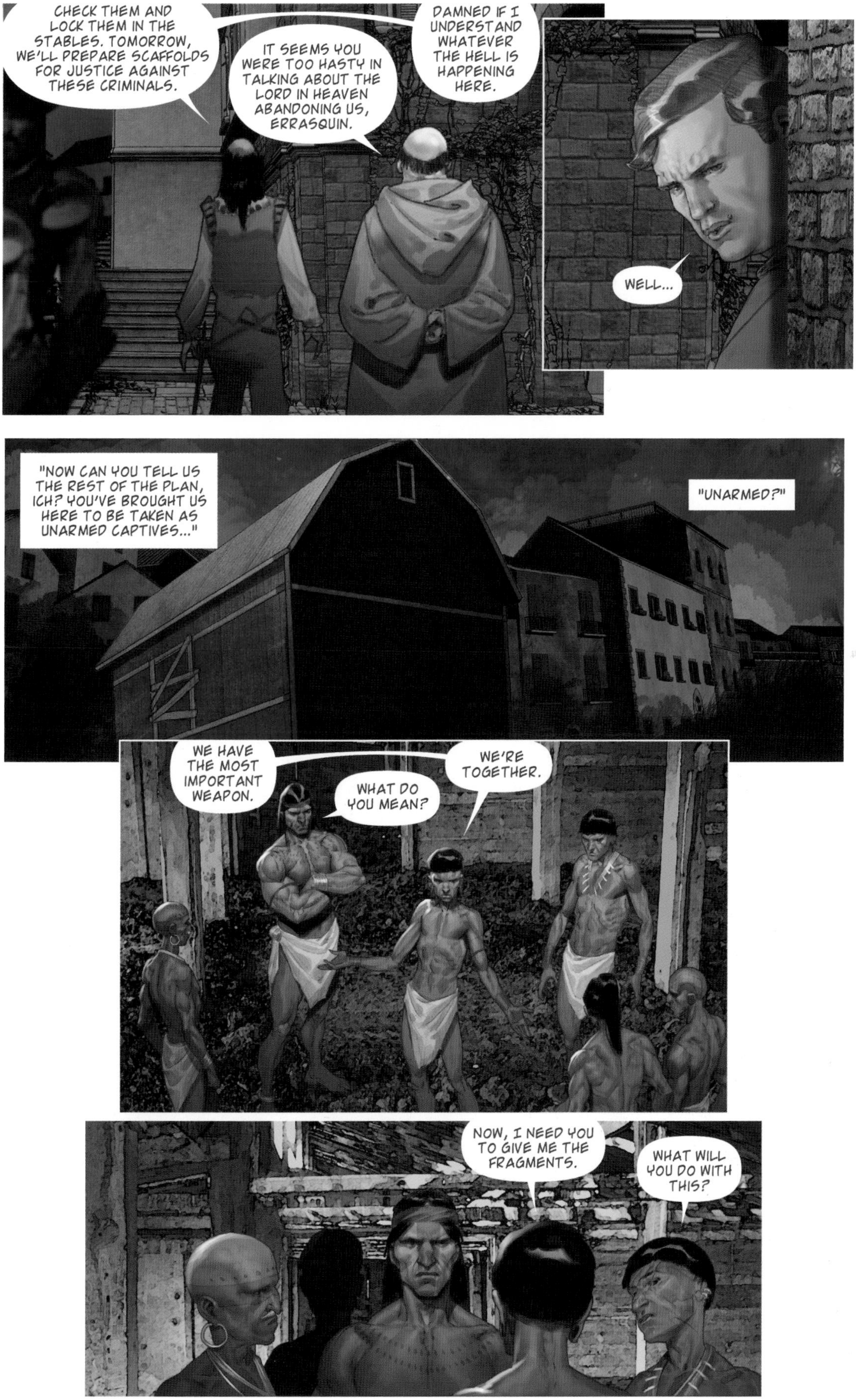
CHECK THEM AND LOCK THEM IN THE STABLES. TOMORROW, WE'LL PREPARE SCAFFOLDS FOR JUSTICE AGAINST THESE CRIMINALS.
DAMNED IF I UNDERSTAND WHATEVER THE HELL IS HAPPENING HERE.
IT SEEMS YOU WERE TOO HASTY IN TALKING ABOUT THE LORD IN HEAVEN ABANDONING US, ERRASQUIN.
WELL...
"NOW CAN YOU TELL US THE REST OF THE PLAN, ICH? YOU'VE BROUGHT US HERE TO BE TAKEN AS UNARMED CAPTIVES..."
"UNARMED?"
WE HAVE THE MOST IMPORTANT WEAPON.
WHAT DO YOU MEAN?
WE'RE TOGETHER.
NOW, I NEED YOU TO GIVE ME THE FRAGMENTS.
WHAT WILL YOU DO WITH THIS?

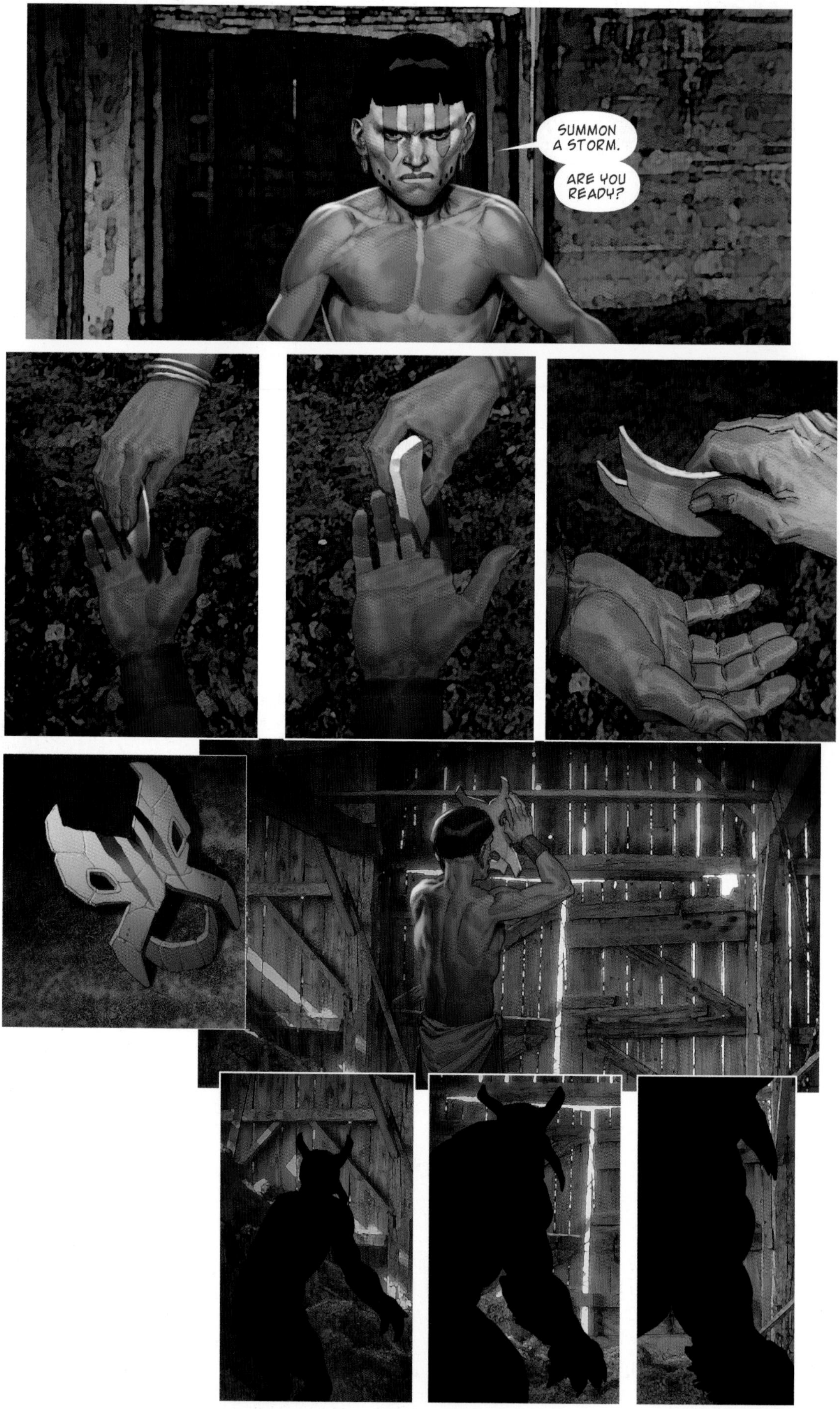
SUMMON A STORM.
ARE YOU READY?

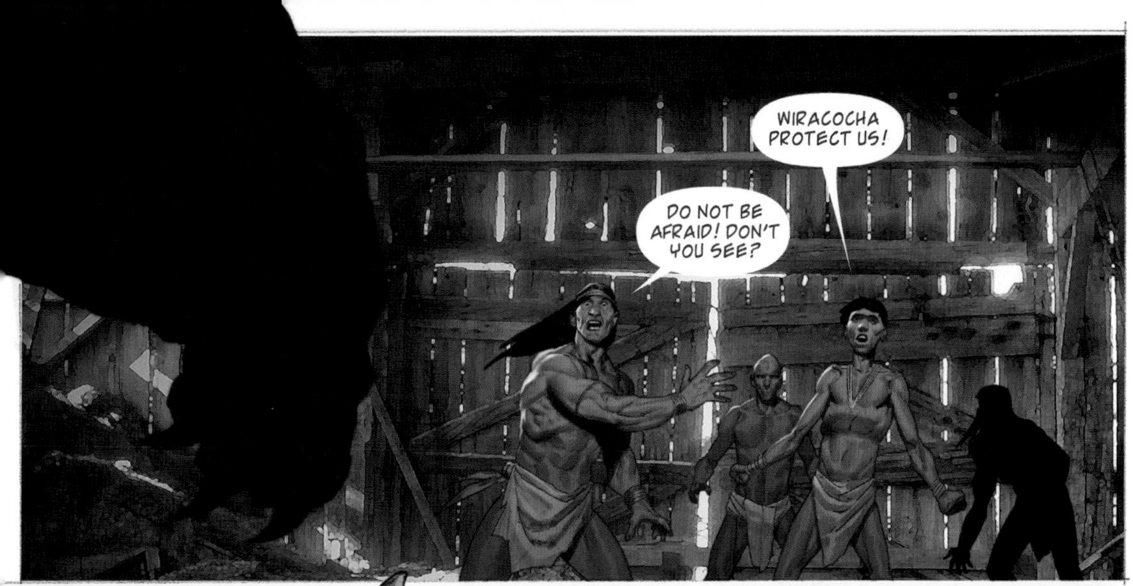
WIRACOCHA PROTECT US!
DO NOT BE AFRAID! DON'T YOU SEE?

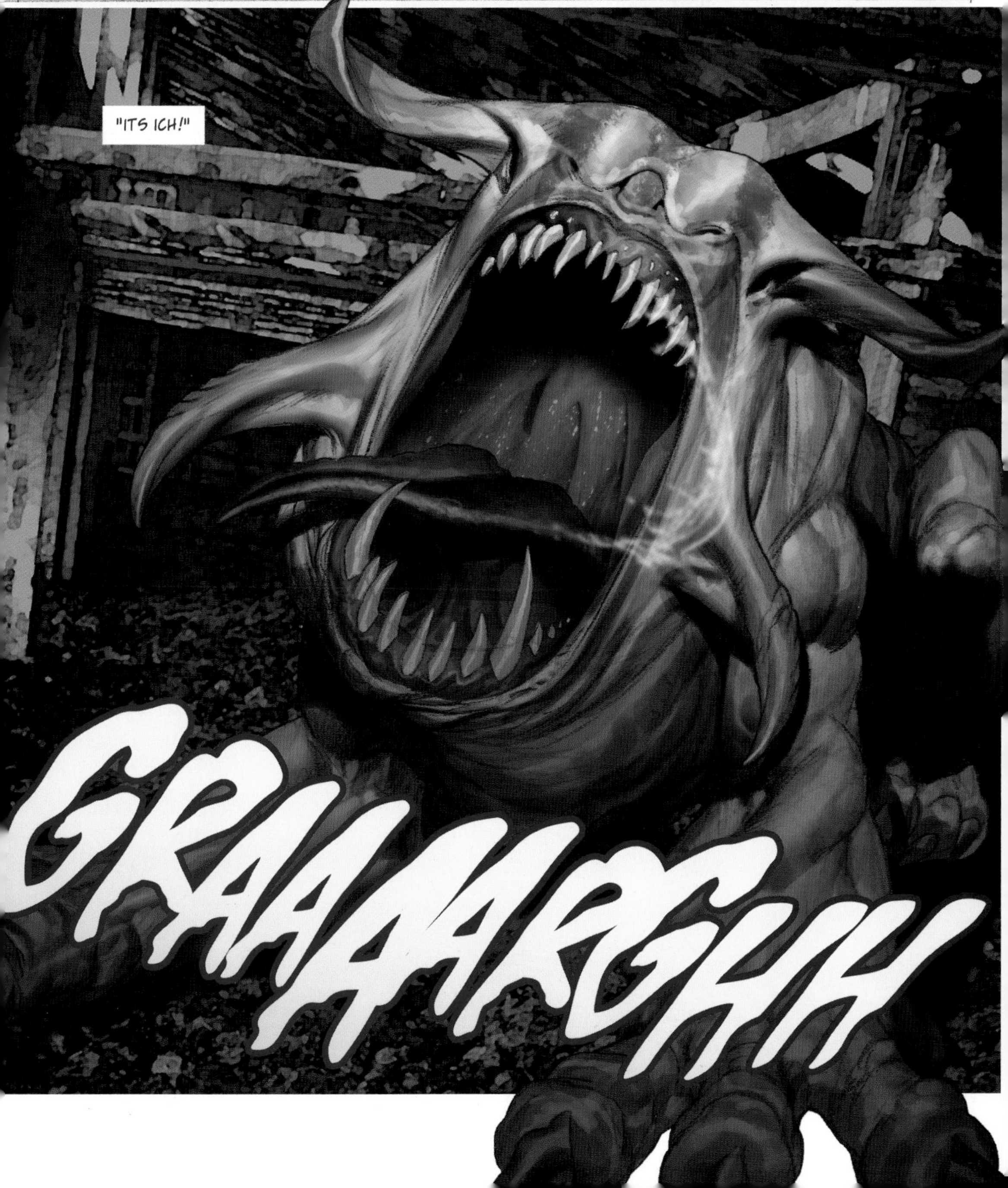
"ITS ICH!"
GRAAAARGHH

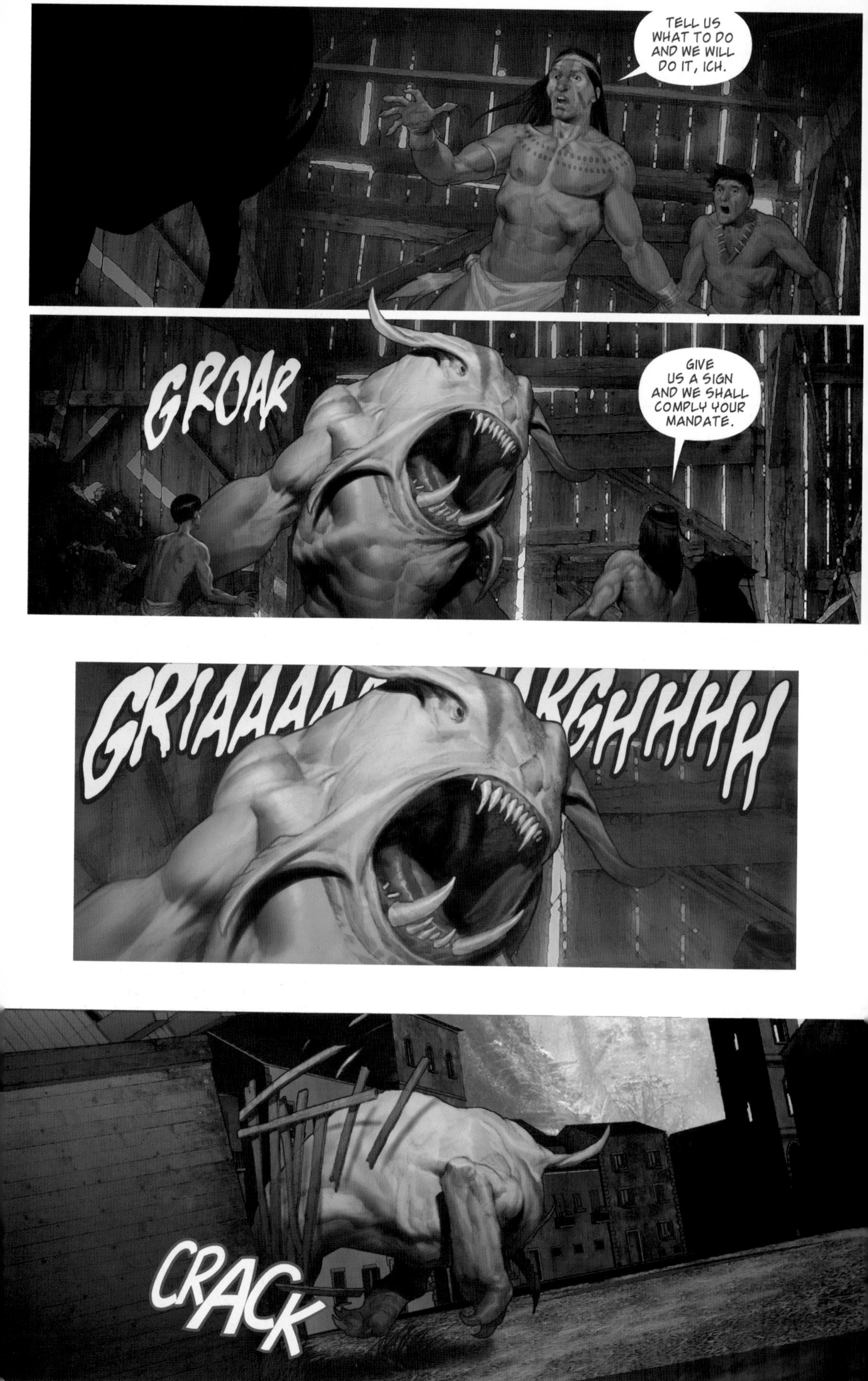
TELL US WHAT TO DO AND WE WILL DO IT, ICH.
GROAR
GIVE US A SIGN AND WE SHALL COMPLY YOUR MANDATE.
CRACK

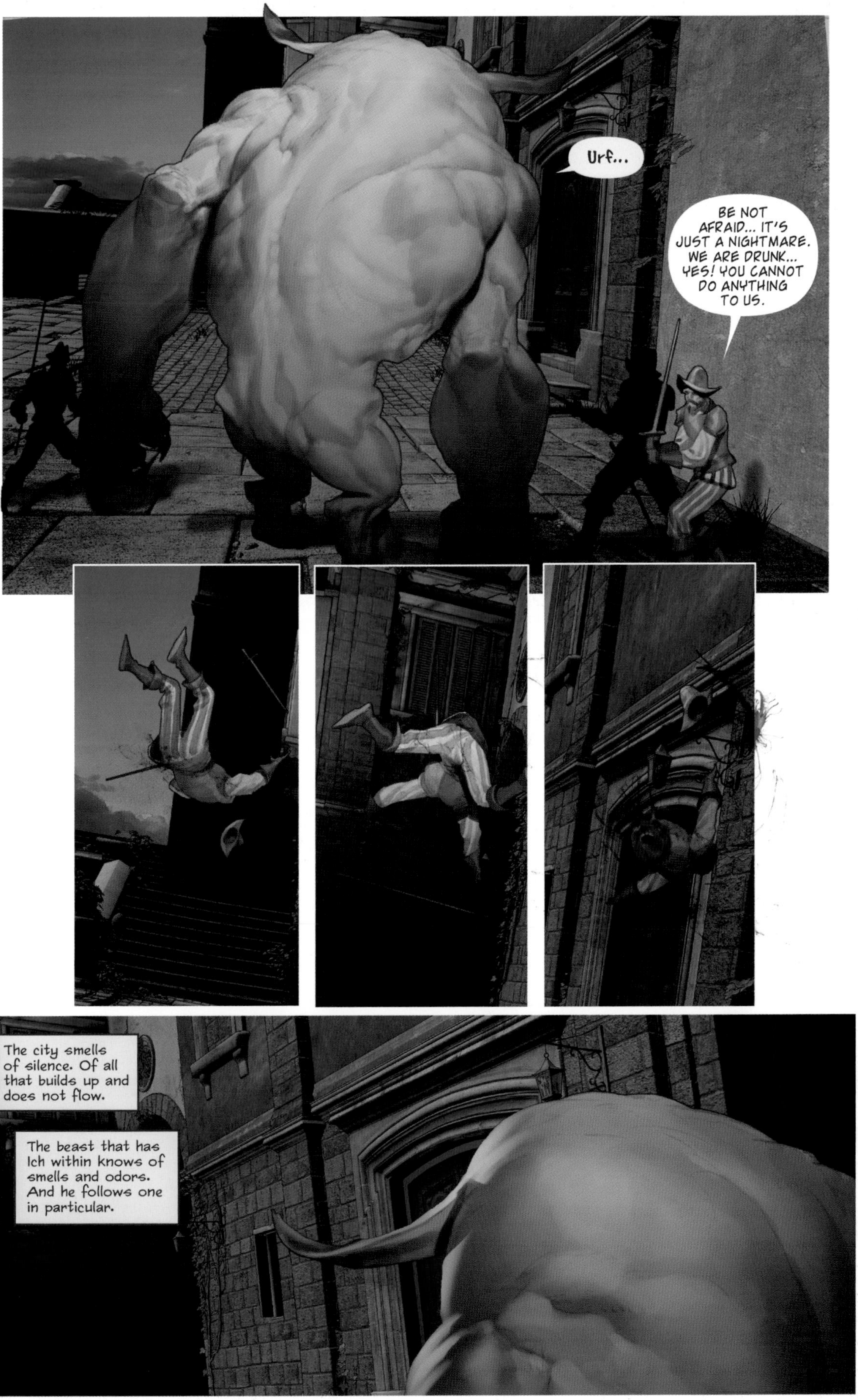
Urf...
BE NOT AFRAID... IT'S JUST A NIGHTMARE. WE ARE DRUNK... YES! YOU CANNOT DO ANYTHING TO US.
The city smells of silence. Of all that builds up and does not flow.
The beast that has Ich within knows of smells and odors. And he follows one in particular.

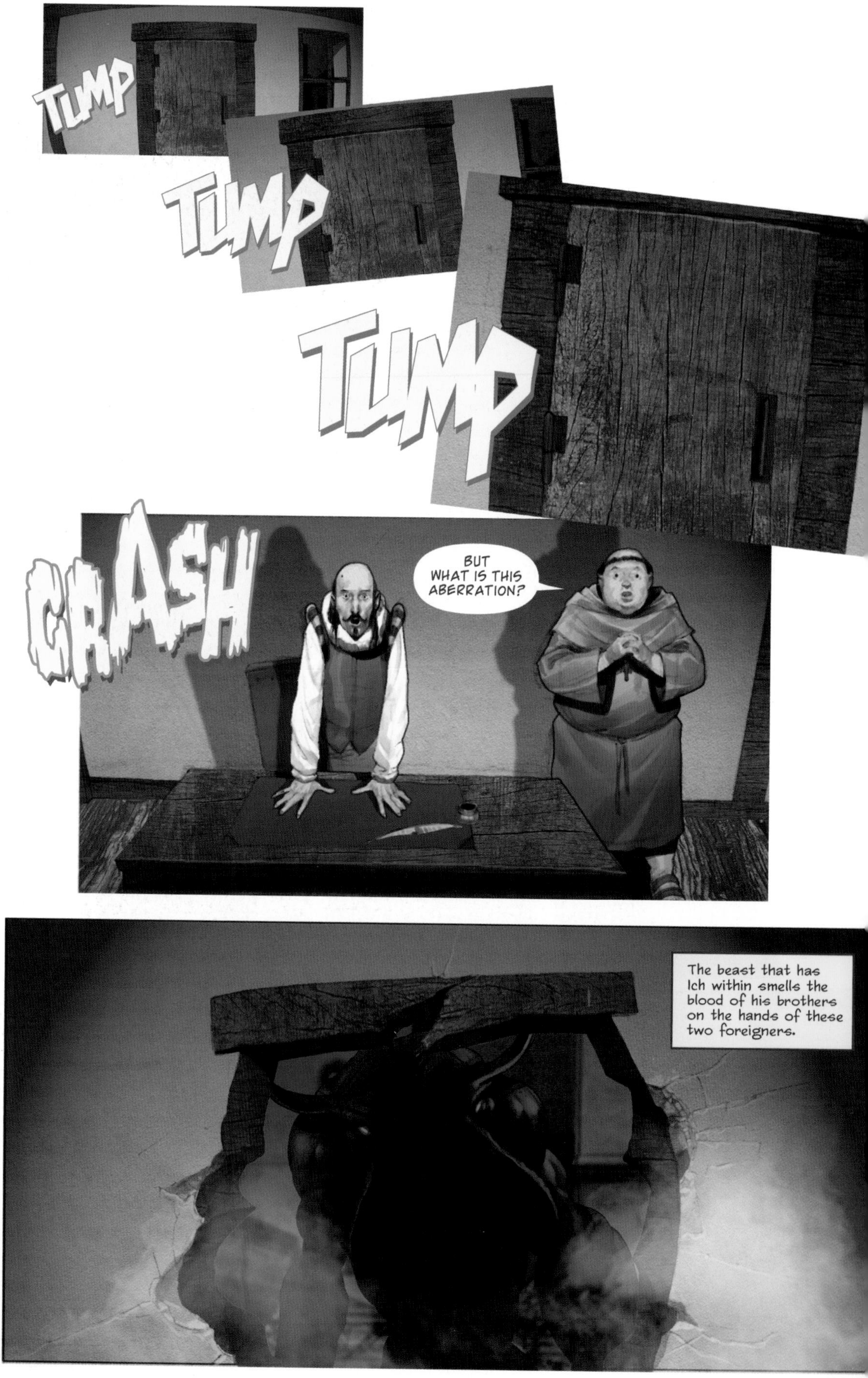
TUMP
TUMP
TUMP
CRASH
BUT WHAT IS THIS ABERRATION?
The beast that has Ich within smells the blood of his brothers on the hands of these two foreigners.

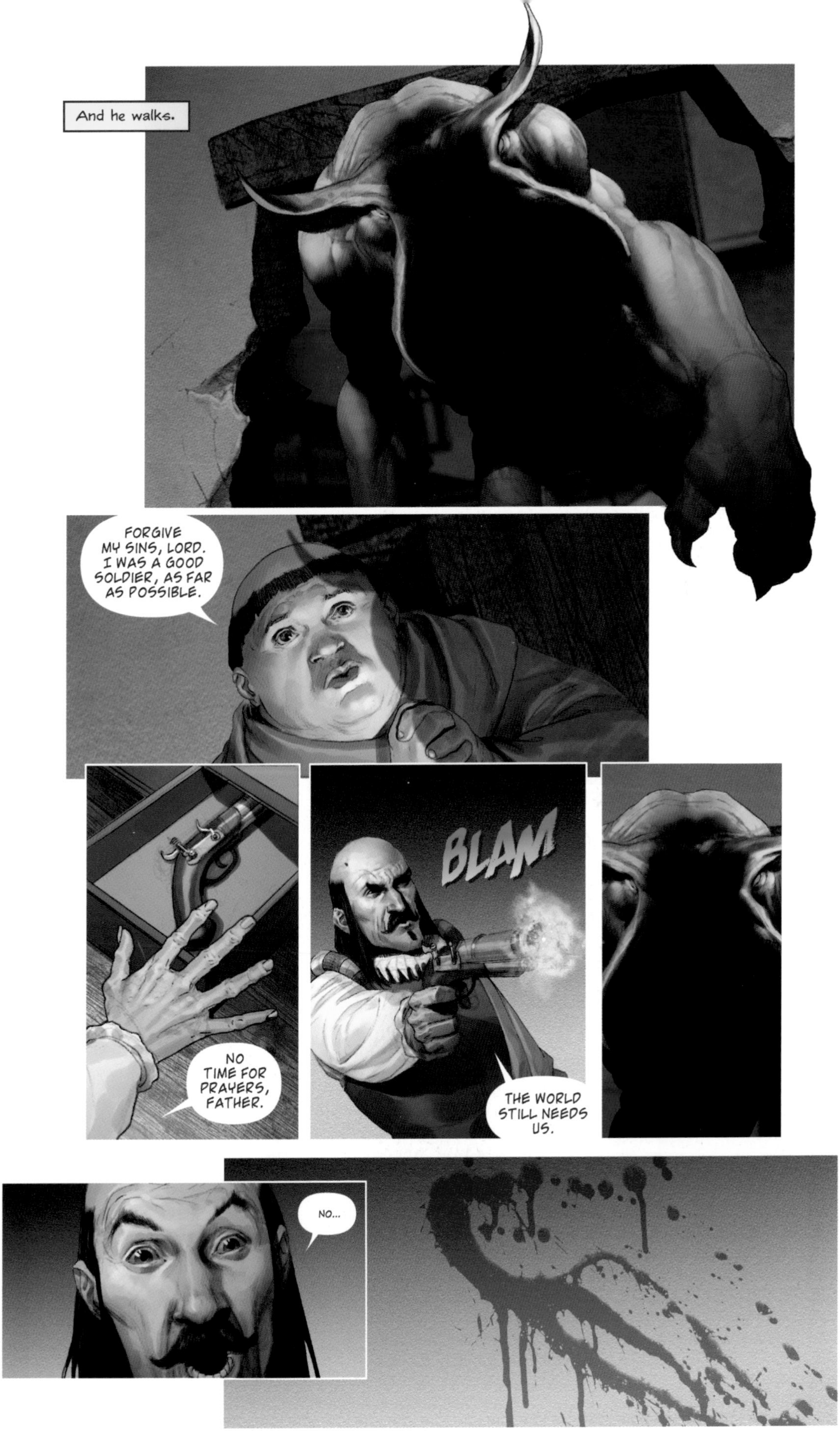

And he walks.
FORGIVE MY SINS, LORD. I WAS A GOOD SOLDIER, AS FAR AS POSSIBLE.
NO TIME FOR PRAYERS, FATHER.
BLAM
THE WORLD STILL NEEDS US.
NO...

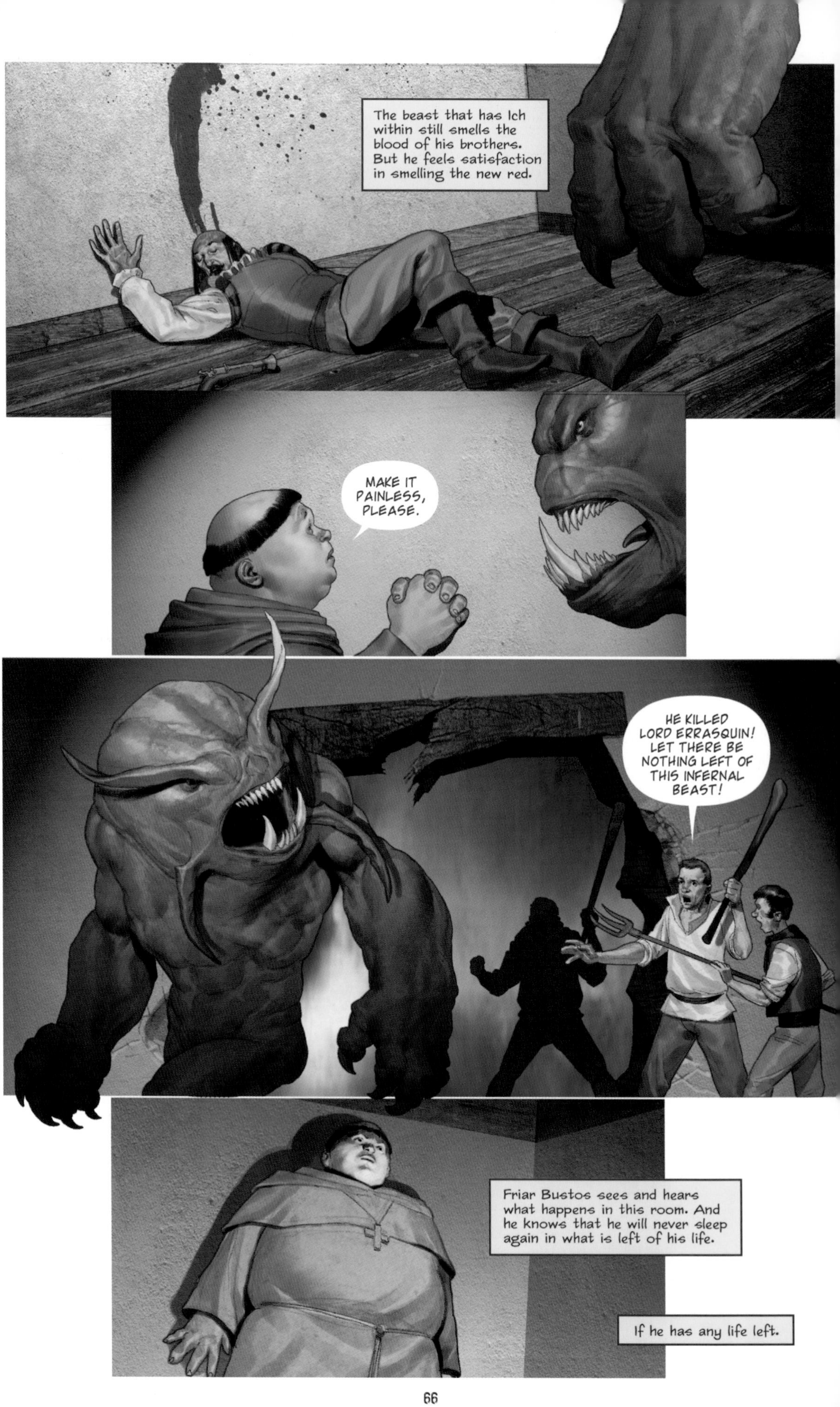
The beast that has Ich within still smells the blood of his brothers. But he feels satisfaction in smelling the new red.
MAKE IT PAINLESS, PLEASE.
HE KILLED LORD ERRASQUIN! LET THERE BE NOTHING LEFT OF THIS INFERNAL BEAST!
Friar Bustos sees and hears what happens in this room. And he knows that he will never sleep again in what is left of his life.
If he has any life left.

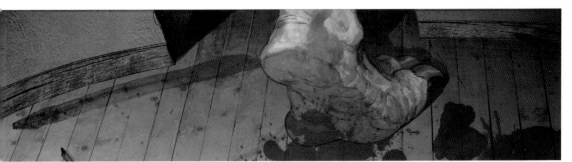

The beast that has Ich within turns once more to look at his work.

And he leaves.

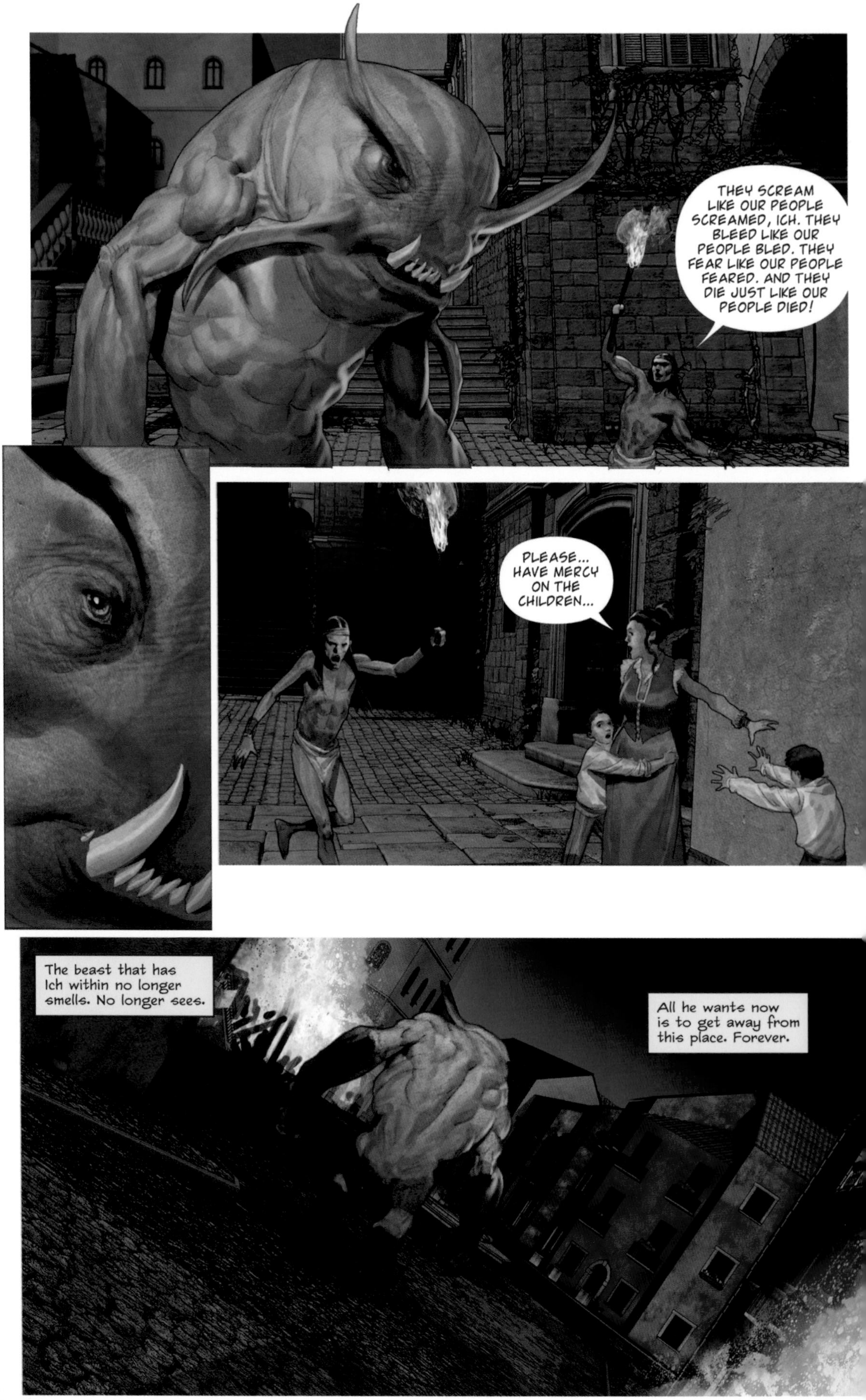
THEY SCREAM LIKE OUR PEOPLE SCREAMED, ICH. THEY BLEED LIKE OUR PEOPLE BLED. THEY FEAR LIKE OUR PEOPLE FEARED. AND THEY DIE JUST LIKE OUR PEOPLE DIED!
PLEASE... HAVE MERCY ON THE CHILDREN...
The beast that has Ich within no longer smells. No longer sees.
All he wants now is to get away from this place. Forever.

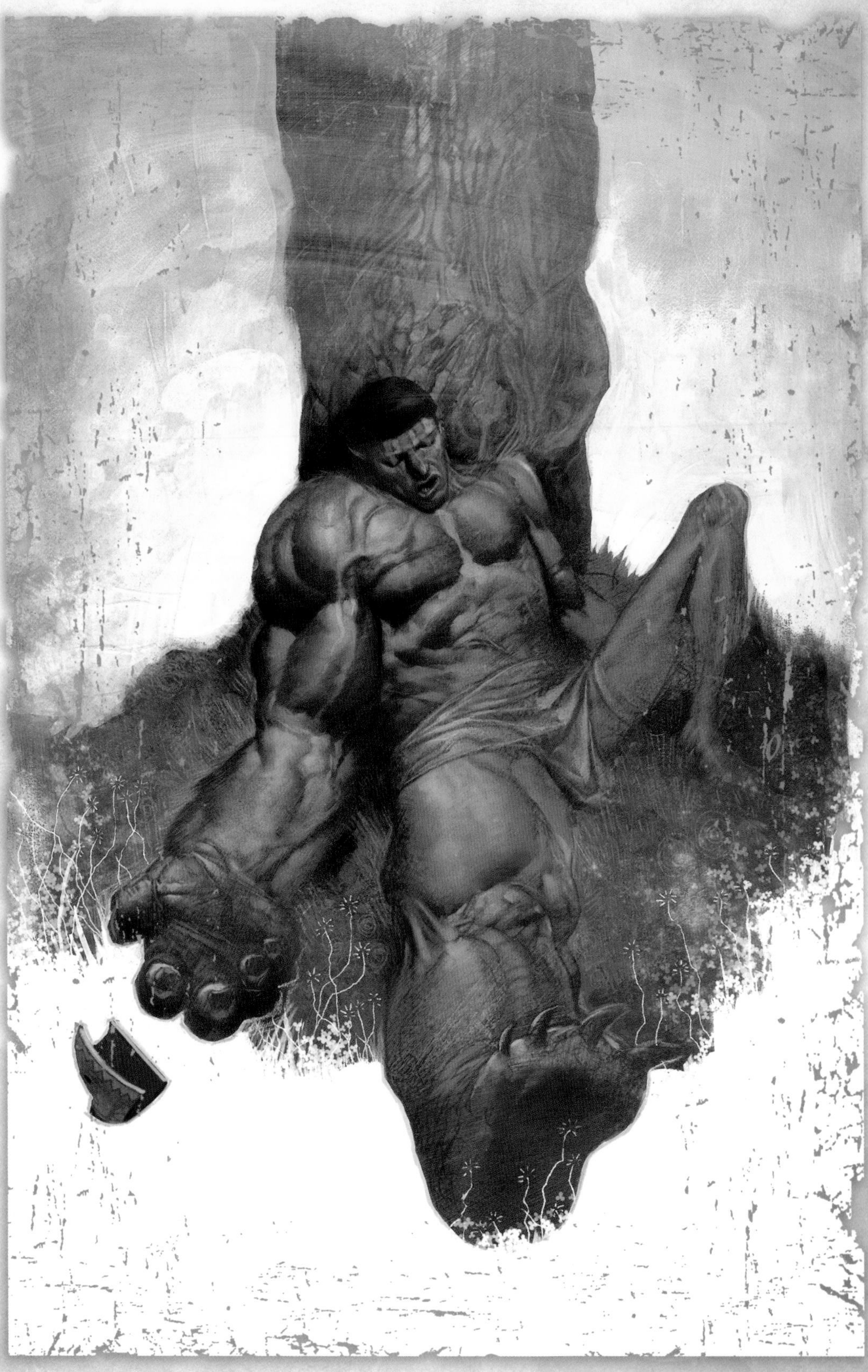

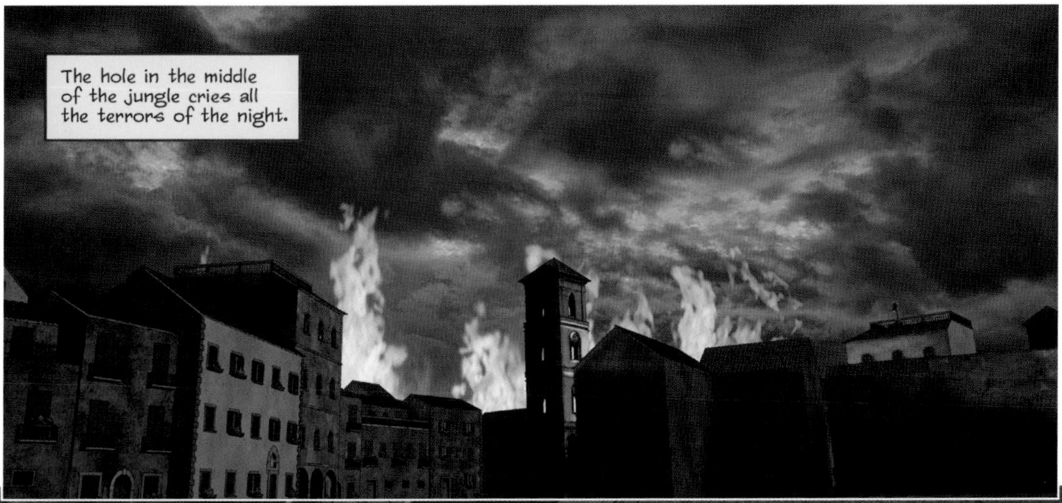
The hole in the middle of the jungle cries all the terrors of the night.

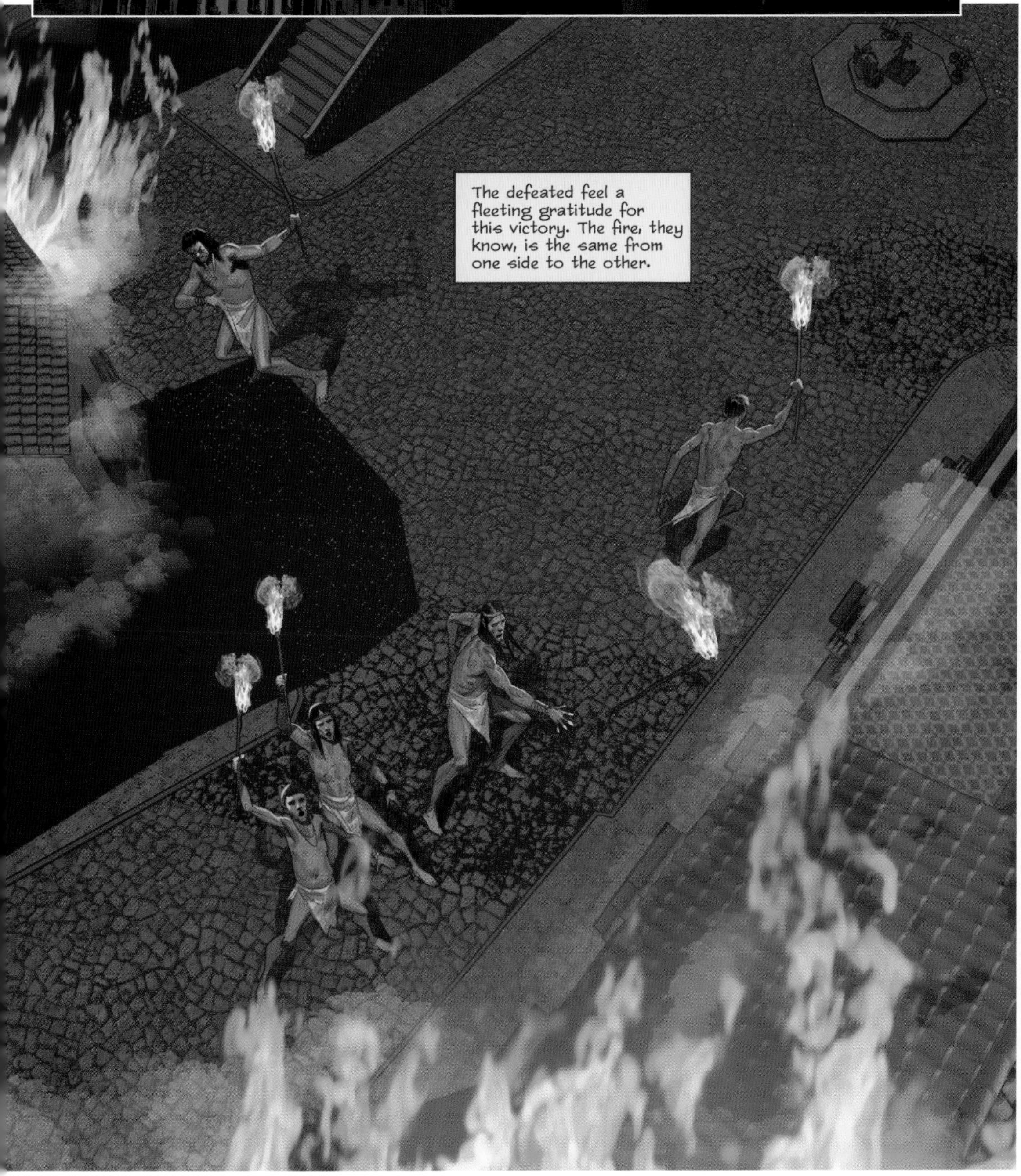
The defeated feel a fleeting gratitude for this victory. The fire, they know, is the same from one side to the other.

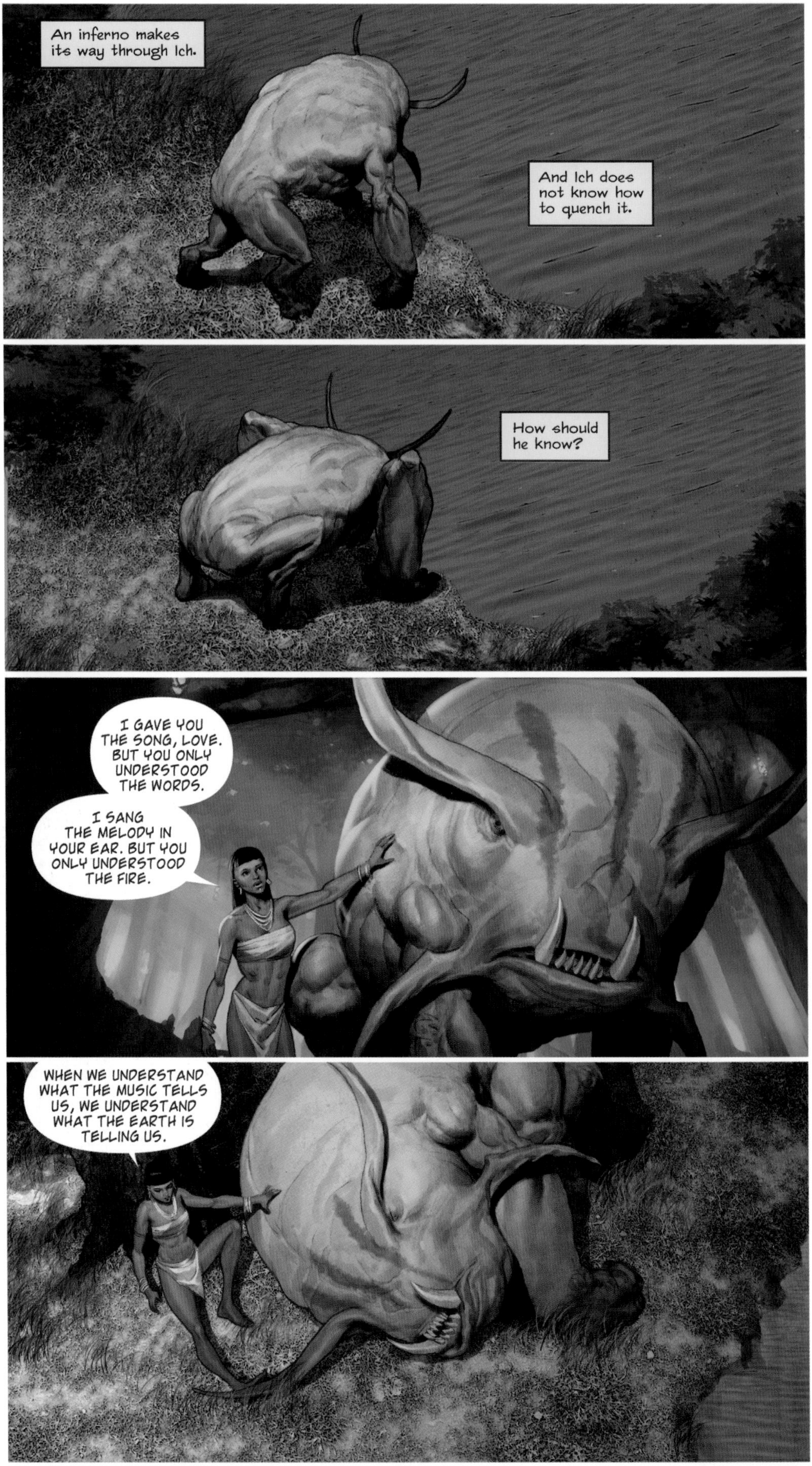
An inferno makes its way through Ich.
And Ich does not know how to quench it.
How should he know?
I GAVE YOU THE SONG, LOVE. BUT YOU ONLY UNDERSTOOD THE WORDS.
I SANG THE MELODY IN YOUR EAR. BUT YOU ONLY UNDERSTOOD THE FIRE.
WHEN WE UNDERSTAND WHAT THE MUSIC TELLS US, WE UNDERSTAND WHAT THE EARTH IS TELLING US.

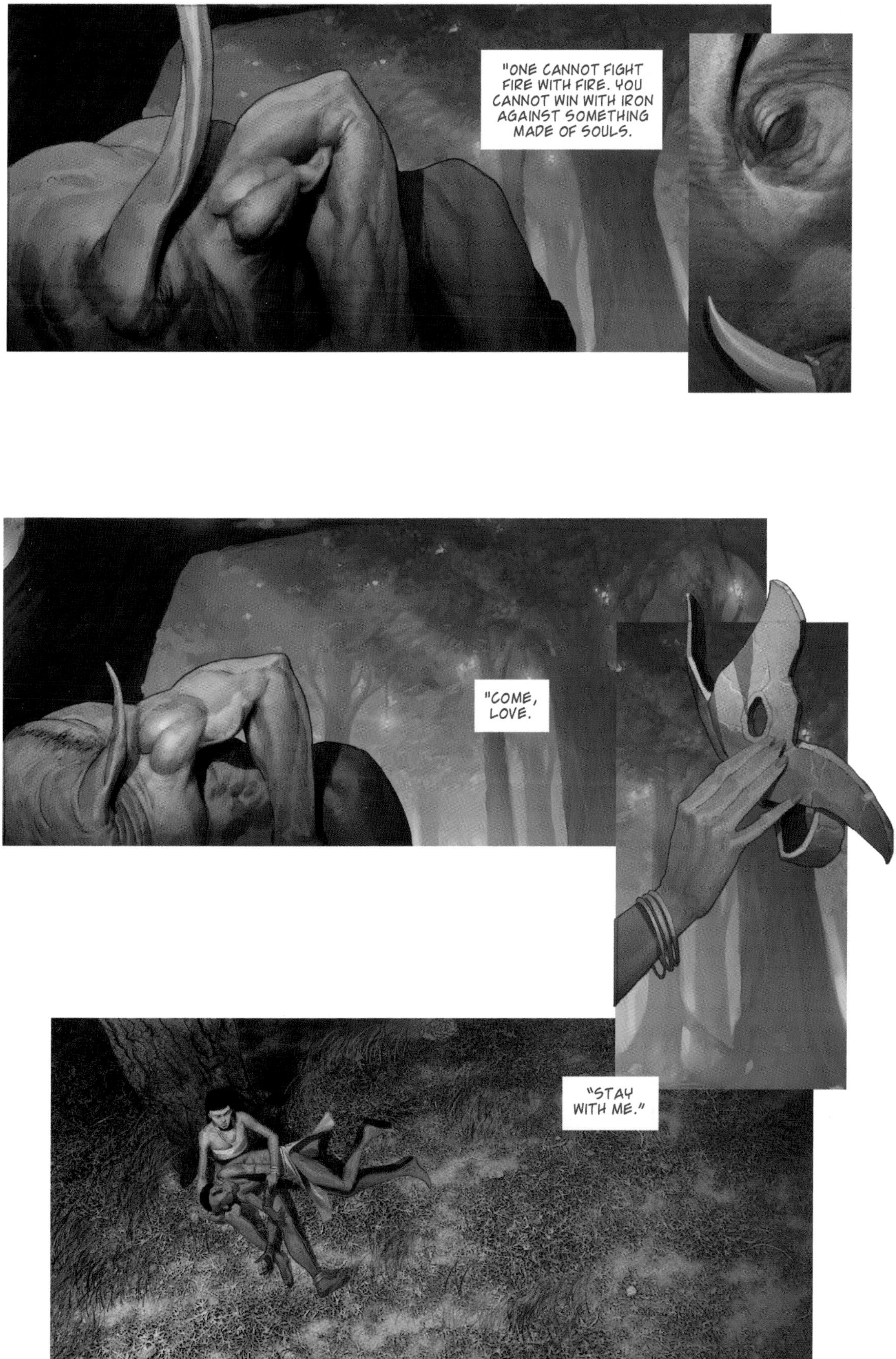
"ONE CANNOT FIGHT FIRE WITH FIRE. YOU CANNOT WIN WITH IRON AGAINST SOMETHING MADE OF SOULS.
"COME, LOVE.
"STAY WITH ME."

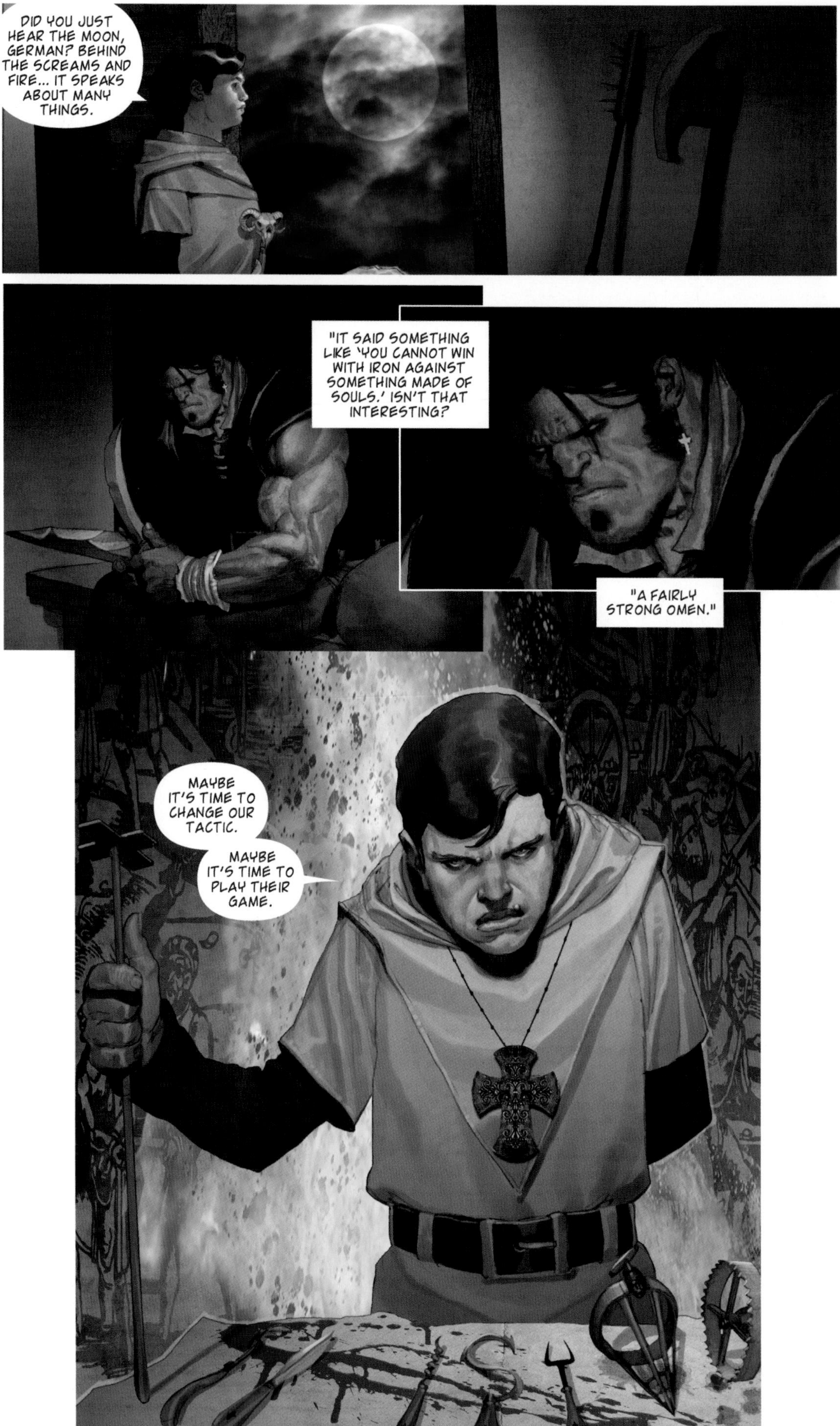
DID YOU JUST HEAR THE MOON, GERMAN? BEHIND THE SCREAMS AND FIRE... IT SPEAKS ABOUT MANY THINGS.
"IT SAID SOMETHING LIKE 'YOU CANNOT WIN WITH IRON AGAINST SOMETHING MADE OF SOULS.' ISN'T THAT INTERESTING?
"A FAIRLY STRONG OMEN."
MAYBE IT'S TIME TO CHANGE OUR TACTIC.
MAYBE IT'S TIME TO PLAY THEIR GAME.

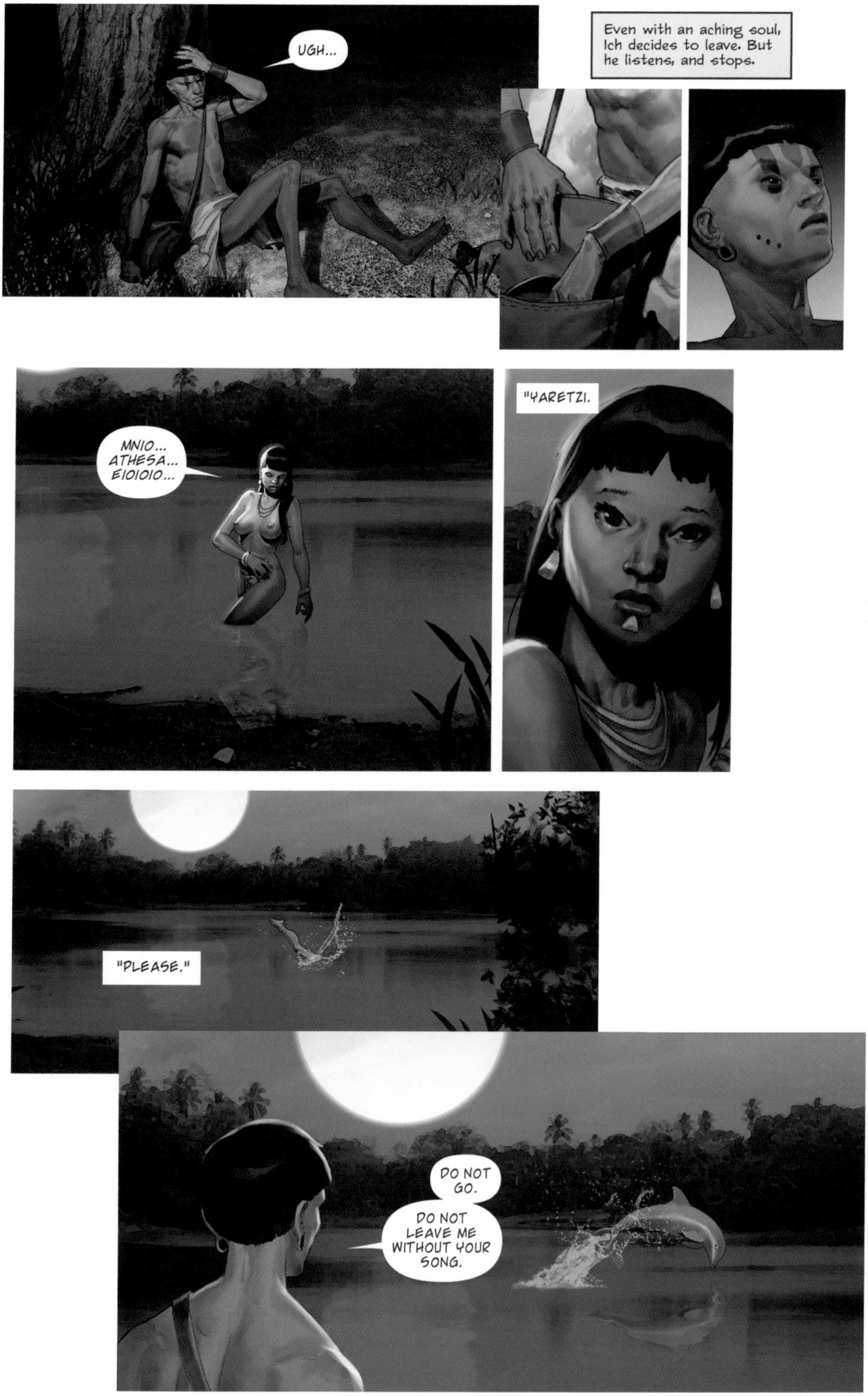
UGH...
Even with an aching soul, Ich decides to leave. But he listens, and stops.
MNIO... ATHESA... EIOIOIO...
"YARETZI.
"PLEASE."
DO NOT GO.
DO NOT LEAVE ME WITHOUT YOUR SONG.

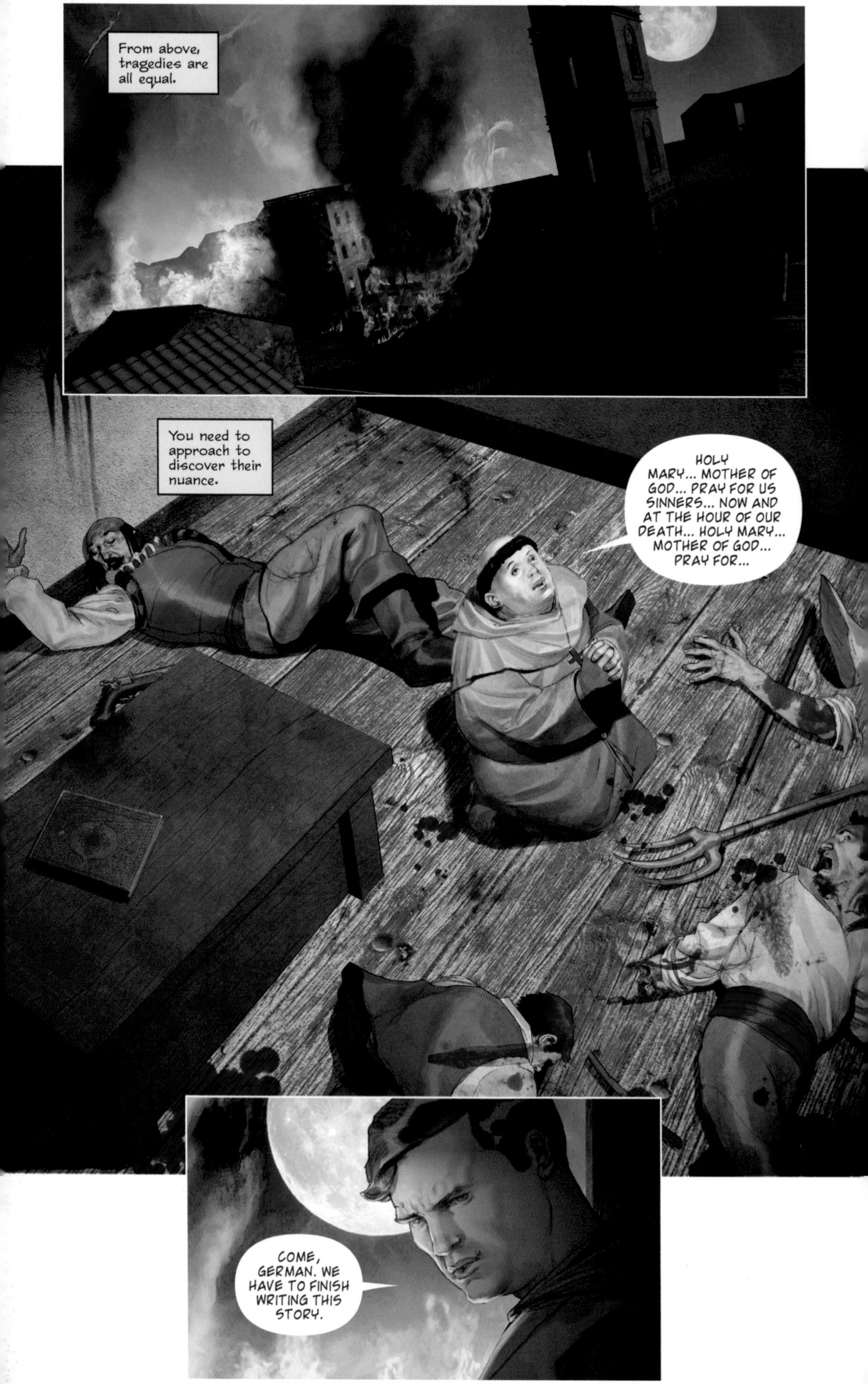
From above, tragedies are all equal.
You need to approach to discover their nuance.
HOLY MARY... MOTHER OF GOD... PRAY FOR US SINNERS... NOW AND AT THE HOUR OF OUR DEATH... HOLY MARY... MOTHER OF GOD... PRAY FOR...
COME, GERMAN. WE HAVE TO FINISH WRITING THIS STORY.

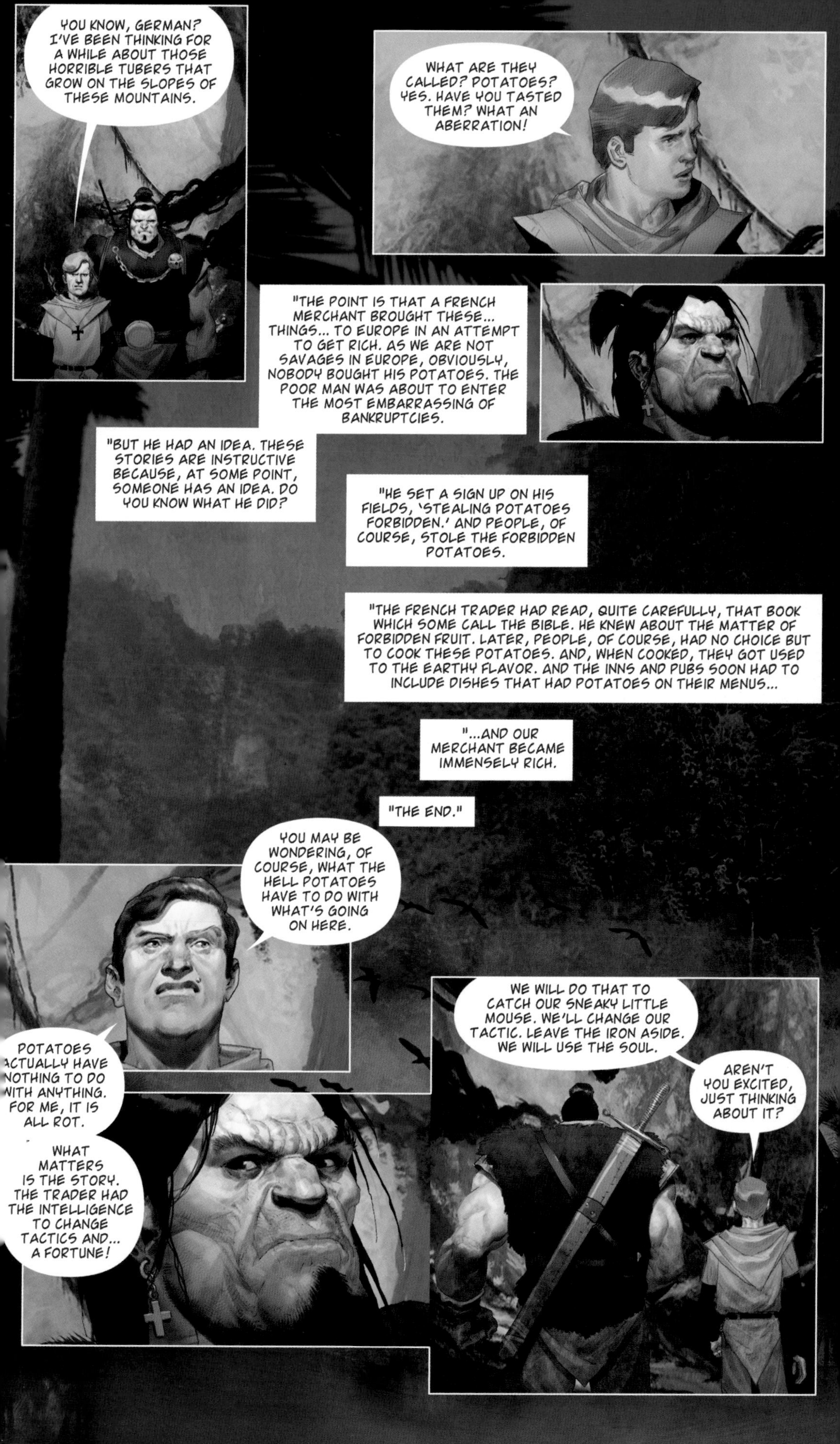
YOU KNOW, GERMAN? I'VE BEEN THINKING FOR A WHILE ABOUT THOSE HORRIBLE TUBERS THAT GROW ON THE SLOPES OF THESE MOUNTAINS.
WHAT ARE THEY CALLED? POTATOES? YES. HAVE YOU TASTED THEM? WHAT AN ABERRATION!
"THE POINT IS THAT A FRENCH MERCHANT BROUGHT THESE... THINGS... TO EUROPE IN AN ATTEMPT TO GET RICH. AS WE ARE NOT SAVAGES IN EUROPE, OBVIOUSLY, NOBODY BOUGHT HIS POTATOES. THE POOR MAN WAS ABOUT TO ENTER THE MOST EMBARRASSING OF BANKRUPTCIES.
"BUT HE HAD AN IDEA. THESE STORIES ARE INSTRUCTIVE BECAUSE, AT SOME POINT, SOMEONE HAS AN IDEA. DO YOU KNOW WHAT HE DID?
"HE SET A SIGN UP ON HIS FIELDS, 'STEALING POTATOES FORBIDDEN.' AND PEOPLE, OF COURSE, STOLE THE FORBIDDEN POTATOES.
"THE FRENCH TRADER HAD READ, QUITE CAREFULLY, THAT BOOK WHICH SOME CALL THE BIBLE. HE KNEW ABOUT THE MATTER OF FORBIDDEN FRUIT. LATER, PEOPLE, OF COURSE, HAD NO CHOICE BUT TO COOK THESE POTATOES. AND, WHEN COOKED, THEY GOT USED TO THE EARTHY FLAVOR. AND THE INNS AND PUBS SOON HAD TO INCLUDE DISHES THAT HAD POTATOES ON THEIR MENUS...
"...AND OUR MERCHANT BECAME IMMENSELY RICH.
"THE END."
YOU MAY BE WONDERING, OF COURSE, WHAT THE HELL POTATOES HAVE TO DO WITH WHAT'S GOING ON HERE.
POTATOES ACTUALLY HAVE NOTHING TO DO WITH ANYTHING. FOR ME, IT IS ALL ROT.
WHAT MATTERS IS THE STORY. THE TRADER HAD THE INTELLIGENCE TO CHANGE TACTICS AND... A FORTUNE!
WE WILL DO THAT TO CATCH OUR SNEAKY LITTLE MOUSE. WE'LL CHANGE OUR TACTIC. LEAVE THE IRON ASIDE. WE WILL USE THE SOUL.
AREN'T YOU EXCITED, JUST THINKING ABOUT IT?

"HERE, GERMAN? DOES THIS SMELL LIKE A GOOD PLACE?"

WE WILL NOT PURSUE HIM, AS WE DO THE WITCHES IN EUROPE...

...WE'LL GET HIM TO COME DIRECTLY TO US.

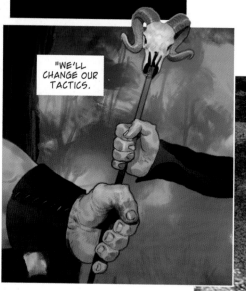

"WE'LL CHANGE OUR TACTICS.

"COME, CHILD."

THE WOLF IS LOOKING FOR YOU.

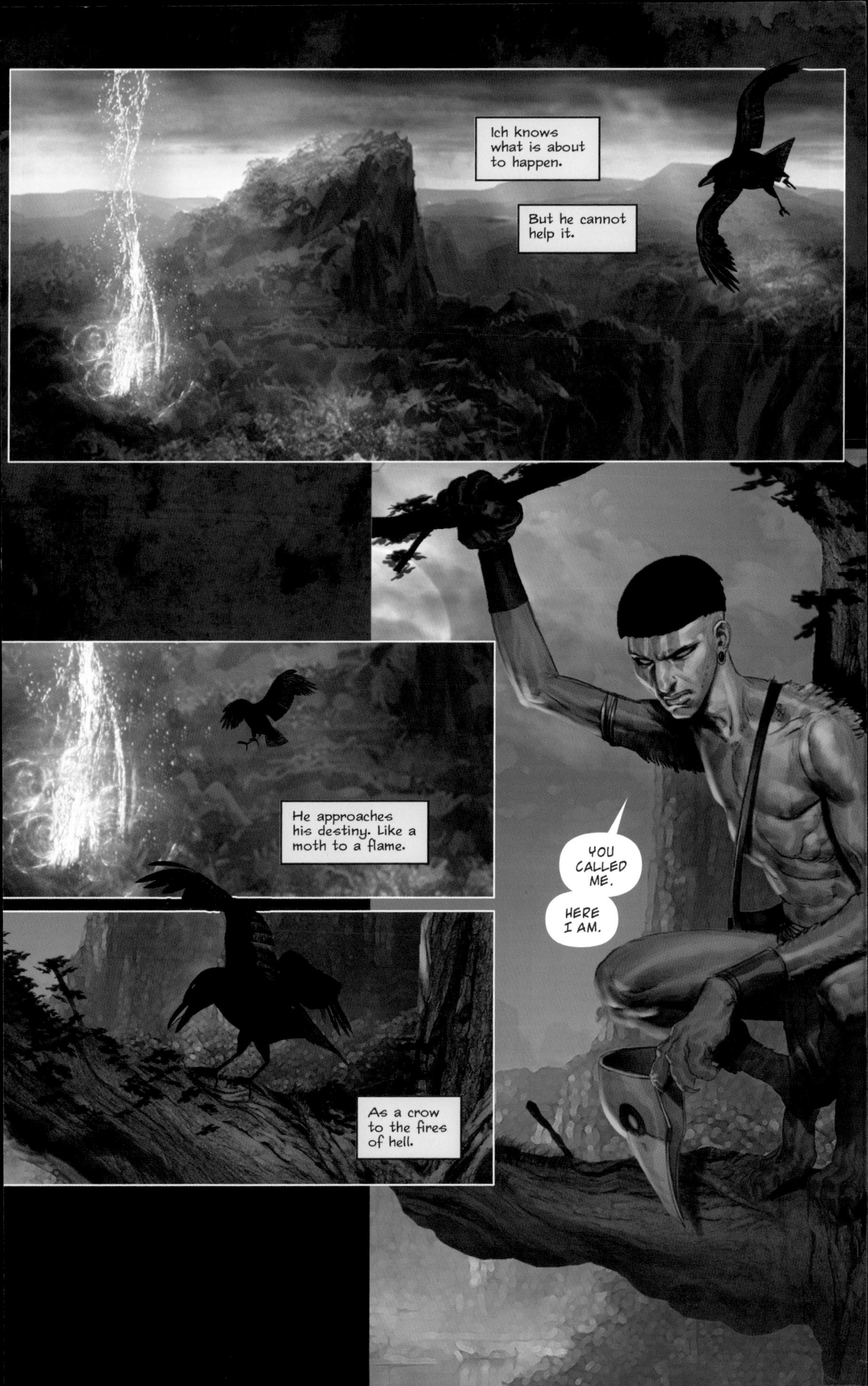
Ich knows what is about to happen.
But he cannot help it.
He approaches his destiny. Like a moth to a flame.
As a crow to the fires of hell.
YOU CALLED ME.
HERE I AM.

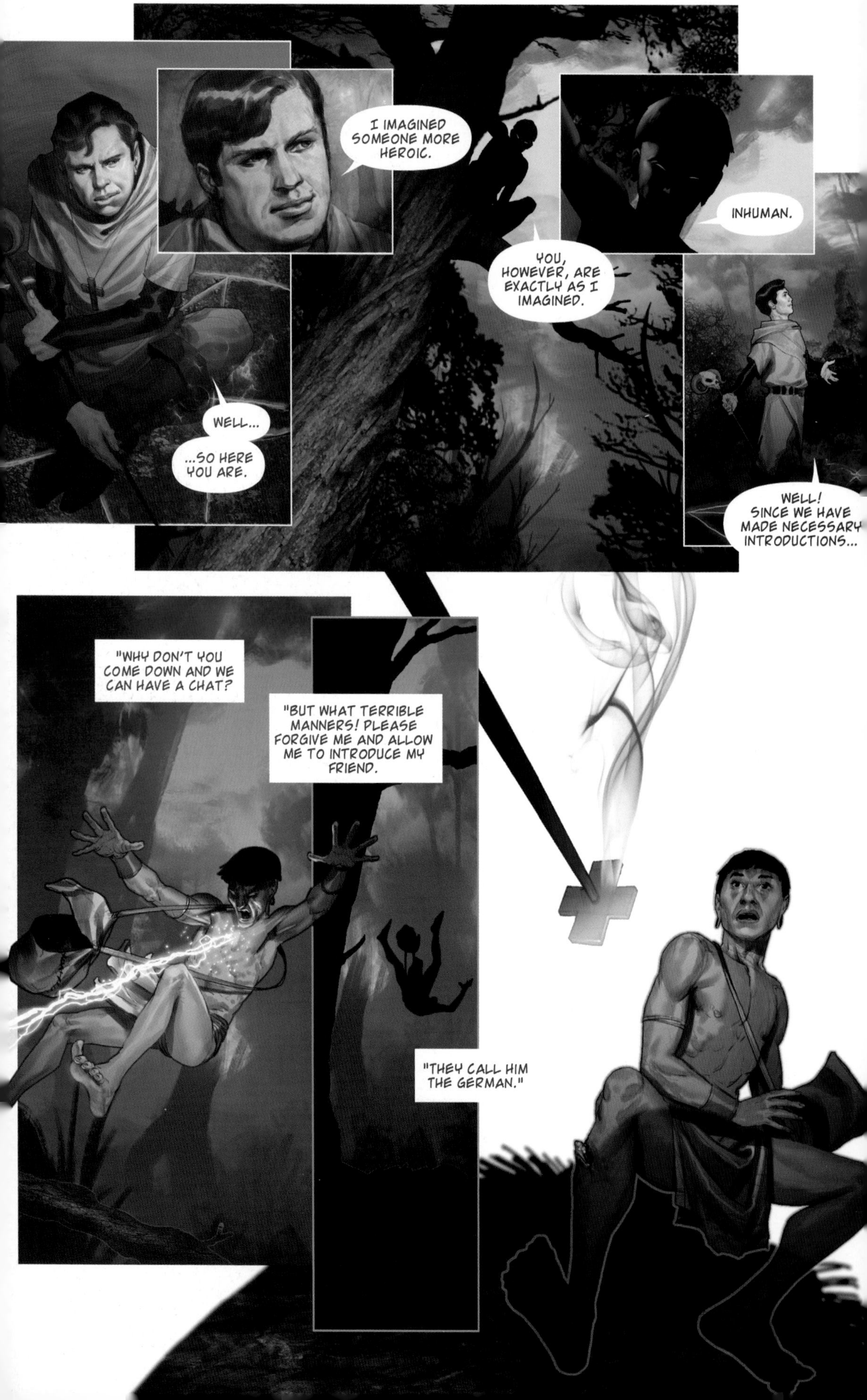
WELL...
...SO HERE YOU ARE.
I IMAGINED SOMEONE MORE HEROIC.
YOU, HOWEVER, ARE EXACTLY AS I IMAGINED.
INHUMAN.
WELL! SINCE WE HAVE MADE NECESSARY INTRODUCTIONS...
"WHY DON'T YOU COME DOWN AND WE CAN HAVE A CHAT?
"BUT WHAT TERRIBLE MANNERS! PLEASE FORGIVE ME AND ALLOW ME TO INTRODUCE MY FRIEND.
"THEY CALL HIM THE GERMAN."

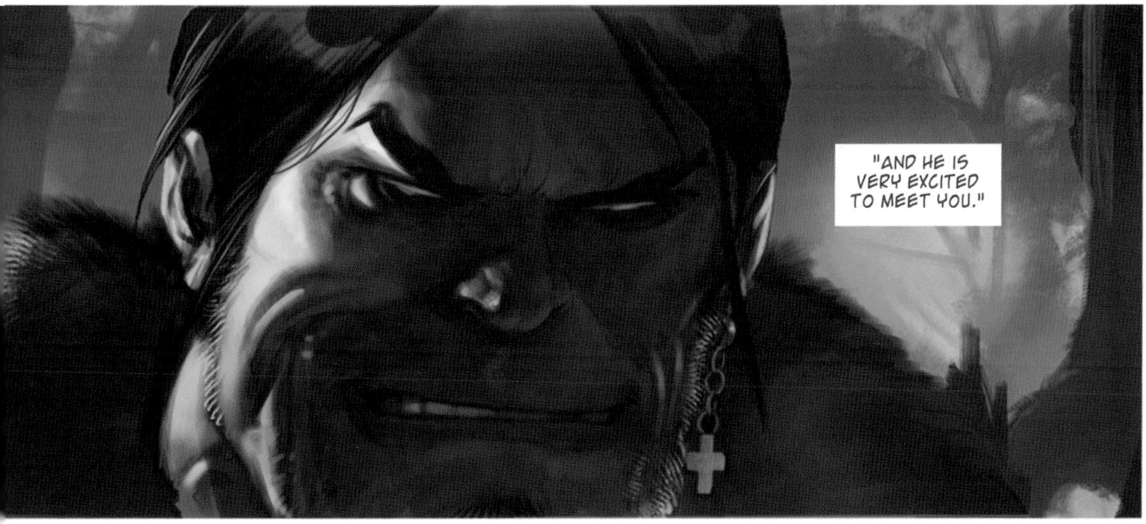
"AND HE IS
VERY EXCITED
TO MEET YOU."

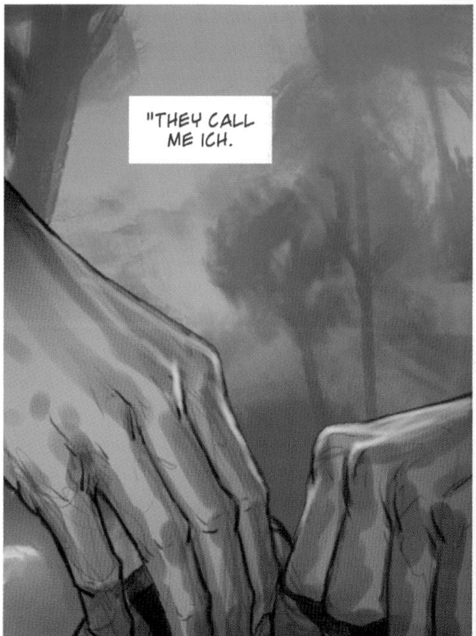
"THEY CALL
ME ICH.

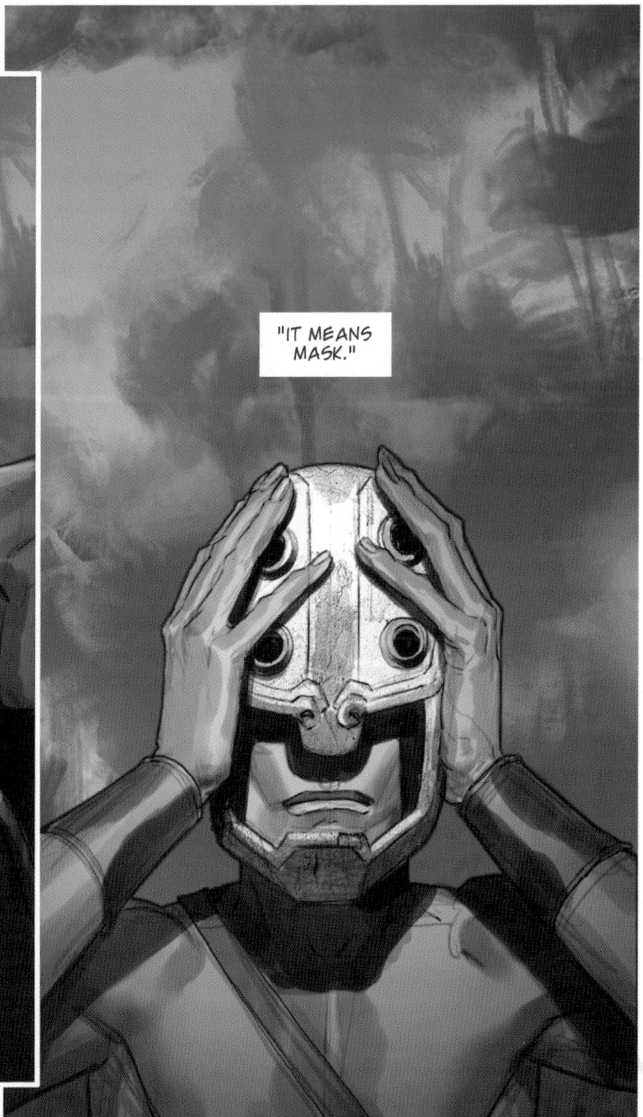
"IT MEANS
MASK."

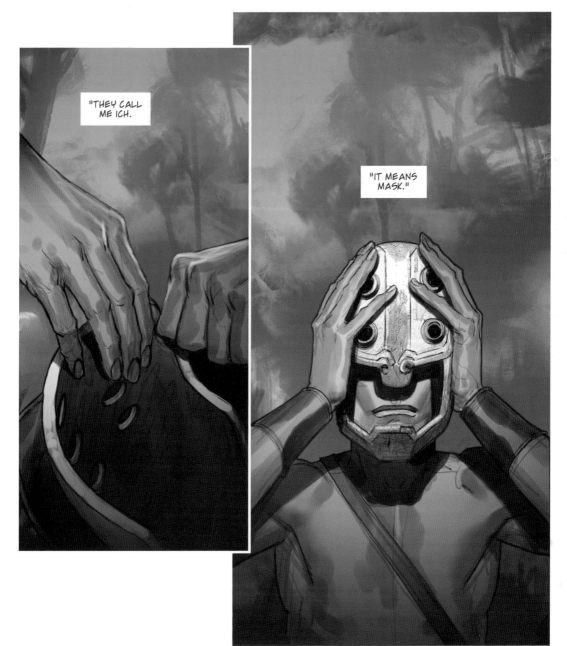

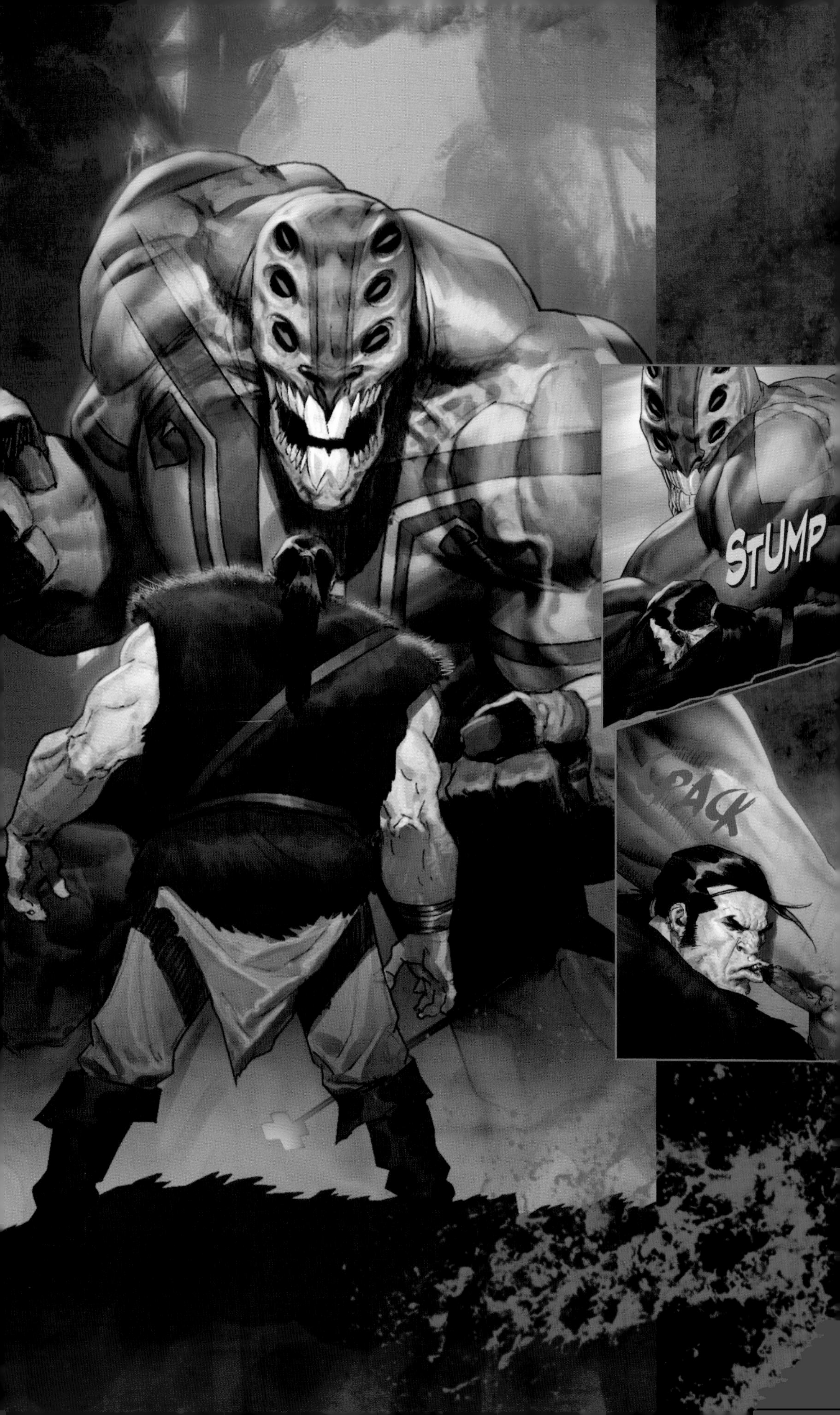
STUMP

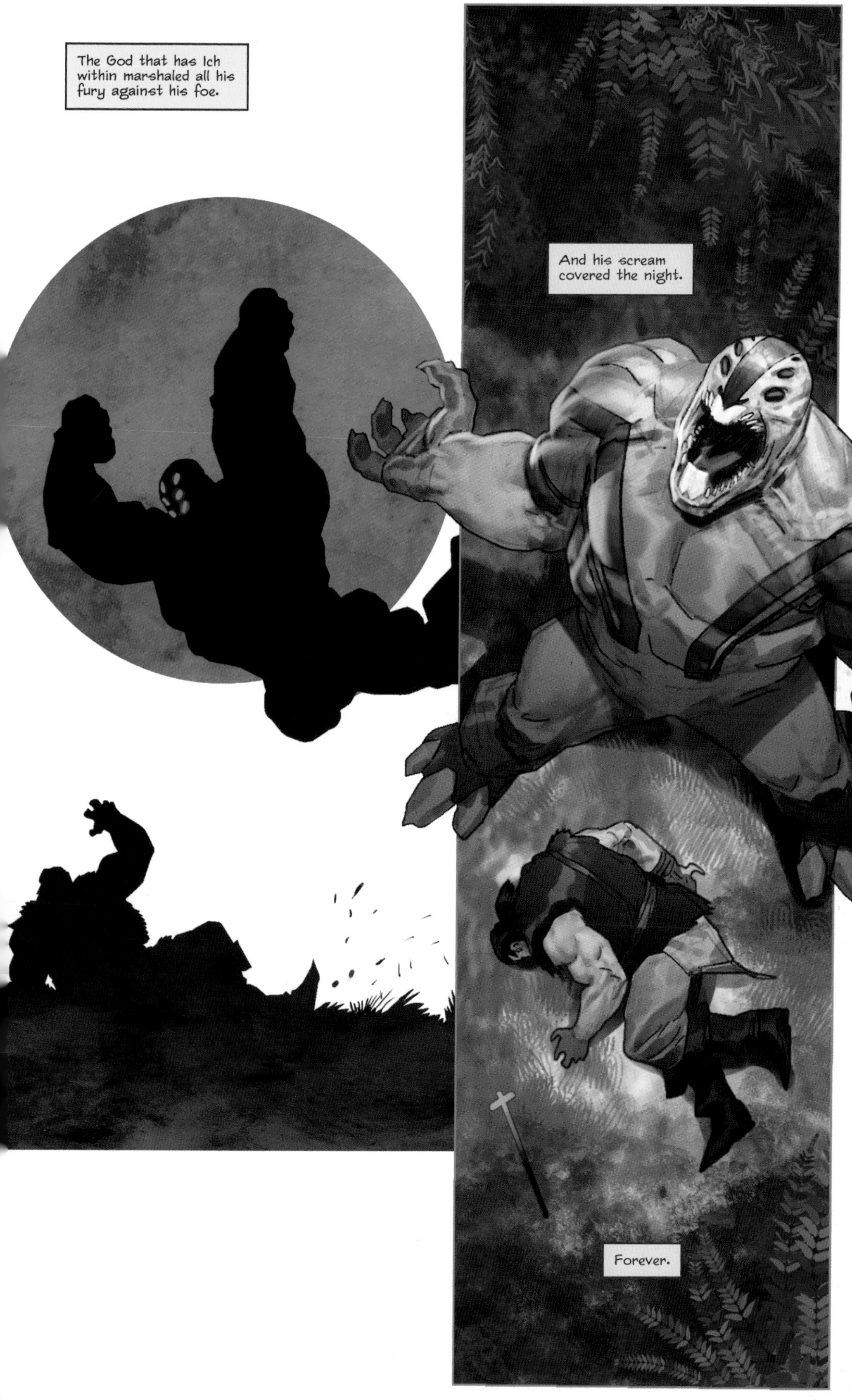
The God that has Ich within marshaled all his fury against his foe.
And his scream covered the night.
Forever.

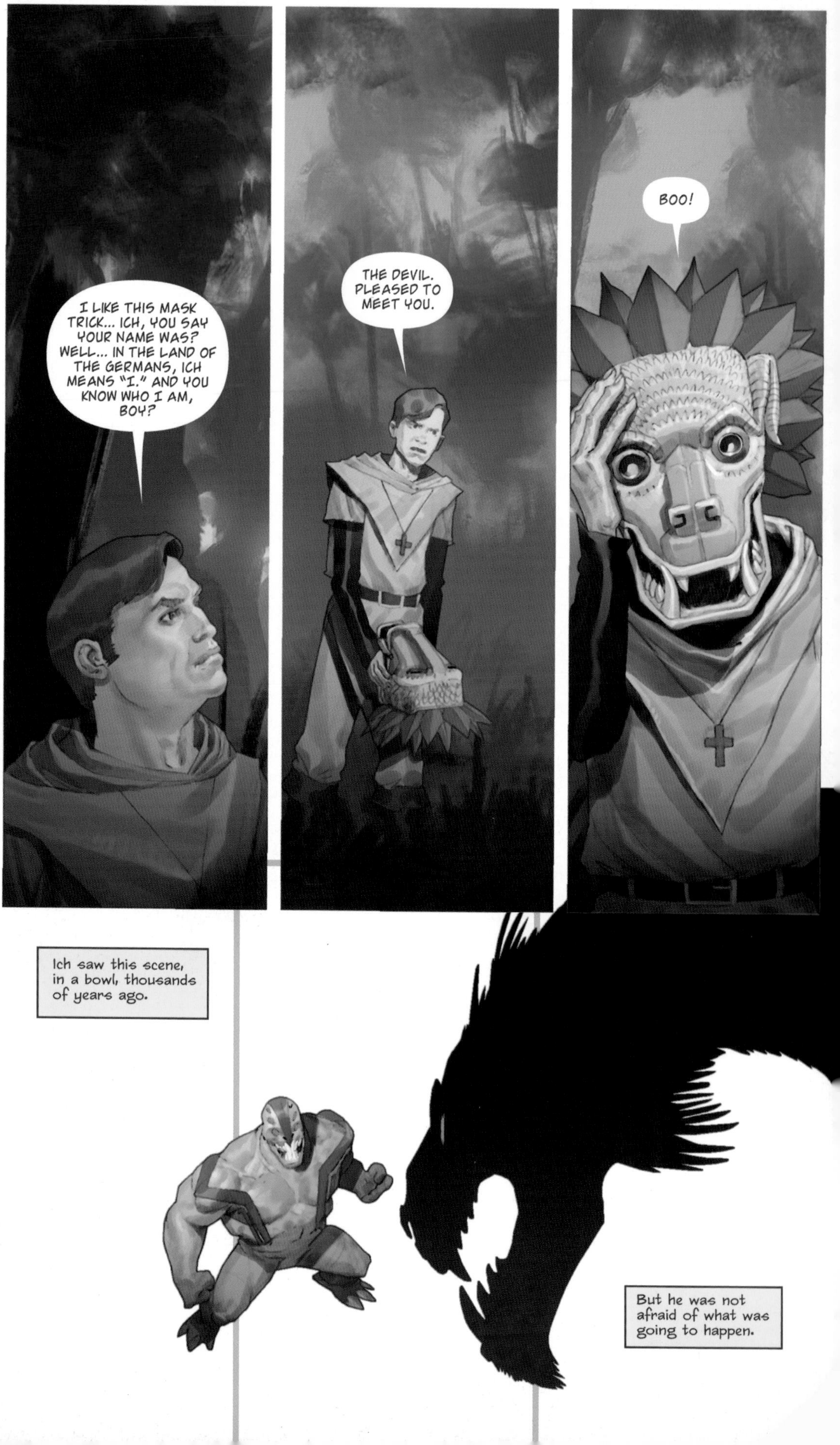
I LIKE THIS MASK TRICK... ICH, YOU SAY YOUR NAME WAS? WELL... IN THE LAND OF THE GERMANS, ICH MEANS "I." AND YOU KNOW WHO I AM, BOY?
THE DEVIL. PLEASED TO MEET YOU.
BOO!
Ich saw this scene, in a bowl, thousands of years ago.
But he was not afraid of what was going to happen.

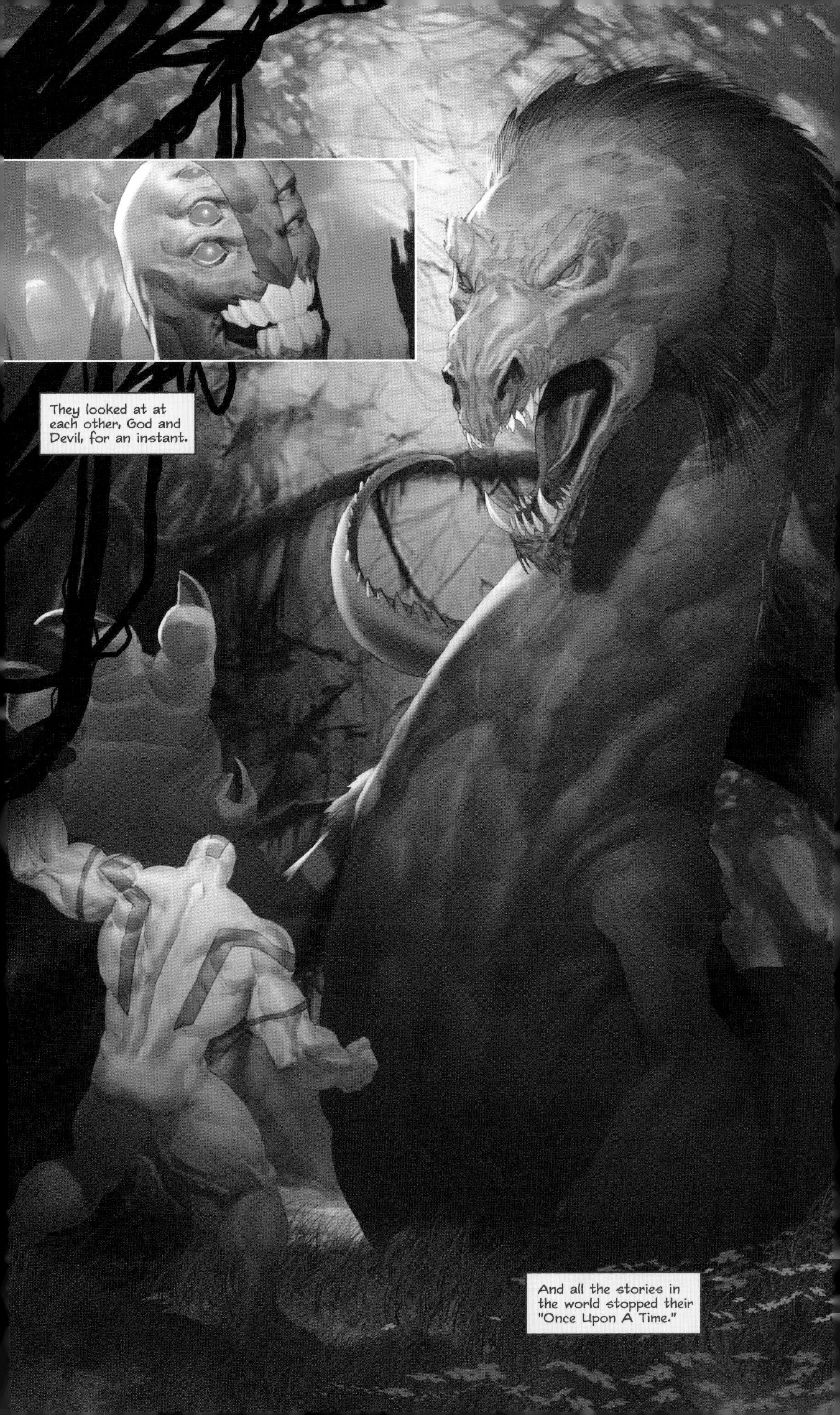
They looked at at each other, God and Devil, for an instant.
And all the stories in the world stopped their "Once Upon A Time."

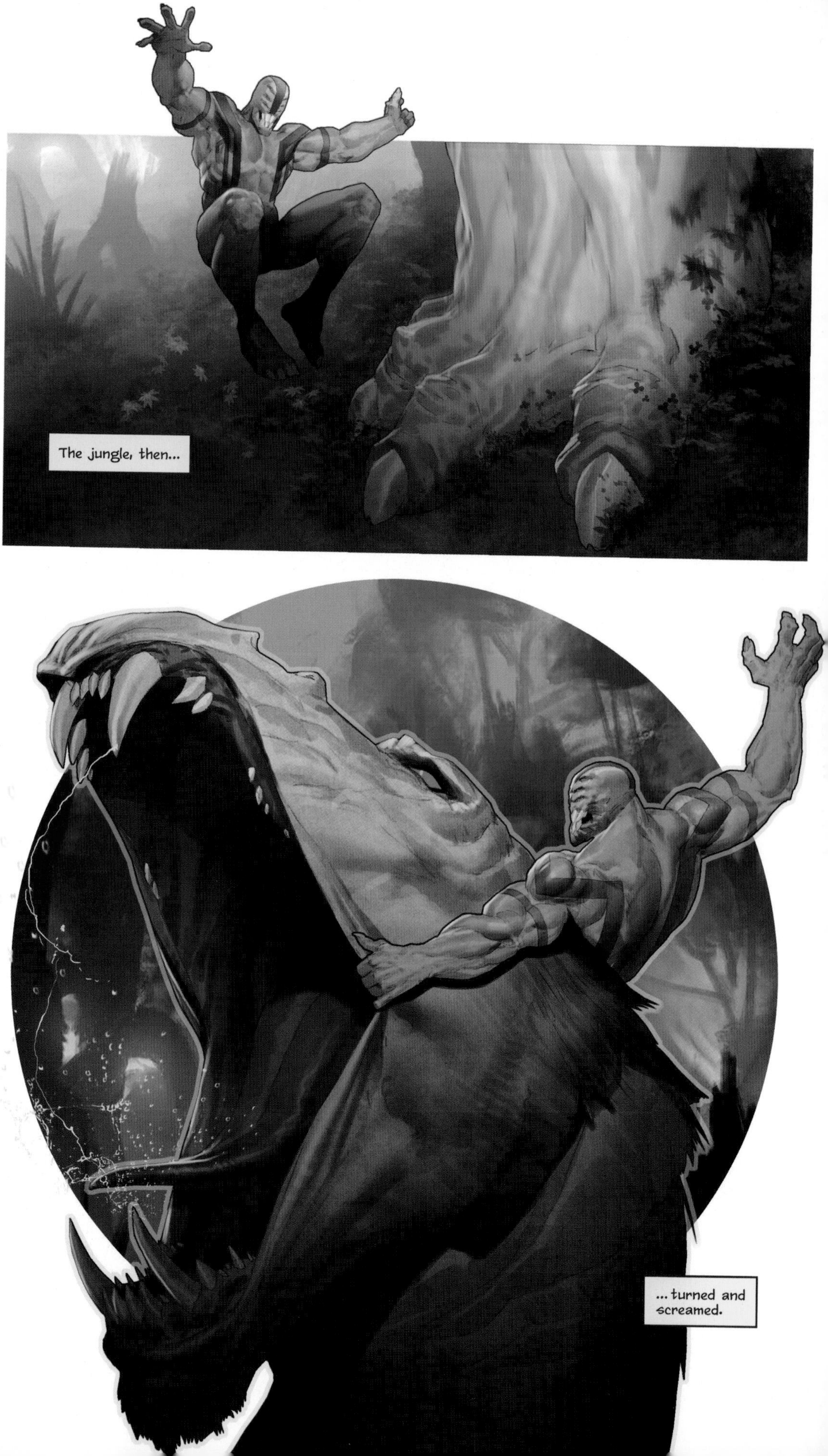
The jungle, then...
... turned and screamed.

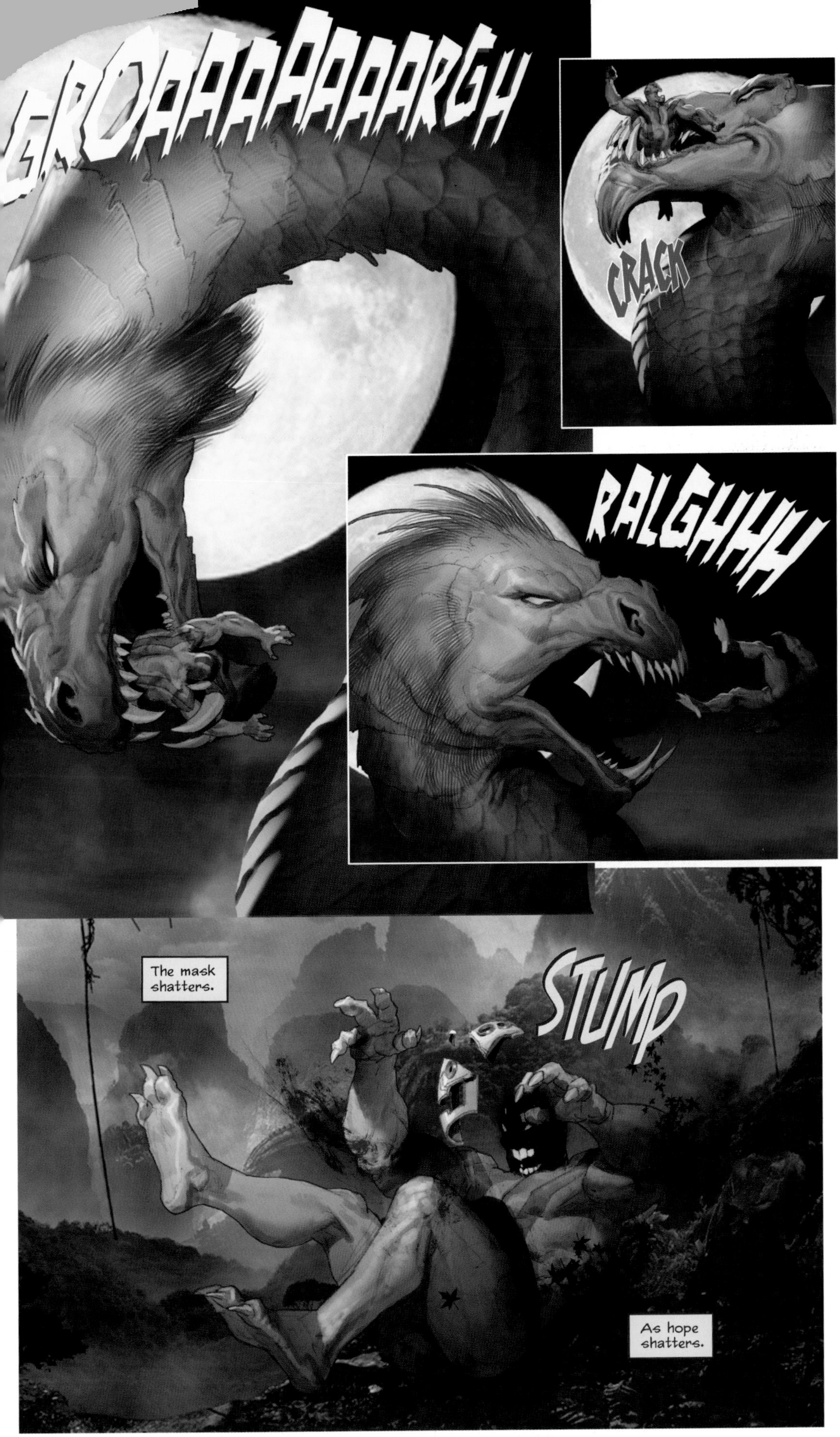
GROAAAAAAAARGH
CRACK
RALGHHH
The mask shatters.
STUMP
As hope shatters.

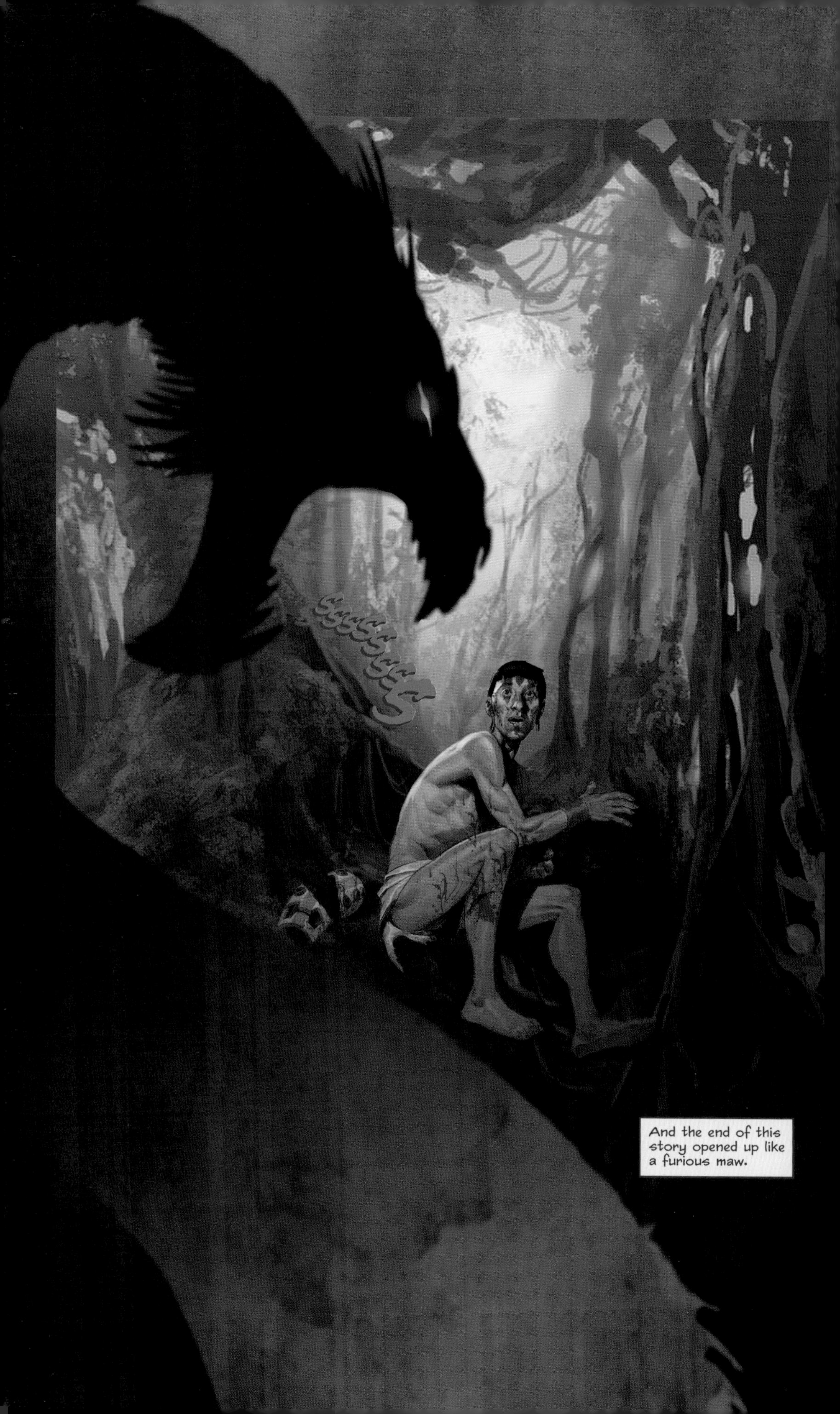
SSSSSSSSS
And the end of this story opened up like a furious maw.

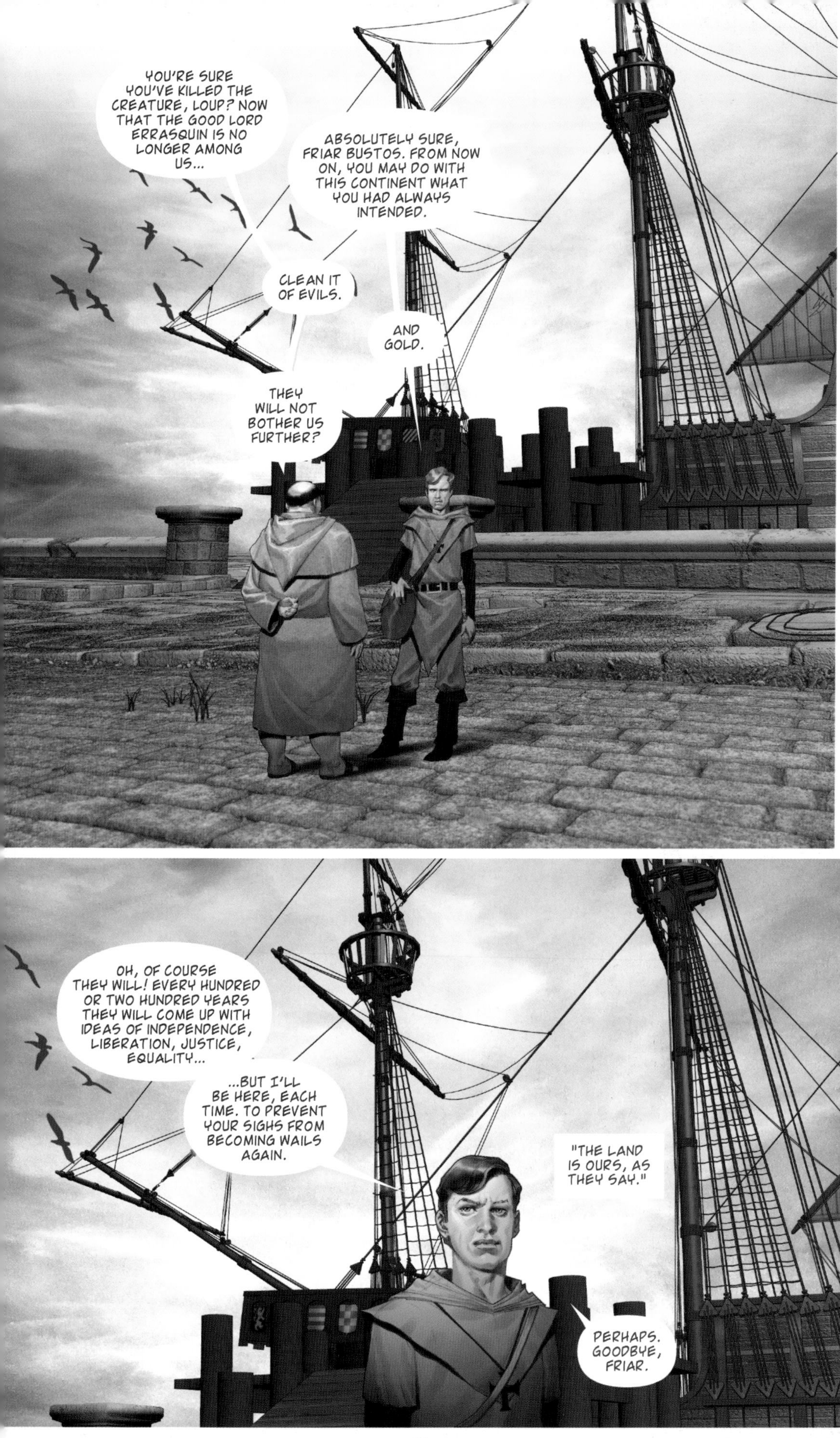
YOU'RE SURE YOU'VE KILLED THE CREATURE, LOUP? NOW THAT THE GOOD LORD ERRASQUIN IS NO LONGER AMONG US...
ABSOLUTELY SURE, FRIAR BUSTOS. FROM NOW ON, YOU MAY DO WITH THIS CONTINENT WHAT YOU HAD ALWAYS INTENDED.
CLEAN IT OF EVILS.
AND GOLD.
THEY WILL NOT BOTHER US FURTHER?
OH, OF COURSE THEY WILL! EVERY HUNDRED OR TWO HUNDRED YEARS THEY WILL COME UP WITH IDEAS OF INDEPENDENCE, LIBERATION, JUSTICE, EQUALITY...
...BUT I'LL BE HERE, EACH TIME. TO PREVENT YOUR SIGHS FROM BECOMING WAILS AGAIN.
"THE LAND IS OURS, AS THEY SAY."
PERHAPS. GOODBYE, FRIAR.

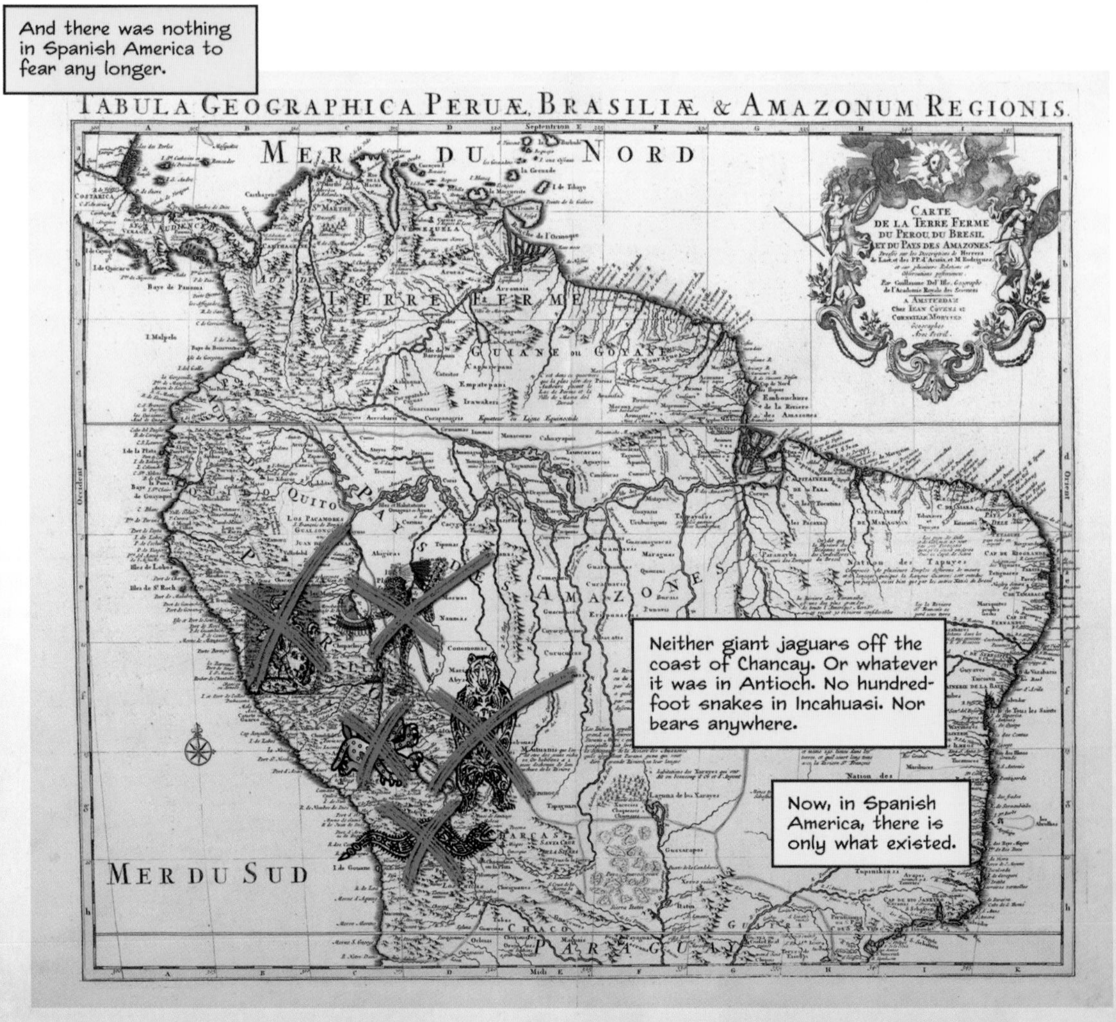
And there was nothing in Spanish America to fear any longer.
TABULA GEOGRAPHICA PERUÆ, BRASILIÆ & AMAZONUM REGIONIS.
MER DU NORD
CARTE DE LA TERRE FERME DU PEROU, DU BRESIL ET DU PAYS DES AMAZONES.
TERRE FERME
GUIANE ou GOYANE
PAYS DES AMAZONES
MER DU SUD
PARAGUAY
Neither giant jaguars off the coast of Chancay. Or whatever it was in Antioch. No hundred-foot snakes in Incahuasi. Nor bears anywhere.
Now, in Spanish America, there is only what existed.

Some endings cannot be rewritten.

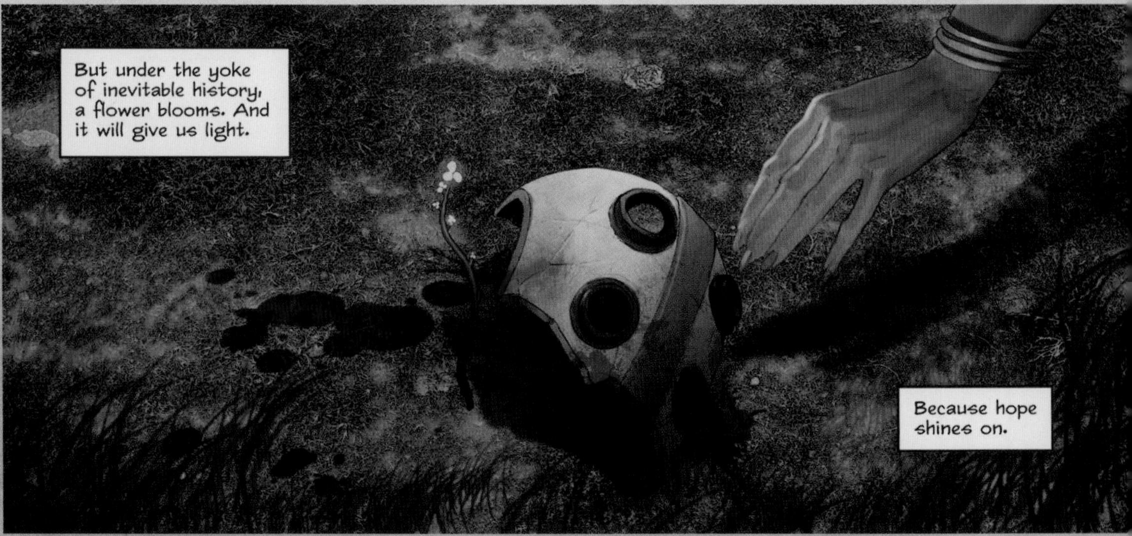
But under the yoke of inevitable history, a flower blooms. And it will give us light.
Because hope shines on.

The End

ART GALLERY

CHUNCHU
SALVAJE

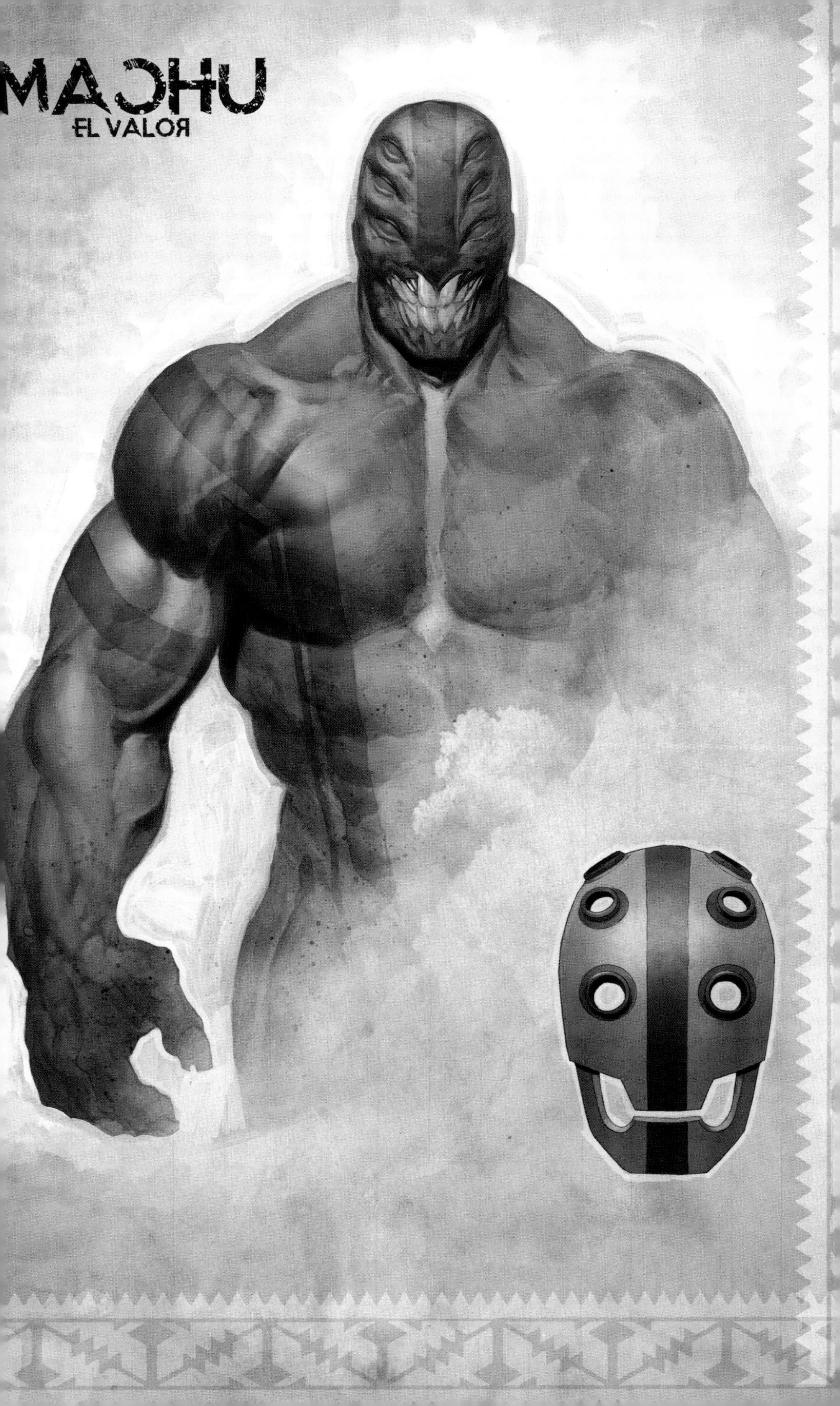
MACHU
EL VALOR

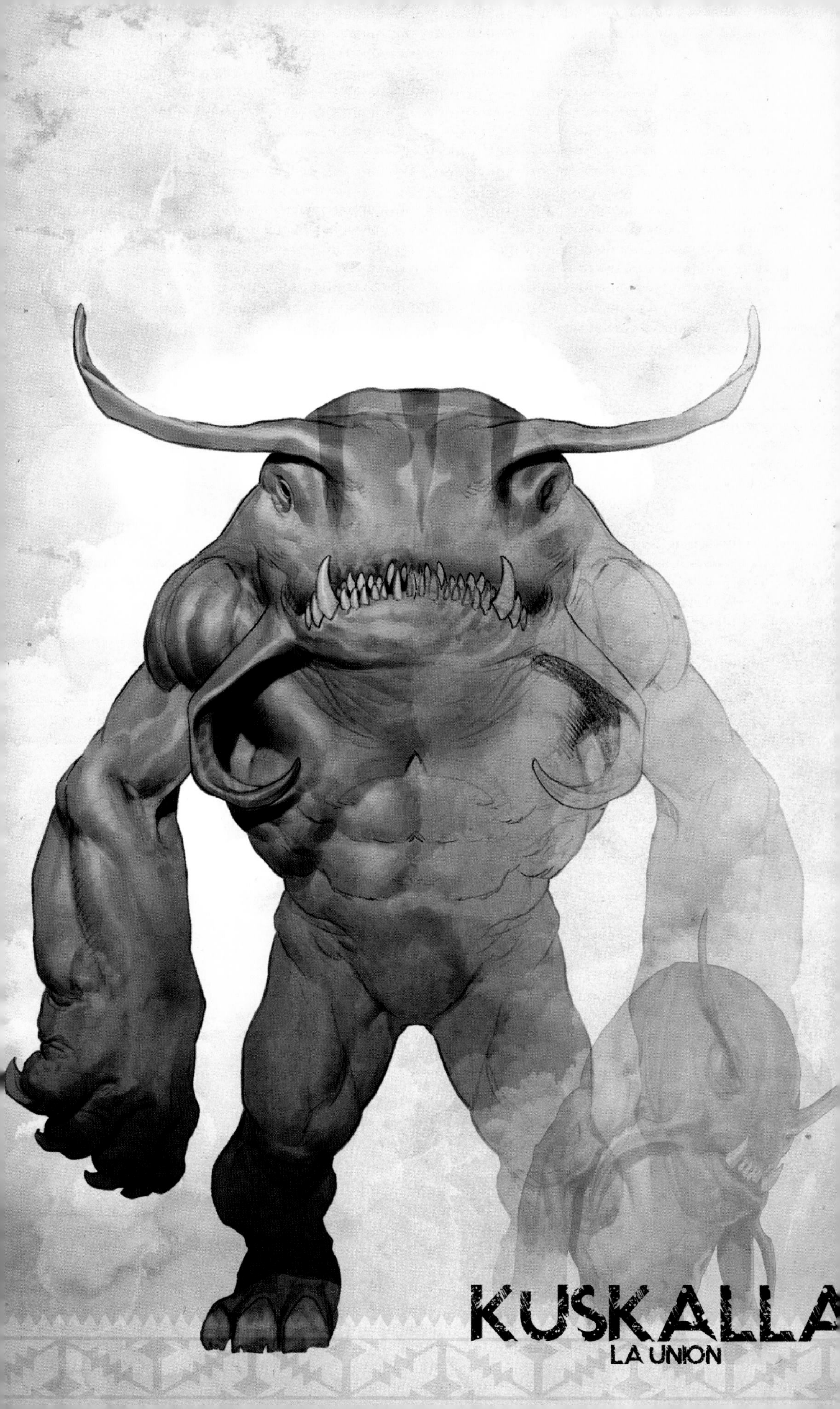
KUSKALLA
LA UNION

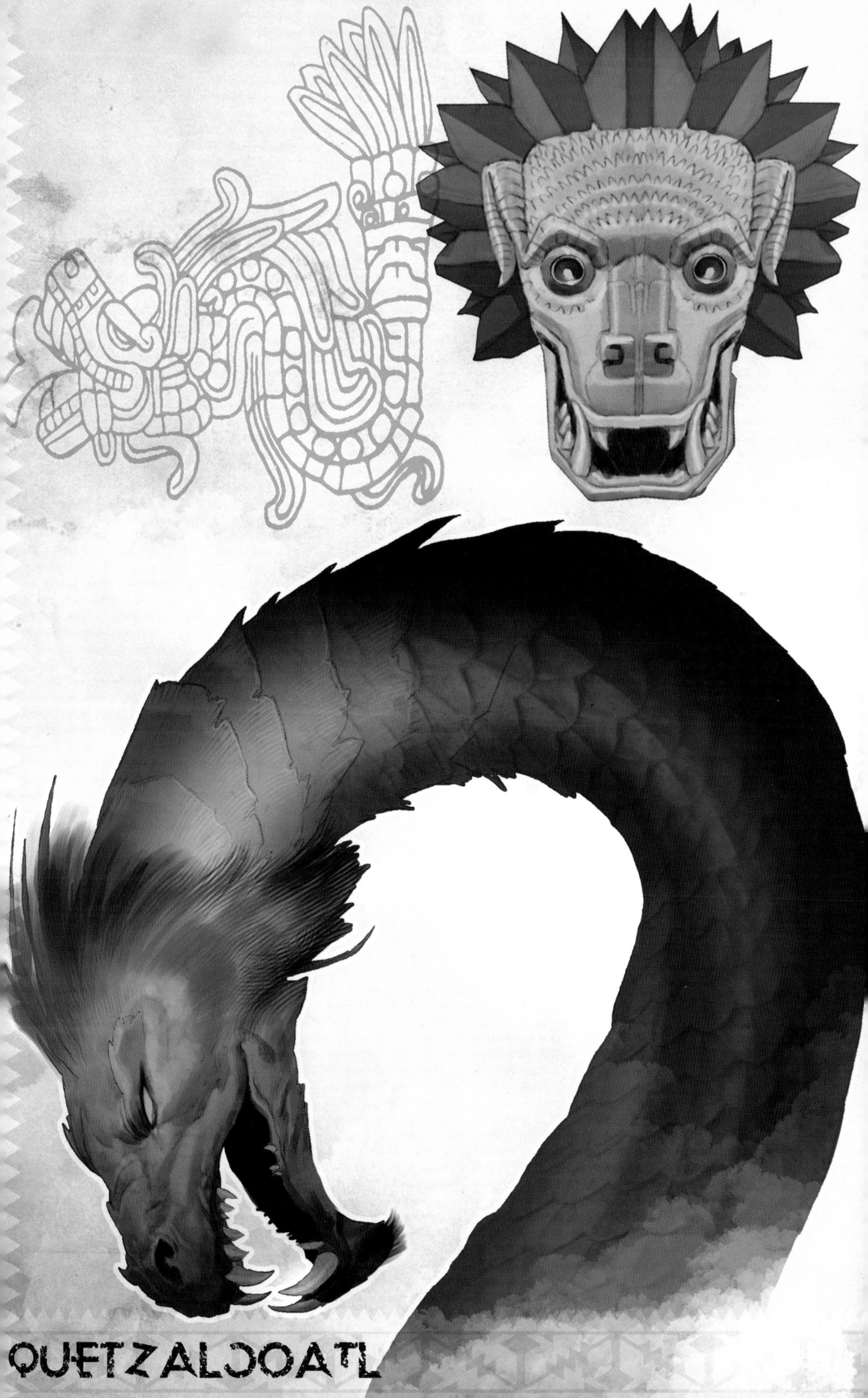

QUETZALCOATL

PHAUANA
EL QUE VUELA

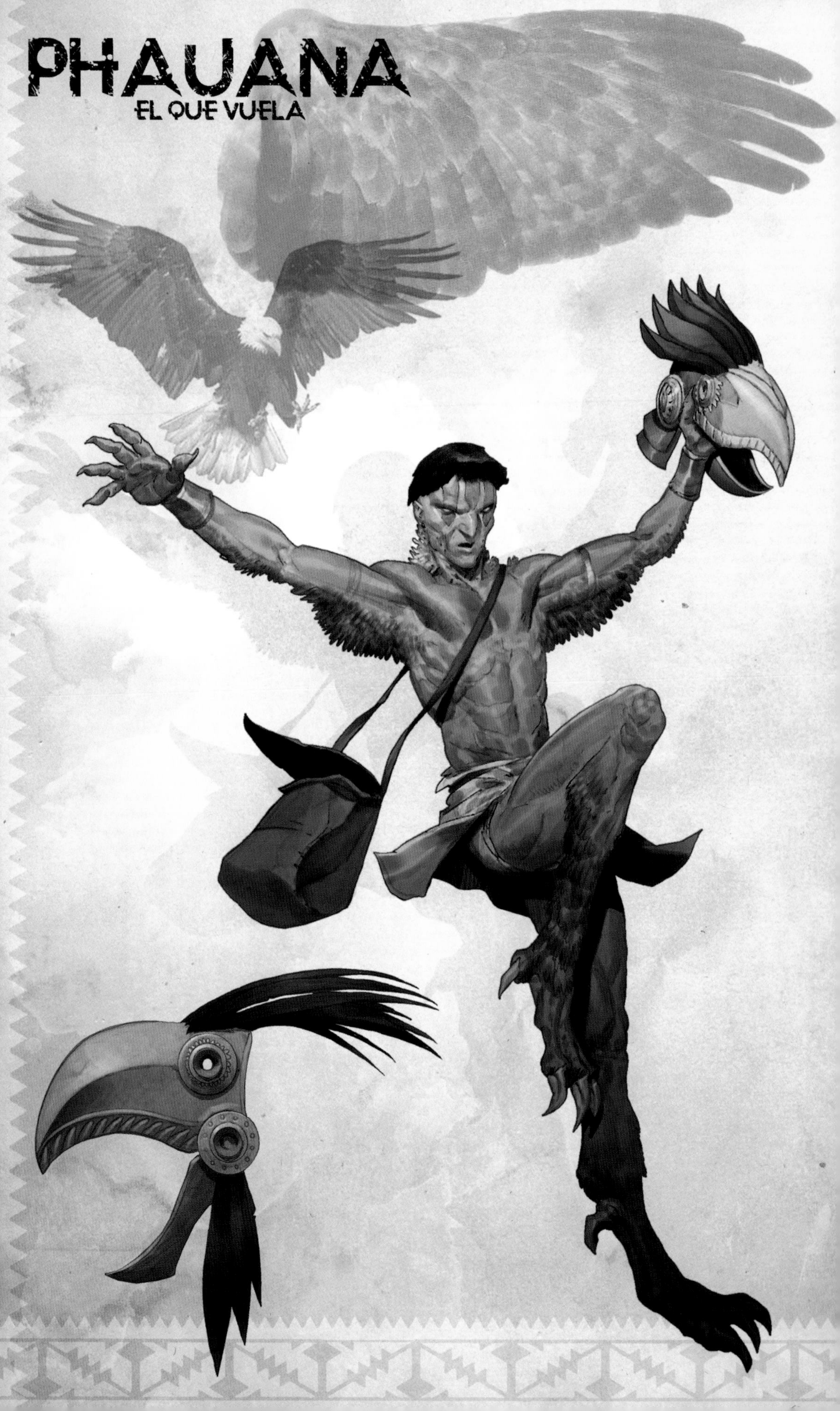

PPAKKINA
EL DESTRUCTOR

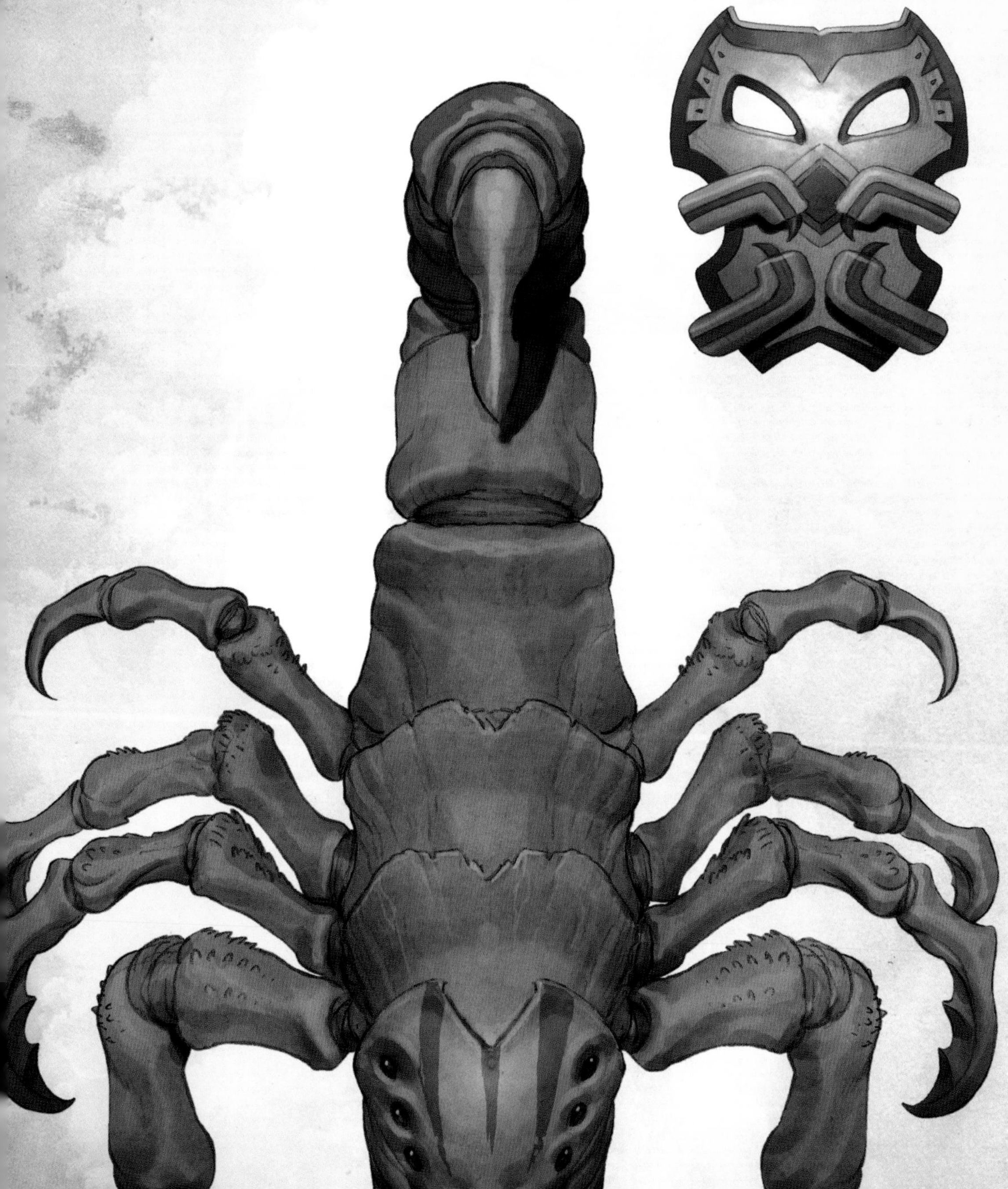

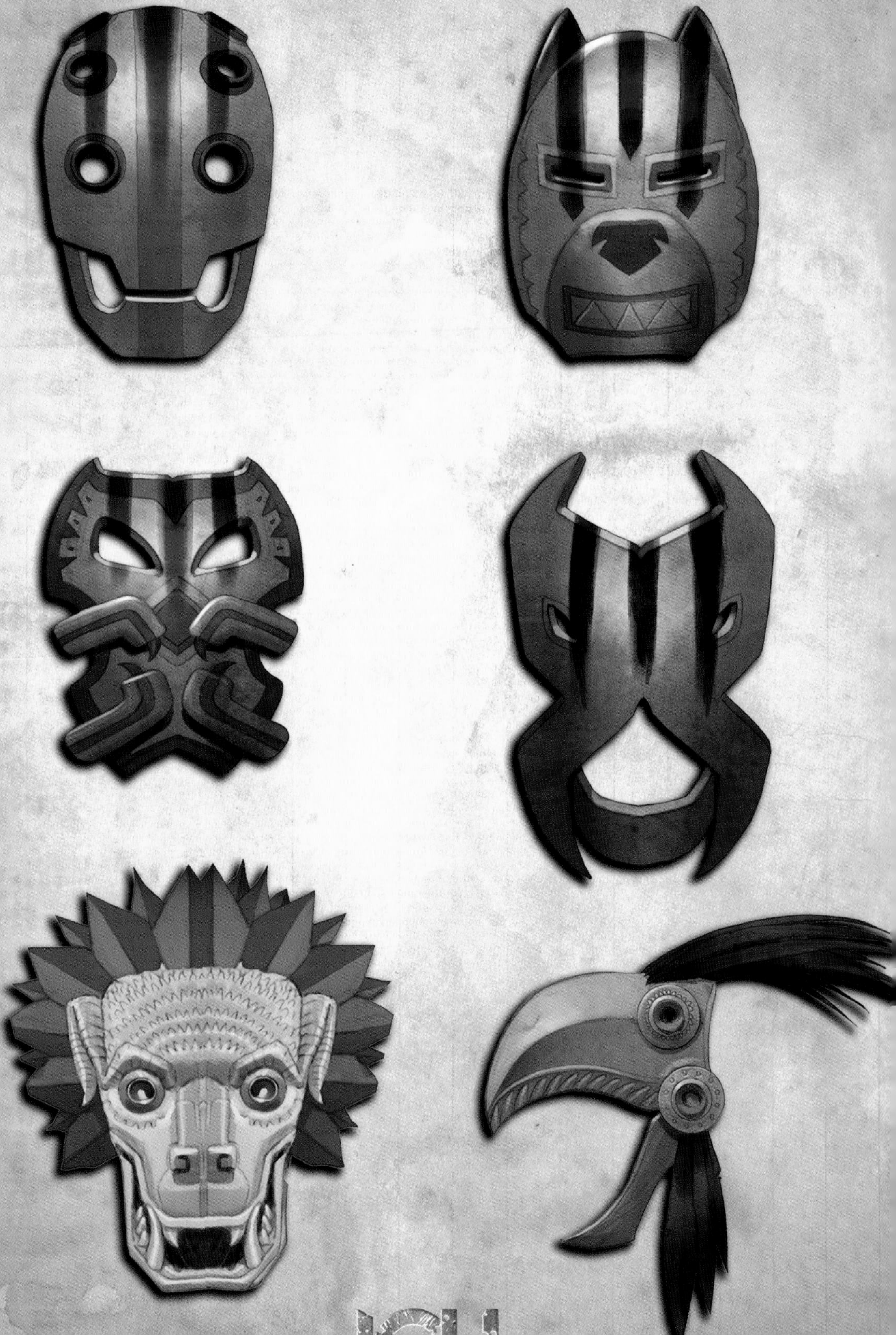
ICH

ICH

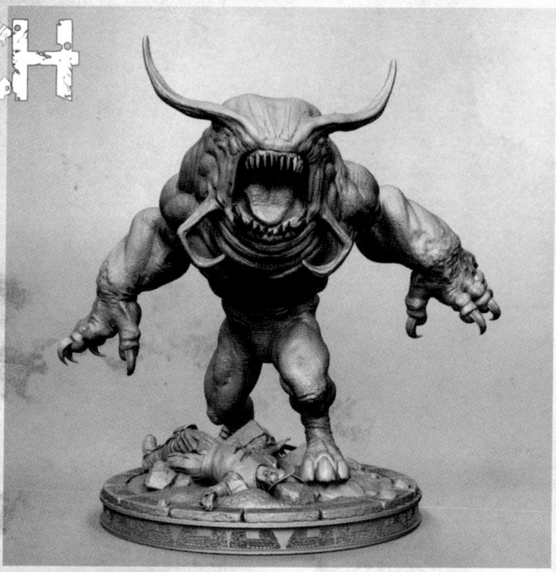

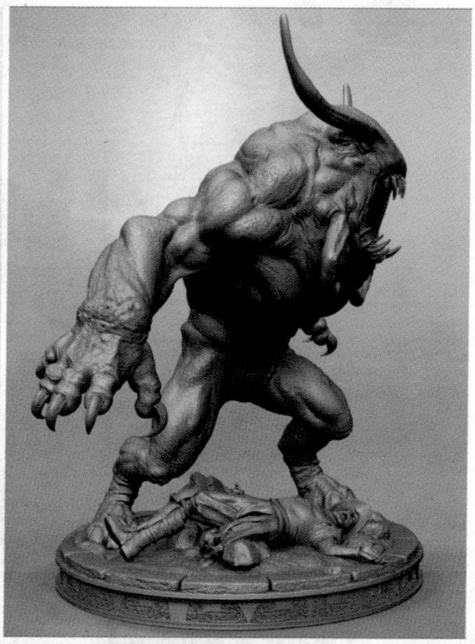

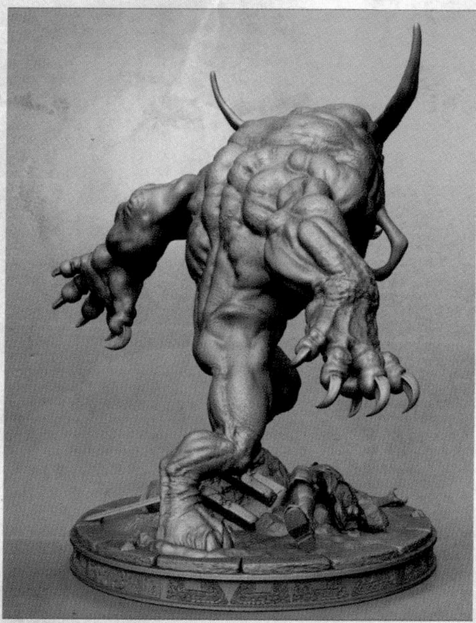

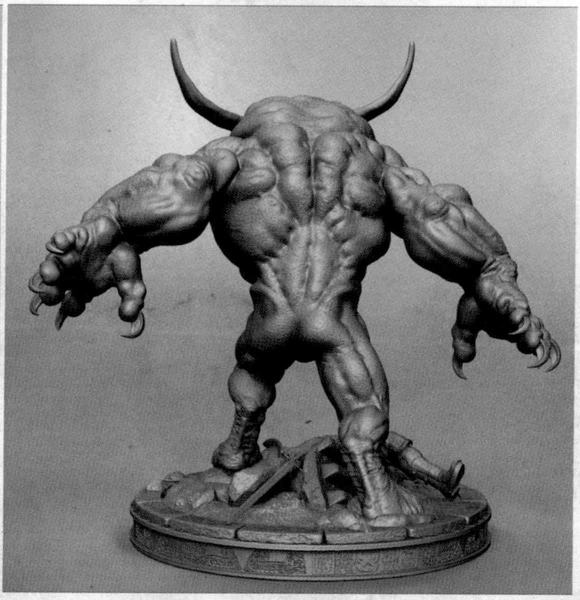

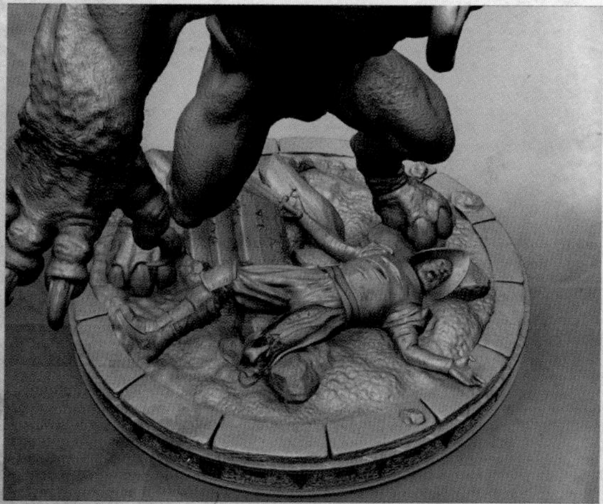

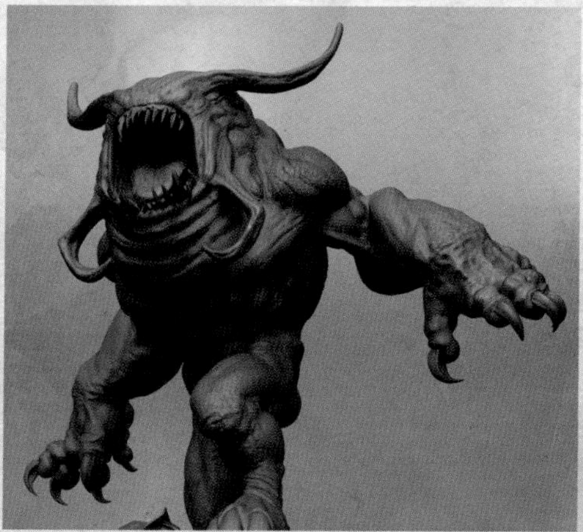

SCULPTURE BY MARTIN CANALE

BRUTAL NATURE

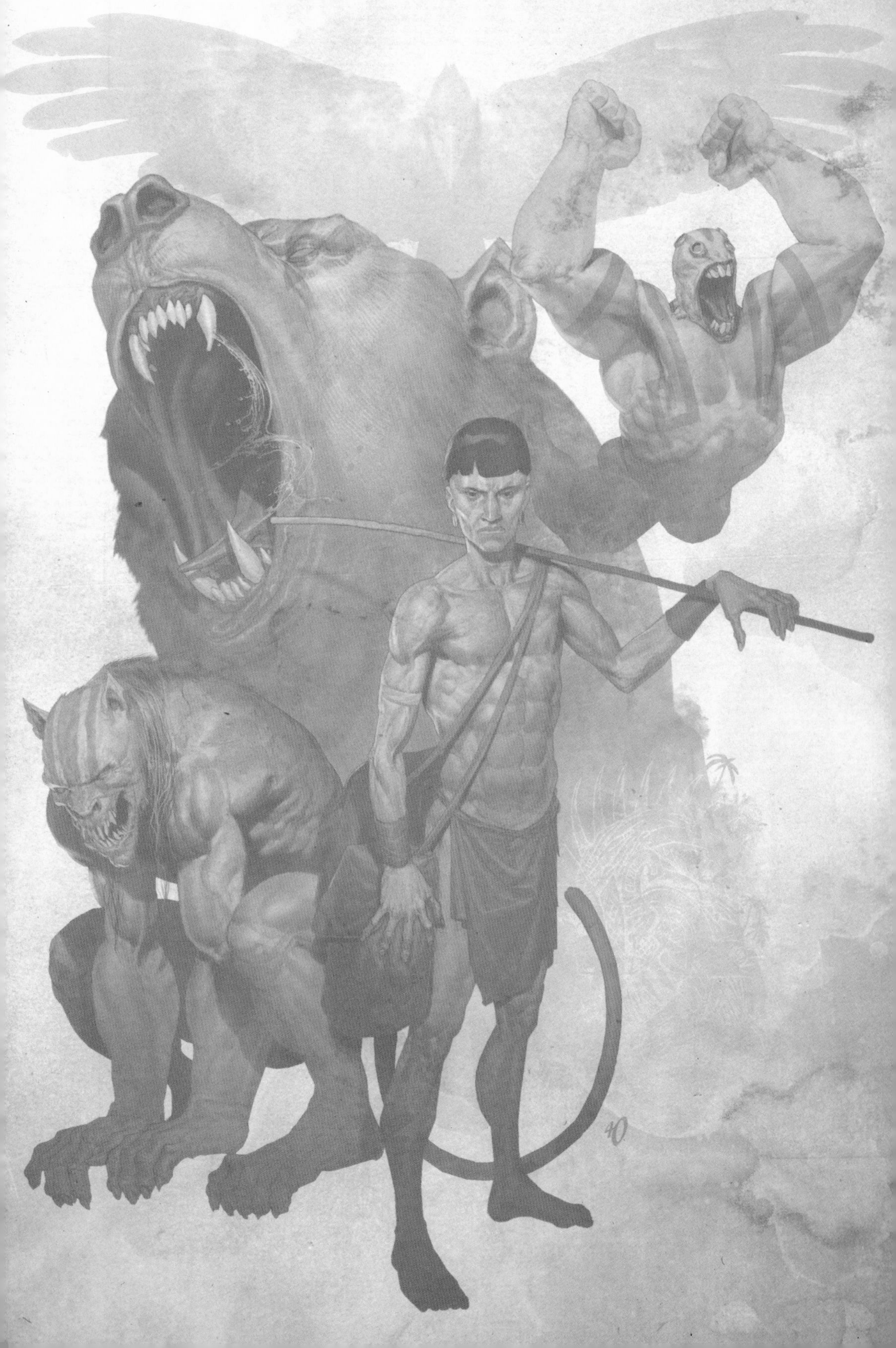